SEEDS OF TROUBLE

Seeds of Trouble

Government Policy and Land Rights in Nyasaland, 1946–1964

Colin Baker

BLOOMSBURY ACADEMIC
LONDON • NEW YORK • OXFORD • NEW DELHI • SYDNEY

BLOOMSBURY ACADEMIC
Bloomsbury Publishing Plc
50 Bedford Square, London, WC1B 3DP, UK
1385 Broadway, New York, NY 10018, USA
29 Earlsfort Terrace, Dublin 2, Ireland

BLOOMSBURY, BLOOMSBURY ACADEMIC and the Diana logo
are trademarks of Bloomsbury Publishing Plc

First published in 1993 by British Academic Press
This paperback edition published by Bloomsbury Academic in 2021

Copyright © Colin Baker, 1993

Colin Baker has asserted his right under the Copyright,
Designs and Patents Act, 1988, to be identified as Author of this work.

All rights reserved. No part of this publication may be reproduced or
transmitted in any form or by any means, electronic or mechanical,
including photocopying, recording, or any information storage or retrieval
system, without prior permission in writing from the publishers.

Bloomsbury Publishing Plc does not have any control over, or responsibility for,
any third-party websites referred to or in this book. All internet addresses given
in this book were correct at the time of going to press. The author and publisher
regret any inconvenience caused if addresses have changed or sites have
ceased to exist, but can accept no responsibility for any such changes.

A catalogue record for this book is available from the British Library.

A catalog record for this book is available from the Library of Congress.

ISBN: HB: 978-1-8504-3615-7
PB: 978-1-3501-8472-5

Typeset by Photoprint, Torquay, Devon

To find out more about our authors and books visit
www.bloomsbury.com and sign up for our newsletters.

Contents

	Page
Note on spelling and currency	vii
List of maps	viii
Preface	ix

Chapter

1	Nyasaland and the origin of private estates	1
2	The problem of Africans on private estates and attempts to solve it, 1900–45	11
3	The Abrahams Commission, 1946, and the Land Planning Committee, 1947	47
4	Sir Geoffrey Colby's early reactions, 1948–53	65
5	The 1953 disturbances and African reaction	97
6	The policy of progressive abolition of *thangata*, 1954	109
7	Negotiations with the BCA Company, 1954–5	135
8	Land acquisition and resettlement, 1955–64	153
9	Conclusion	173

Maps	189
Notes	193
Sources	213

Note on spelling and currency

The spelling of place names follows that used at the relevant time and no attempt has been made to render place names into their present form; e.g. Cholo and Mlanje are so spelled, as in colonial days, rather than in their modern form, as Thyolo and Mulanje.

The term *thangata* is so spelled, in its modern form, rather than in its previous form of *tangata*, except when the word is used in quotations, in which case it remains in its original form.

The currency used is the pound sterling, undecimalized, with reference in some cases to shillings and pence; there were 12 pence to the shilling and 20 shillings to the pound. No attempt has been made to render the amounts into their Malawian equivalent in *kwacha*.

Maps

Maps drawn by Russell Townsend

		Page
1	Nyasaland in Africa	188
2	Nyasaland in Central Africa	189
3	Nyasaland	190
4	Southern Nyasaland, showing the Shire Highlands	191

Preface

If, in 1946, observers had been able to foresee the end of the colonial era in Nyasaland in less than twenty years as a result of a few years of strong, unified, and often violent African opposition to the government and its policies, they might confidently have forecast that those leading this opposition would use for attack an issue which was readily available, and which could rouse mass emotions, unite the African people, form a rallying point, and threaten the security and economy of the country, thus helping to bring the colonial government to submission. That issue, the cudgel with which to beat the government, was private estates.

In essence, there were huge estates, privately owned by Europeans, in the southern part of the country, many of which were both undeveloped and unoccupied, located in some of the most densely African-populated land in the continent. Africans on Trust Land, with its depleted fertility, looked with envy on the unoccupied, frequently fertile, areas of private land. Those on private estates resented the social and economic restrictions placed upon them as tenants, the obligation to pay annual rent in either cash or labour, and the insecurity of their tenure. The resentment was aimed at the European estate owners and was intensified by the connection, in the African mind, of land issues with white domination from Southern Rhodesia.

The final assault on colonialism was launched in 1958 when Dr Banda returned to Nyasaland. He had been away from his homeland since he was a teenager, first in Southern Rhodesia and South Africa, where he worked in hospitals and mines, then in the USA, where he studied medicine, and finally in Britain and the Gold Coast, where he practised medicine. When he returned, as a politician, after over 40 years' absence, he had three publicly avowed intentions in each of which, although he did not say so, land was involved: to secure independence; to abolish federation; and to improve race relations.[1] In the case of independence, one of the greatest fears of Europeans was that an African government would expropriate their land. Concerning federation, one of the greatest fears of Africans was that white Southern Rhodesians would deprive them of large areas of their land. With regard to race relations, the normally good relations were endangered by friction between European estate owners and Africans who lived on or near their estates.

Observers might also confidently have forecast that the cudgel would be picked up and wielded in precisely that compact area of southern Nyasaland where more than two-thirds of the country's Europeans and almost one-third of its Africans lived, and where most of the active politicians of both races resided: an area also which contributed massively to the country's non-subsistence economy, and whose vulnerability would endanger the whole of that economy.

Such forecasts as to the instrument, and the location, for attacking the colonial government would not have required any great intimacy of knowledge or exceptional powers of prediction: the factors were well known and obvious.

Yet, when the time came, land, and especially the question of Africans on private estates, was not a significant issue; it featured little, if at all, in the nationalist politicians' armoury of attack. It had been deprived of its explosive potential and was no longer a focus of acute conflict or the source of opposition and violence. Why was this? What part did government policy play in removing this potential source of conflagration in the years between 1946 and 1964? That is the question which this book sets out to answer.

1
Nyasaland and the origin of private estates

Nyasaland, the pre-independence name for Malawi, is situated in the south-eastern part of Central Africa, 130 miles from the Indian Ocean. In its northern half it is bordered to the west by Zambia (formerly Northern Rhodesia) and to the east by Tanzania (formerly Tanganyika), and in its southern half by Mozambique both to the west and to the east. It is a long, narrow country, 560 miles north to south and 30 to 100 miles west to east. A quarter of its 46,000 square miles is covered by lakes.[1]

Its northern two-thirds are comprised of Lake Malawi (formerly Lake Nyasa) to the east, 11,000 square miles in extent, at 1,500 feet above sea level; and of high plateaux to the west, generally at 4,000 feet above sea level but rising to 8,000 feet in the Nyika Highlands. The southern one-third is comprised of the Shire River valley, descending from 1,500 feet to 100 feet, with the 3,000 feet Shire Highlands Plateau to the east, rising to over 10,000 feet in the Mlanje Mountains, and the 3,500 feet Kirk Range to the west. It is a country of varied landscapes, some with great natural beauty.

The climate is monsoonal, with a warm to hot main rainy season from November to March, followed by late rains during April and May, and a cooler dry season from June to October. Mean temperatures vary with season and altitude. At Fort Hill (4,200 feet) in the extreme north the January mean is 69 degrees F and the July mean is 62 degrees F, whilst at Port Herald (190 feet) in the extreme south the means are 81 degrees F in January and 68 degrees F in July. Over 90 per cent of the rainfall occurs during November to March, although there are 'chiperone' mists and light rains during the 'dry' season in certain mountain areas, notably in the Shire Highlands. Annual rainfall varies from over 80 inches in the far north, the Nkata Bay area, Zomba and Mlanje mountains, to less than 30 inches in the Mzimba and Kasungu plains and the Shire valley.

By African standards the country enjoys a relatively high proportion of fertile, intrinsically good, soils, although their nutrient status varies widely, being more fertile in the south – especially in the Shire Highlands – than in the north. The steep terrain of many areas and the intensity of tropical rainstorms render soils very susceptible to erosion.

Given the absence of economically exploitable minerals, the economy has always been overwhelmingly based on agriculture, as the export trade history demonstrates.[2] The period 1891 to 1904 was characterized by the rapid rise and then fall (due to disease) of coffee and the similar fate of rubber, and by the decline of ivory as a significant export. During this period these three items contributed over 90 per cent to the country's export earnings. In 1904 the export trade was valued at £27,500, of which 65 per cent (£18,000) was derived from coffee, as compared with peaks respectively of £78,500 and £62,000 (79 per cent) in 1900. The period 1905 to 1922 began to set the pattern which to a large extent has persisted ever since: competitors were eliminated until tobacco contributed £316,000 (70 per cent), cotton £73,000 (16 per cent) and tea £20,500 (5 per cent) in a total of £450,000. The decade 1923 to 1932 saw tobacco contributing an even greater share to export earnings, and tea increasing as cotton declined: tobacco rose to £550,000 (84 per cent), tea rose to £43,000 (7 per cent) and cotton declined to £35,000 (5 per cent) in a total of £656,120. During the 1930s and 1940s, tea grew further to rival tobacco so that, by 1951, tobacco contributed £2,733,430 (47 per cent), tea £2,028,866 (35 per cent) and cotton £330,000 (6 per cent). In the remaining years of the colonial era, tobacco and tea continued to dominate and were joined by groundnuts and tung oil, whilst cotton continued to decline. In 1963 tobacco exports were valued at £4,098,588 (39 per cent), tea £3,464,737 (33 per cent), groundnuts £1,876,006 (17 per cent), tung oil £321,424 (3 per cent), and cotton £188,707 (2 per cent), out of a total of £10,515,574. The economy thus came to be dominated by two major crops: tobacco from the Southern and Central Provinces, grown on European estates and on African village lands; and tea, which was exclusively grown on European estates in the Shire Highlands. African village smallholders occupied 95 per cent of the country's agricultural land, predominantly producing maize as the staple food.

The African population grew from 900,000 in 1901 to 3,000,000 in 1964; the European from 600 to 9,500; and the Asian, with those of mixed race, from 500 to 14,500. In the post-Second World War period, the vast majority of the Africans were subsistence farmers; the Asians were overwhelmingly engaged in trading and storekeeping; while about a quarter of the Europeans were engaged each in government service, mission work and agriculture, with the remainder in commerce or living as dependants. The Euro-Africans and Indo-Africans were primarily occupied in trading, transport and agriculture. The population density was one of the highest in Africa, being particularly high in the Shire Highlands – where overall density exceeded 200 to the square mile, reaching over 800 in a number of areas – and growing at a rate which doubled it every 25 years.

There were three categories of land-holding: before the Native Trust Land Order in Council of 1936, land was classified into freehold land, land leased from the Crown, and Crown Land. After 1936, the term Crown Land applied simply to the land acquired by the government, whilst freehold and leasehold land, together with forest reserves and townships, became known as Reserved Land, and the remainder became Native Trust Land.[3]

European influence developed after David Livingstone first reached Lake Malawi in August 1859. He was followed by the initially abortive Universities Mission to Central Africa at Magomero in the Shire Highlands in 1861, by the Free Church of Scotland at Cape Maclear on the southern Lake shore in October 1875, and by the Church of Scotland Mission at Blantyre, also in the Shire Highlands, in September 1876. The first resident British official was Captain Foot who, in October 1883, was appointed 'Consul ... in the districts adjacent to Lake Nyassa'. Other consuls succeeded him and in September 1889 Buchanan declared a protectorate over the Shire Highlands to forestall a Portuguese advance into that area. This protectorate was extended in 1891 to cover the whole area which became British Central Africa, whose first Commissioner was H. H. Johnston.[4]

In 1904 responsibility for the protectorate passed from the Foreign Office to the Colonial Office. Three years later, the name of the country was changed to Nyasaland, the Commissioner was restyled Governor, and Executive and Legislative Councils were created. Minor adjustments to the Councils were made, and in 1946 Executive Council had five official and two non-official members, all European, whilst Legislative Council had six official and six non-official members, also all European. In 1960 Executive Council had five officials, all European, and two African and two European non-officials; Legislative Council had fourteen officials, all European, and seven African and six European non-officials. Between 1960 and independence in 1964, rapid changes to increase African and non-official membership of both Councils occurred.[5]

In summary, then, Nyasaland may be described as a relatively small country, somewhat off the beaten track, with scenery, climate and soils varying from the excellent to the indifferent or hostile. At the end of the Second World War the country relied overwhelmingly on agriculture: peasant subsistence maize farming, with an export economy based almost exclusively on tobacco and tea, much of the value of both being the result of European enterprise on alienated land. The country was densely populated and the soils were susceptible to heavy erosion. Of its 23,500,000 acres, 5.1 per cent was freehold, 7.65 per cent was other Reserved Land, an insignificant proportion was Crown Land, and 87.25 per cent was Native Trust Land. The Executive and Legislative Councils were exclusively European in composition, and officials formed a majority in both. Few governors before 1948 had been development-minded, the funding available to the government was severely limited, and the country – this Cinderella among the Protectorates[6] – was sorely in need of development.

Within this general scenario, the Shire Highlands had a number of important features. It was a highland region in which Europeans had settled, finding the climate pleasant and healthy. Much of the land was fertile and, with the adequate rainfall and 'chiperone' mists, was suitable for growing tea. The European-owned estates produced tea and tobacco which were vital to the protectorate's economy. The more peaceful conditions which European government and settlement brought attracted large numbers who settled on both Trust Land and estates, many from Mozambique early in the twentieth century. The Shire Highlands also contained the expatriate urban centres of Blantyre and Limbe, with the offices of the local headquarters of major companies, including land-holding companies. In 1945, a total of 652,718 Africans, 31 per cent of the African population, lived in the Shire Highlands, which comprised only 11 per cent of Nyasaland's land area; 173,028 of these lived on private estates. Population density on both Trust Land and estates was high, and much of the land was heavily congested. Density would have been even higher had not a further 29,699 African emigrant workers been absent in southern Africa.[7] Congestion, steep slopes and heavy rainfall resulted in serious soil erosion which reduced subsistence crop yields and exacerbated the problem of population density. Even so, there were significant areas of alienated land which were both undeveloped and unoccupied. Many leading political figures, both European (including most of the early non-official members of Legislative and Executive Councils) and African,[8] lived in this area. It was a favoured area: the transportation system was more advanced than elsewhere, for this was the area which was first served by the railways, where the early road system was first developed[9] and where the first macadamized road surfaces were made. The Shire Highlands were of considerable economic and political significance to the government and to the country.

From the early 1880s, a number of European individuals, companies, missionaries, traders, hunters and planters acquired land from African chiefs,[10] most of which was then sparsely inhabited. Between 1887 and 1891, just under a million acres in the Shire Highlands passed into European hands, mainly unoccupied and uncultivated, and were registered by Consul Buchanan. Of this land, 372,000 acres passed to Sharrer (later to become British Central Africa (BCA) Company property), 176,448 to A. L. Bruce, 168,000 to Buchanan and his brothers (later to become the property of the Blantyre and East Africa (B&EA) Company), and 55,000 to the Moir brothers for the African Lakes Company (ALC).[11]

The proclamation of the protectorate was followed by a marked increase in European settlers, from 57 in 1891 to 237 in 1894,[12] and by what Johnston called:

> wholesale grabbing of land or, where it is not fair to describe the acquisition of land as 'grabbing', at any rate huge tracts had been bought for disproportionate amounts from the natives.[13]

The settlers knew that Johnston would have to enquire into and settle their claims and that he was unlikely to sanction some of them, either wholly or in part.[14]

The position of the ALC's large areas of land was well illustrated in a memorandum written by F. L. Moir, General Manager, scarcely a month after the declaration of the extended protectorate:

> The [Company] claims certain lands ... on account of Agreements made with the Chiefs ... Treaties whereby for assistance promised in protecting them from aggression they handed over to the Company their supreme power as Chiefs. ... On the refusal of Government to grant protection then, the Company spent several thousand pounds [and] much time and trouble in attending to the interests of the Chiefs [and] undertook heavy and grave responsibilities, which resulted in securing for the Chiefs British protection.[15]

On receiving this memorandum, the Foreign Office instructed Johnston to report on all land claims and made clear that the sovereign rights ceded by the Treaties were now vested in the Crown as a result of the declaration of a protectorate. On 18 July 1891, Johnston asked every European in the country to submit land claims to him and said that, whilst claims were being settled, no further purchases could be made without his sanction.[16]

In September 1892, Johnston began an enquiry into land alienation and gradually he, or Sharpe, his deputy – who did the major part of the work – or Sclater, his engineer, visited and examined every estate. Evidence of long occupation and improvement in the way of cultivation or buildings – which was rare – sufficed even in the absence of a properly authenticated document. However, in other cases confirmation of the grant depended upon there being no valid counter-claim; the chief admitting sale; the deed being authentic; proper provision being made for non-disturbance of existing African villages and gardens; the boundaries described in the deed according with the area of land claimed; and fair value having been paid. Where fair value had not been paid, an additional payment or a reduction in acreage was required before Johnston confirmed the grant.[17]

He dealt with the claims pragmatically, using a variety of reasonings and solutions to achieve, as he saw it, the most just, reasonable and economically advantageous outcome available in each case. In some cases he granted land where there was no real claim to it, while in others he secured the withdrawal of spurious claims. In a number of cases, especially where those who had purported to sell the land had no right to do so, he completely rejected the claim.[18] Only in the most outrageously unfair cases[19] did he deprive the claimant of all the land claimed: 'Even where flagrant deception had been attempted ... he always provided land somewhere on easy terms for a man who meant to develop it.'[20] In a large number of cases, he was able to ratify the claims in full.

The Rev. Alexander Hetherwick, for many years Head of the Church of Scotland Mission in Blantyre, who took a deep and active interest in land matters, especially from the African point of view, expressed the position well:

> Previous to the advent of the Administration, certain chiefs had appended their hand to documents, by which, in return for a certain stated sum paid in cloth or other trade goods, they made over to the European purchasers a slice of their territories, extending from a few hundred acres in some cases to a good many thousands in others. Apart from the question as to whether the chief was entitled to dispose in this way with any part of his territory, which he undoubtedly held only on behalf of his people, there is no doubt that the consignor did not realise or understand what he was doing – in many cases believing that he was granting only leave to plant, not making over a freehold of the estate in perpetuity ... These questions involved many intricacies which the Commissioner wisely avoided. He determined, where there was evidence of a bona fide transaction, not to go back on these agreements, but to grant to those who held such title deeds, 'Certificates of Claim' which would have the value and force of a copy hold.[21]

Johnston, aware that the chiefs by custom had no right to alienate the land,[22] considered that they had assumed that right and that it was tacitly accepted by their people, although 'it may well have been that some peasant rights or claims were disposed of in the process'.[23] In order to secure the people from their chiefs' 'heedlessness' and to avoid them becoming 'serfs' of the new European owners,[24] Johnston made it clear that their villages and plantations were not alienated when the surrounding land was alienated:

> Except on very small estates the existing native villages and plantations were exempted from all these purchases, and the natives were informed that the sale of the surrounding land did not include the alienation of their homes and plantations.[25]

One of the results of the land settlement, therefore, was to completely free the natives from any dependency on the white settlers, by restoring to them the inalienable occupancy of their villages and plantations.[26]

He purported to do this by including in most of the deeds, which he styled 'Certificates of Claim' when he confirmed the alienation, a non-disturbance clause:

> That no native village or plantation existing at the date of this Certificate on the said Estate shall be disturbed or removed without the consent in writing of Her Majesty's Commissioner and Consul-General, but when such consent shall have been given the sites of such villages or plantations shall revert to the Proprietor of the said estate. No natives can make other and new villages or plantations on the said Estate without the prior consent of the Proprietor.[27]

This clause was the only restriction on what in English law is a fee simple absolute, and was to be resented, or rather ignored, by the owners of private estates.

Johnston said that his objectives in settling the land claims were: firstly, to protect the rights of the Africans, to see that their villages and plantations were not disturbed and that sufficient space was left for their expansion (that is, presumably, their natural increase and traditional shifting cultivation); secondly, to discourage land speculation; and thirdly, to secure the rights of the Crown. He added that:

> [Where] land . . . is thickly populated and . . . bought 'over the heads' of the people by a bargain between the Chief and the purchaser . . . I have (usually) insisted that the native occupants should remain in undisturbed possession of their land and villages, and have only allowed the purchaser to make use of the waste land.[28]

The difficulties associated with alienated, densely populated land were, therefore, understood at a very early date.

A later commentator said that 'Johnston . . . made sense of a very difficult situation and tried very hard to be fair', although another believed that the Commissioner had 'kept the options open whilst giving the edge to the European planters'.[29] Johnston himself was pleased with his settlement, which registered 66 Certificates of Claim[30] covering 3,705,255 acres, saying that it was well accepted by the Europeans, gave distinct satisfaction to the Africans, and was agreed without modification by the British government. Having dealt with the Certificates of Claim, he secured Crown control over the remaining land, which then became inalienable without his sanction.[31] It was accepted that the government thus became owners in fee simple and Sharpe later claimed that the chiefs clearly recognized this.[32]

The essential intentions of Johnston's intervention were three-fold. Firstly, in the interests of the Europeans and of economic development, he confirmed the alienation of land not heavily populated, genuinely agreed by the chiefs, for which fair value had been paid; and he made it clear that the opening of new villages and gardens on these alienated areas required the prior consent of the landowners and was no longer at the disposal of the chiefs. Secondly, in the interests of the Africans, such alienations excluded the areas then devoted to village settlements and gardens and space for their expansion: he confirmed the non-alienated status of these areas and their inalienability save with his written consent. In heavily populated areas he endorsed the alienation only of waste land, that is undeveloped land, a concept later of great importance. Thirdly, in the interests of both Europeans and Africans, he reserved to himself the exclusive right of further alienation, thereby nipping a dangerous development in the bud as much as was then possible. Even so, there was already the fear of further alienation in the minds of the Africans: 'They are going to take away our land and give it to the Europeans.'[33]

2

The problem of Africans on private estates and attempts to solve it, 1900–45

Johnston's steps were adequate for the late nineteenth century: further uncontrolled alienation of land was prevented, the rights of non-disturbance of residence on estates were secured, and there was plenty of space for both Africans and Europeans.

In practice, neither side enforced the non-disturbance clause and little hindrance was placed on Africans moving within an estate every few years with shifting cultivation. When this happened, the estate owner took over the abandoned sites – quite unlawfully it would appear. Until about 1902 there was no opposition to this movement: either the owners consented – expressly or implicitly – to 'other or new villages or plantations' in accordance with the clause;[1] or more likely they believed, genuinely or otherwise, that when the original occupants moved from their original site they forfeited its protection.

The turn of the century saw a change in the protectorate's economy, as the pioneer collecting stage, based on ivory and rubber, gave way to cultivation. From planting coffee in the 1890s, the Shire Highlands estate owners began, in the very early 1900s, to plant considerable acreages of cotton and, a little later, tobacco. This required far more labour than formerly, much of it residential, because tobacco, an annual crop, needs more continuous attention than does coffee, a tree crop. In response to this demand for labour, large numbers of Anguru migrated from Mozambique into southern Nyasaland where many of them settled. There had been a trickle of Anguru immigration for a number of years but now 'this movement became a mass flight when the Portuguese colonial government ... introduced a new Labour Code for Mozambique': all males between the ages of 14 and 60 were legally obliged to work to grow foodstuffs, cotton or sugar, and 'Africans in their thousands crossed the border into British Central Africa'. Whether they settled on Crown Land or on private estates, they were a captive labour force because if they refused to work they lost their right to settle in British Central Africa.[2]

The relationship between European landowners and African residents now changed from being one concerning simply residence to one additionally concerning labour. Since many of the Africans were newcomers whose residence relationships were not covered by the Certificates of Claim, and since the labour relationships of the original occupants were also not covered by the Certificates, some landowners tried to place these new relationships on a contractual footing by written agreements with headmen on their estates. The B&EA Company, which held 167,829 acres in the Shire Highlands under Certificates of Claim,[3] took a lead and seems genuinely to have been trying to achieve a relationship which was satisfactory to all parties, which spelled out the residence conditions in more detail than had the Certificates, and which also dealt with the labour conditions.[4]

The B&EA Company agreements were signed by the Company's manager and marked by eleven headmen on behalf of their people on 26 September 1902. Presumably for simplicity and clarity, and realizing the practical difficulties in differentiating between original occupants and newcomers, the Company sought the renunciation of the non-disturbance clause protection. In exchange for being allowed to change their village and garden sites and 'to enjoy various privileges as tenants', the headmen agreed to give up all non-disturbance clause rights and to occupy their villages and gardens as tenants of the Company. They also agreed to cut timber only in demarcated areas; to build new houses, open new gardens and admit newcomers only with the estate owner's permission; and to move gardens and houses if asked, with adequate notice given, on the assurance that 'the new sites will be ample as regards garden room, water etc and suitable in all respects for their occupation'. The Company guaranteed 'the peaceful and undisturbed possession of [tenants'] houses and villages and gardens'. In respect of African residence conditions, the agreements were at least as favourable as were the non-disturbance clauses, save for the crucial point that the agreements could be terminated, on five months' notice, whereas the Certificate of Claim rights were in perpetuity.

With regard to labour conditions, the headmen agreed 'on behalf of their people and with the full consent of their people' to give two months' work during the rainy season, if asked, in lieu of six shillings rent a year. In return, the Company agreed to pay the taxes of their tenants for the first month worked and to pay normal wages for the second. Breaches of the agreement by the tenants entitled the Company to issue a notice to quit. In respect of labour conditions, the agreement seemed to be fair: residence, tax, and a month's wages in exchange for two months' labour and agreement not to work for other employers.

The practice embodied in these agreements became known as *thangata*, the traditional labour service rendered to chiefs. Although to have voiced objection might have jeopardized their chances of being given work (and consequently their ability to pay tax), and might also have run the risk of their being returned to Mozambique, the Africans did not appear to be aggrieved by this arrangement. The work did not seem more onerous or unreasonable than that which the newcomers had performed for the local chief when they first arrived,[5] and none relied on the non-disturbance clauses. Nonetheless, worried by the removal of the clause protection, the Supervisor for Native Affairs petitioned the High Court to set the agreements aside.

In giving his judgment on 28 April 1903, Judge Nunan said:

> The present agreement ... appears to me to be exceedingly unfair and one-sided. The natives ... surrender a freehold or claim of freehold, and receive a tenancy at will with the super-added condition that if they do not work for the land owner ... they are bound to pay six shillings annual rent for their holdings ... As these conditions are neither fair nor reasonable the Court has no hesitation in setting them aside.

Having disposed quite quickly of the labour aspects of the agreement, Nunan turned to what was for him the more interesting and 'far wider question of the right of natives under the old Certificates of Claim [which] must be decided once and for all'. Indeed, his decision on the labour aspects must have related to the original occupants who were entitled to protection under the Certificates, because the agreement could not reasonably have been called 'exceedingly unfair and one-sided' in the case of newcomers with no rights of residence. He was, he felt, required to determine three questions.

First, he asked, 'To whom were the [non-disturbance] rights secured by the Certificates of Claim? To the tribe, to the village community, or to the individual native?' Johnston had not expressed a view on this question, presumably because he considered the areas in question to have the same status as other African-held, unalienated, land. Nunan ruled that the rights were conferred on the village communities.

His second question was 'What was the nature and extent of the rights so secured?', and here he was in no doubt that Johnston had confirmed to the landholder an estate in fee simple. 'There was, on the other hand, no idea of conferring upon the village communities an estate in fee simple over the villages and plantations expressly reserved.' He was, however, highly ambiguous for he immediately went on to say, 'But the intention of the Crown was to reserve to the villagers a freehold right as a community to the said villages and plantations.' He did not explain the difference between 'an estate in fee simple', 'a freehold right', and, later, the rights of 'native freeholders'. As to the extent of the right, he ruled that at least eight acres per hut would allow 'a sufficiency of land to obviate the necessity of migration and to allow of a proper rotation of gardens and a proper fallow period': like Johnston, he accepted that the lands reserved to African original occupants were larger than those currently used for villages and gardens.

Nunan's third question was 'How are the persons or bodies in whom the rights inhere to be ascertained, and upon whom [is it that] the onus of proof lies?'. He first noted 'a most serious difficulty' because many villages had moved or greatly expanded, many new villages had sprung up, and 'in these last three years have come the great Anguru immigrations wiping out old landmarks and producing a situation of the greatest complexity'. He then ruled that: firstly, if the 'native freeholders' (the judge's expression) were permitted to move from their original sites without objection, they could not be treated as tenants; secondly, settlers other than Anguru could not be treated as tenants unless the estate owner satisfied the Commissioner that they were not original occupants; and thirdly, proof that original sites were voluntarily abandoned would be required before they reverted to the proprietor. In respect of this last point, he confused disturbance or removal with the opening of new villages or gardens; only in the former case was reversion to the estate owner mentioned in the Certificates of Claim.

At the very end of his judgment, Nunan returned to the labour question and suggested 'a new arrangement' whereby, from the Africans' point of view, without distinguishing between original occupants and newcomers, they paid a 'moderate rent' of perhaps three shillings (which should be commutable if they worked for a month during the rainy season) 'in return for a fixity of tenure and for the grant of an allowance of land sufficient to prevent frequent migration of the village community'. From the European's point of view, it would 'probably be in the interests of the proprietor not to attempt to make a sharp division between old occupiers and new tenants'. For the Africans, however, the unfair distinction was not between old occupants and new tenants, but between those on estates and those on Crown Land.[6]

Nunan's decisions may be effectively summarized as follows. Firstly, that the B&EA Company agreements were unfair and unreasonable because they removed the non-disturbance clause security from the original occupants. Secondly, he re-affirmed that the non-disturbance clause rights were vested in the village communities, were freehold rights, and extended to eight acres per family; and that the burden of proof that a resident was not an original occupant rested with the landowners. Thirdly, he suggested that the Africans, whether original occupants or newcomers, might find it in their interest to agree to pay a rent, or work, in exchange for 'a fixity of tenure', and that the Europeans might in their turn find it in their interest not to distinguish between original and new occupants. Save for a difference over the amount of work to be performed and its equivalent in rent, and the question of long-term security of tenure for original occupants, Nunan does not seem to have accomplished any more than the B&EA Company agreements would have done.

Whilst this case was being heard, the Commissioner appointed a Land Commission under Nunan's chairmanship to consider how best to give effect to it, and particularly to deal with the two differences between Nunan's judgment and the estate owners' agreements with Africans on their estates. Nunan recognized that his ruling on the law – that the original occupants were protected and that the onus of establishing an African's status rested with the landowner – conflicted with the practical fact that the owners could not reasonably be expected to prove this. He therefore made the point – significantly more in his Vice-Consular role than in his judicial role – that if the owners did not enter into discussions 'in a spirit of compromise', the Government might well impose a 'drastic land tax [and resume] large tracts of land . . . for public purposes' which would 'help to loosen the mortmain of the great proprietors'. He was threatening them with penal taxation and expropriation in order to secure their cooperation.

As a result of Nunan's recommendations,[7] the Lands (Native Locations) Ordinance of 1904[8] was enacted, which empowered the Commissioner to direct landowners to set aside for Africans locations of up to 10 per cent of undeveloped land, and to allot this land to estate residents on the basis of eight acres per family.[9] The land was to be vested in the male tax-paying heads of families as joint tenants upon a lease forever without power to mortgage, sell, or pledge their interest in the land.[10] In this way, the long-term security of tenure of original occupants, which the Company agreements would have removed, was reaffirmed, albeit not in respect of the original sites and not without payment of rent. Every tenant was required to pay an annual rent of four shillings to the landlord or be liable to have his crops, goods and chattels distrained. Where rent remained unpaid for a year the defaulter's interest in the land could, at the Governor's discretion, be forfeited and the defaulter could be evicted;[11] presumably, if the Governor declined to exercise this discretion, the long-term security of original occupants was as sound as under the Certificates of Claim. The effect of this Ordinance was to extend to all Africans on private estates some of the non-disturbance clause benefits and the liability to pay rent or be evicted; the original occupants suffered a duty – to pay rent – whilst the new tenants gained a right – to occupy eight acres of land. *Thangata*, labour rent, which Nunan had ruled invalid in the B&EA Company agreements, was not mentioned in the 1904 Ordinance.

For reasons later not entirely clear, the Ordinance was never brought into effect. Perhaps the assimilation of the two types of Africans on private estates was recognized to be unfair on the original occupants. The large landowners later claimed that the reason was that the Africans did not like being confined to a small area of land, the locations,[12] and Sir George Smith's opinion in 1917 was that it would operate with undue harshness on the smaller estate owners and 'would certainly carry in its wake many of the inconsistencies and undesirable consequences of a system of native compounds or locations'.[13] In any case, save for giving long-term security of residence – which the B&EA Company agreements did not give – it did little but provide for giving legal effect to a well-established practice. The owners wanted labour and the practice provided it because, notwithstanding the Ordinance's silence on labour rent, in order to pay the rent the Africans had to work. They did not publicly object, presumably, principally because they wanted to work in order to also pay their tax and purchase trade goods. The Ordinance was capable of giving the non-disturbance rights, or something very like them – a perpetual lease – statutory force because it would have been open to the Commissioner to allot locations only to original occupants, who then, as a community – notwithstanding the individual requirement to pay rent – would have security of tenure. It would also have been open to the Commissioner not to exercise his discretion to order eviction for rent default in the case of the original occupants. This statutory force could have clarified the position of the original occupants; but for Africans it was not then a pressing matter, and for Europeans it was a restriction they would resist. In not bringing the Ordinance into effect, Sharpe missed the opportunity to resolve a dangerous problem which was to worry his successors for the next half-century. In 1904, a total of 3,618,000 of the protectorate's 26,000,000 acres was alienated: 2,700,000 in North Nyasa, 387,000 in Zomba, 364,000 in Blantyre, 94,000 in Ruo, and 73,000 in Upper Shire. Only 32,809 acres of private land were under cultivation and 156,727 acres were occupied by Africans.[14] Sharrer had developed only 5,000 of his 367,000 acres, the B&EA Company only 3,000 of its 160,000 acres, and the Bruce Estates only 500 of their 160,000 acres.[15] If the full powers of the 1904 Ordinance had been used, the BCA Company would have had to give up 36,200 acres to become African locations, the B&EA Company 15,700 acres, and the Bruce Estates 15,950 acres.

In the early twentieth century, then, the question of Africans on private estates emerged: under what conditions were estate owners to secure labour from resident Africans without infringing the non-disturbance rights of original occupants? Allied to this central problem were other problems which grew in severity over the years: difficulties in identifying original occupants; of giving tenants no choice to pay money rather than labour rent; of conserving natural resources against the damage caused by traditional African forms of cultivation; of increasing population pressure; and of withholding from development large areas of land in the hands of absentee landlords (large companies based in Great Britain).

A very large extension of alienated land was agreed by the government in its 1902 and 1908 contracts with the Shire Highlands Railway (SHR) Company.[16] In exchange for constructing a railway, the government agreed to grant lands in fee simple by way of a subsidy to the Company at the rate of 3,200 acres (the Company had originally asked for 6,400 acres[17]) for each completed mile of rail. 243,634 of the 361,600 acres to be granted in this way[18] were held in reserve in the Chiradzulu, Blantyre and Mlanje Districts where 'the land is in fact so thickly populated and so denuded of timber that it can be of no use to any private owner except for the control of the labour supply'.[19]

The Associated Chamber of Agriculture and Commerce[20] now became deeply concerned about the shortage of Crown Land available for lease or purchase, since 'the greater part of the Shire Highlands [was already] taken up by private companies' and they resented the large grants being made to the SHR Company.[21] They seized upon the fact that the Company had not completed its contract on time to press the government to withdraw its grants of subsidy lands. The cause was taken up not only by the planters, but also by Hetherwick, who in 1908 pointed to the very large holdings held, and shortly to be held, by the BCA Company, the company formed to succeed the SHR Company, and added:

> What was to be done to get these large tracts . . . now in private hands, developed, or if not developed brought into the market?
> . . . The planting companies can only develop certain portions of their lands; why do they hold up their land when planters are crying out for new ground to settle on?[22]

Although his arguments were directed at acquiring land for Europeans rather than for Africans, the basic point was one to become important later from an African point of view: it was unwise to allow large alienated areas to be unused rather than open them up for development. In 1908, only 86 Europeans were engaged in agriculture, and consequently their ability to develop the land speedily was extremely limited.[23]

The BCA Company responded that it was wrong to assume their lands would lie idle, for they were ready to 'sell or lease land at a reasonable figure' or to develop it themselves. When the General Manager produced a map showing the BCA Company's Shire Highlands estates in red or pink, the Chairman of the meeting exclaimed, 'The map seems to be all red and pink!'.[24]

Pressure continued, however, and Hetherwick raised the issue at the November 1909 meeting of Legislative Council,[25] still basing his arguments on the failure of the SHR Company to complete its contract on time. He pointed out that on the subsidy lands 'were settled a large native population. Their position and their rights were very important features of the whole case'; and he asked the government to 'secure some re-arrangement of the terms as regards the disposal of land. The question of the native living on this tract of land was becoming more and more serious.'

The Governor recognized that the subsidy lands were an 'important question' and, although the contract with the SHR Company preserved the rights of Africans living on the subsidy land, he feared the Company might refuse to recognize the rights of the many newcomers since the contract was signed.

The Deputy Governor admitted that shifting cultivation was now damaging the estates' natural resources and the owners were reluctant to allow it to continue, especially since the population was increasing at a fast rate (in the Shire Highlands by 121 per cent between 1901 and 1908 – from 95,000 to 210,000) and it was becoming extremely difficult to distinguish the original occupants from newcomers.

The Governor said that he knew of 'no question more difficult which an Administrator of an African State had to confront than this matter of land where there were both black and white populations'; what the country needed 'more than anything else' was to deal with the question of land in a 'comprehensive and suitable manner'. Hetherwick took these remarks as an indication that the matter was under active consideration by the government and 'would be dealt with at an early date', so he did not then press his points further.

At this same meeting of Legislative Council in November 1909, an Employment of Natives Bill was discussed and agreed to. Although it provided that 'the wages of every employee shall be paid to him in cash', which almost certainly meant that payment in the form of residence rights was illegal, this particular aspect was not raised in the legislature, nor by the Chamber of Commerce which made representations to it.[26] The estate owners circumvented the difficulty by continuing the B&EA Company practice of paying their tenant-labourers' tax directly to the government. Had the government insisted on enforcing the 1909 Ordinance, they would have lost the considerable financial and administrative benefits of having the tax collected for them.[27] Later, owners overcame the legal difficulty by paying wages for the work which they continued to insist on.

Hetherwick kept the land question in the public eye, and at the May 1910 meeting of Legislative Council[28] he initiated a debate on 'Native Land Tenure' in which he claimed that the Lands (Native Locations) Ordinance was a 'dead letter'. He attributed its failure, on the European side, to it not being in their interests to encourage disalienation of their land; and, on the African side, to ignorance of the existence, let alone the content, of the law. He argued that African agriculture would expand, benefiting the economy, only if Africans had secure tenure; and thus not only should the Ordinance be used to create secure locations, but also Crown Land should be used to create reserves. He also argued that the government should re-acquire land in districts where 'Government land was scarce, by purchase or by treaty with private . . . owners to lease it out to . . . natives'. There had been many recent changes of private land ownership, so that the question of the rights of Africans living on the estates arose, and Hetherwick concluded that:

> the only policy Government could adopt was to find some means by which some of the lands which the native disposed of years ago were returned to him.

In this way he went further than had Nunan, who merely recommended that the government should require estate owners to set aside locations, recommending instead that the government should itself purchase private land and set aside part of its own land for African settlement.

A month after this Legislative Council meeting, the Governor asked the Chamber of Commerce for its views on a tax on undeveloped private land. The idea, originally mooted in 1897, had been repeated by the Land Commission in 1903 when the government had decided to take no action, but they now wished to consider it again. The Chamber advised against it, but the government became influenced by the sharp increase in the number of Europeans settling in the country, mainly in the Shire Highlands. The support of the Secretary of State was secured and, at the November 1911 meeting of Legislative Council, a Land Tax Bill was introduced.[29]

It was a short Bill but the officials introducing it argued their case at unusual length and with unusual strength, pleading for the three non-official members to support it since:

A unanimous vote ... would ... indicate to the Home Government that the Nyasaland European was ... willing to take a responsible interest in the country. It meant that future representations for works of development ... would be considerably strengthened ... and it would tend eventually to financial independence.

Conversely, dissent would weaken the country's position 'and it would be the planting community who would eventually suffer'. In every previous year Britain had met Nyasaland's budget deficit – some £750,000 in twenty years – and it was felt it was high time that Nyasaland stood on its own financial feet. Yet the non-official representatives in Legislative Council all had a deep personal interest in land and were unlikely to agree readily to a land tax, particularly one which was aimed primarily at large estates such as their own. Metcalfe was General Manager of the BCA Company; Bruce owned the Magomero estates; and Kidney was General Manager of the ALC.

The government's argument was that, since the Africans already contributed 70 per cent of the revenue and were about to have their hut tax increased, the Europeans should pay more so as to maintain the 30 per cent which they currently contributed to public revenue. At half a penny an acre the land tax, which would fall almost exclusively upon Europeans, would raise £8,000 a year, and since half of this would fall upon the British South Africa Company's North Nyasa holdings, and another £2,000 would derive from land north of Fort Johnston, only £2,000 would be taken from Shire Highlands owners, in exchange for which the Governor gave an assurance that £8,000 would be devoted exclusively to 'the benefit of the planting and commercial community in the Shire Highlands' by macadamizing roads and constructing feeder roads from the plantation areas to the railway. There was to be no attempt to distinguish between the values or cultivability of land; although this was put forward on grounds of simplicity and cheapness, the government was well aware that if they taxed the poorer and undeveloped land equally with other land, the large owners might be induced to part with the poorer land and develop the better areas. Of the non-official members, Kidney and Bruce saw no necessity for additional revenue but were won over by the promise that the £8,000 would be devoted to the Shire Highlands. Bruce believed that the European planters should make the 'sacrifice' 'in order to assist and hasten on the bettering of existing lines of communication and genuine development'. This belief was related to the fact that the Bruce estates were located across one of the two routes which the northward extension of the railway system was most likely to take; Bruce, consequently, had a deep personal interest in the matter. Metcalfe, however, was not won over, notwithstanding the fact that his company owned land astride the other probable route.[30] He also saw no necessity to raise additional revenue, nor could he see the economic necessity:

> if the large landowners ... were holding up their lands there would perhaps be some excuse for this tax, but this was not the case; on the other hand, they were doing their utmost to develop them as opportunity occurred by selling and leasing, and by opportunity occurring he meant by cultivation as far as the supply of labour went.

He distinguished between land capable of development and land not capable of development either because it was 'naturally uncultivable' or because – revealingly at this early stage – it was 'occupied by thousands of natives', for whom he could see no reason why the owner should pay land tax.

The Governor attempted to win Metcalfe over with a final plea for unanimity. However, he had no great hope of success, and Metcalfe voted against the Bill. Everyone else voted for it, and the Bill eventually became law, taking effect on 1 April 1912.

Hetherwick returned yet again to the land question in Legislative Council in November 1912[31] and argued for African reserves in every district because 'there might be natives living on European lands who ... might feel themselves occupying a situation which they desired to be relieved of'. The only satisfactory solution, he felt, was to reserve 'sufficient for the needs of the natives' of each district. In reply, the Deputy Governor said that, especially in the Shire Highlands, 'suitable Crown lands for the natives were scarce and scattered' and it would be difficult to set aside land for reserves. Indeed:

> Government was ... compelled to inform District Residents where Anguru immigration was taking place that no further immigrants would be allowed to come and settle on Crown lands in the Shire Highlands, but could be directed to the

Estates of private land holders who still desired them as settlers.[32]

This encouragement of immigration onto private land was to exacerbate a problem which was later to become very difficult to solve, but it is clear that the government was aware of the general dangers and was taking steps to control immigration, at least onto Crown Land. The occasion for this debate was the introduction of the Crown Land Bill which included a requirement that a fixed proportion of the land leased should be developed within a stated period or that a certain sum should be invested in its development. Had the government been able and minded to apply similar conditions to freehold land this would significantly have stimulated the development of private estates.[33]

In 1913, the government negotiated with the BCA Company to redeem the railway subsidy lands as a result of pressures by the Chamber of Commerce and by other Europeans, especially the smaller landowners, to secure more land for themselves, and by Hetherwick to secure land for the Africans. Also, the fast growth of population in the Shire Highlands made it extremely difficult to claim that the Africans did not need the land: in the Shire Highlands, the African population increased by 64 per cent (from 168,584 to 275,738) between 1905 and 1913.[34] The government redeemed the subsidy lands for £180,800 – ten shillings an acre – with a loan from the imperial treasury.[35] In this way, the BCA Company Shire Highlands holdings became 361,600 acres less than they would otherwise have been: to that extent, what was later to become a problem of very serious dimensions and a source of grave concern was lessened.

In March 1914, Legislative Council debated a Bill to make 'general a practice which has obtained in the past on several important estates'.[36] The Bill was designed to require landlords to enter into written agreements with tenants on their land, stipulating the payment of a money rent but permitting, in lieu, labour for a specified period and at a stated wage. Tenants collectively or individually would be required to declare and adhere to their preference for payment of rent in money or labour. These agreements, which original occupants protected by the non-disturbance clauses could, but need not, enter into, would be terminable on six months' notice – but only if and when accommodation elsewhere had been provided. In his opening remarks, the Attorney General said that the government wished to arrive at an 'arrangement in regard to the conditions upon which the native population, and especially the [large] immigrant native population, should be allowed to settle and remain upon landed estates', and he referred to the different attitudes of Africans from those of Europeans towards 'land as a species of private property'. On the one hand 'the native mind has no conception of individual tenure', whilst on the other were the 'Europeans with this highly developed sense of value of individual tenure'. He then spoke of the great increase in population and asked:

> How are we to deal with this growing population, which we do not wish to discourage? ... was it seriously proposed that the only condition on which we would admit them is that they are bound to work for the particular landlord on whose land they happened to settle? ... The only alternative then was to provide some fixity of tenure and give them the opportunity to pay their rent either in money or by service in lieu of money rent.

He hoped the large landowners 'on whose land these increases chiefly occurred' would agree, because it was largely owing to their 'holding up' practically the whole of their land that the situation had arisen: these owners were developing only a minute percentage of their holdings. If immigration was not to be discouraged, and the usefulness of the Africans on the estates was to be increased, it was important to have fair conditions of employment, a choice of employer, and 'fixity of tenure which should not be removed at the caprice of an individual owner'.

Bruce first replied that the Bill had been sprung upon them with insufficient time to give it adequate examination, and then described the system which had worked for many years on his estates: all tenants, by oral agreement, worked for one month for the owner who, in exchange, paid their hut tax. In addition, they worked for one month for wages, and:

> the thousands of natives who had settled, and were settling, on the land with full knowledge of these conditions bore witness to the fact that there was no hardship in such an agreement.

He was convinced that the option to pay rent, rather than to work, would upset the labour supply and damage development because the extension of cultivation 'largely depended on the number of new tenants who annually settled on the land'. Because high yields of cotton could be maintained only by cultivating freshly cleared fields, the demand for labour for clearing bush land was continuous and expanding: 'More labour was used to clear more bush each year to maintain productivity.'[37] Principally as a result of complaints about the lack of time given to examine the Bill, further consideration was postponed until the next meeting, although, in the event, it was not then proceeded with.

Even so, the 1914 debate was important. On the government side, there was recognition of the fundamentally different views of land holding in the European and the African minds: private ownership versus communal use. There was also acknowledgement of the large immigration and of the government's wish not to discourage it; and the belief in some security of tenure for Africans and the choice of working or paying money rent in exchange for security. The government was also clear that it was the large landowners who accepted most immigrants and who were retarding development by 'holding up practically the whole of their land'. On the estate owners' side, there was the argument that work in exchange for residential rights was so widely acquiesced in that, logically, it must involve no hardship. In addition, Bruce claimed that the fuller development depended on the work – not the rent – of new African settlers to open up further areas of land: a point hinted at by Metcalfe earlier.

The Report on the 1915 Chilembwe Rising at Magomero – on Bruce's land in fact – disapproved of the agreements to provide labour in return for residential rights.[38] It recommended that work in lieu of money rent be abolished except at the tenant's choice, that fair rents be established, that reasonable notice to quit be given, and that eviction be only by the order of a court. As a consequence, the Governor discussed the 1904 Ordinance, and the need to modify both this and the 1914 draft Bill, in Executive Council in the middle of 1916.[39] He concluded that the 1914 proposals for written contracts were 'unworkable' and should be replaced by an ordinance regulating the accommodation and obligations of estate Africans. A new draft Bill omitted written agreements and provided for: first, banning compulsory labour in lieu of rent; second, a monetary payment in all cases, to be determined by the landlord within government-set maxima; and third, the landlord's power to evict tenants within safeguards. Governor Smith, ignoring Nunan's 1903 ruling on the *onus probandi*, inserted a section in the draft Bill to abrogate the non-disturbance rights on the grounds that:

> With the many changes in the population which have occurred ... and the practice of breaking new ground for native gardens at short intervals, it would be practically impossible for a claim to be now sustained on behalf of any individual or group of natives.

In giving these proposals to the Secretary of State, Smith acknowledged that the question of Africans on private estates was 'one of no little difficulty and complexity' but he was optimistic that his proposals would 'do much to regularise the position'. The Colonial Office accepted his proposals but required him to remove the section which purported to abrogate the non-disturbance rights of original occupants.

The Bill, published on 30 September 1916,[40] was discussed, *inter alia*, by the Blantyre Scottish missionaries and by the Chamber of Commerce. The missionaries were particularly worried by the shortage of African land in the Shire Highlands and concluded, in their journal *Life and Work in Nyasaland*: 'We see no way out of the present impasse than that the Government should buy over some of the undeveloped land in European hands'.[41] The Chamber emphasized that the only reason for owners having Africans on their land was as a supply of labour and that the rent charged was but a minor consideration.[42] The government replied that the 1909 Employment of Natives Ordinance forbade payment for work in anything other than cash and that rent-free residence in exchange for labour was probably illegal. The Chamber objected that the Bill took away the right of free contract with estate Africans and in effect cancelled existing contracts. They believed that the destructive nature of traditional African cultivation rendered any rent 'quite inadequate' to cover the damage to the soil and woodland; consequently labour – *thangata* – was the only real return to the estate owner and was not an onerous requirement. They were deeply concerned that the provision that tenants could not be removed until the District Resident was satisfied that accommodation elsewhere had been provided or was available, would amount to expropriation if the removal was to a new area on the estate, since there was hardly any Crown Land available in the Shire Highlands to which they could be moved.

The Chamber summarized their objections: freedom to contract to pay rent in labour should be maintained; the level of rents should be fixed locally, to reflect varying land values; the extent of land to which a resident African was entitled should not be precisely specified, but stated simply as sufficient for a dwelling and subsistence; the Resident should be obliged, without discretion, to eject Africans who failed to fulfil their obligations and to whom due notice had been given; and that:

> it [was] inopportune to raise questions affecting relations between proprietors and natives at the present time when a number of men whose interests [were] affected [were] absent on active service.

These objections were raised again when the Governor discussed the proposals with the Chamber early in 1917. He secured agreement on several points but two cardinal points remained: the method of fixing rents, and the necessity for accommodation to be provided or be available before eviction was permitted. During the Bill's passage through Legislative Council, he stood firm on the former objection and conceded the latter.

In reporting this progress to the Colonial Office in April 1917,[43] the Governor dealt with hardships which might fall upon the Africans resident on private estates, having first distinguished between the large landowners, the bulk of whose land was undeveloped, and the 270 smaller owners with less than 5,000 acres each, 197 of whom owned less than 1,000 acres each. Unrestricted squatting on the larger estates had not so far interfered with their economic exploitation, but on the smaller estates it was likely to 'become a burden and result in considerable interference with the interests of the proprietor'. Since smaller estate owners needed the labour, it was unlikely that they would be harsh or unreasonable with their tenants.

Next, Smith wrote of the hardship resulting from Africans being 'turned off the estate at a moment's notice' and felt that this was now to be covered by requiring fair and reasonable notice to quit. Unlike the Chamber, the Governor believed that there was still sufficient Crown Land in the Shire Highlands and adjacent areas for Africans to settle. If there was 'undue expulsion' from estates, the 1904 Ordinance could still be used to create locations on government land.

The Governor, anxious to set matters right as far as possible, 'reserved' the Bill for viewing by the Colonial Office after it had been approved by Legislative Council and before it finally became law.[44] The Colonial Office were worried that, 'in deference to local opinion', the stipulation had been removed that six months' notice of eviction was to start only when the Resident was satisfied that accommodation was provided or available elsewhere; but were reassured by the retention of the non-disturbance clause, by the Governor's view that Crown Land was available, and by the 1904 powers to create locations. A further change was to remove the Resident's discretion in evicting defaulting tenants following due notice.[45]

Although the Colonial Office accepted the Bill, they were clear that it had 'been modified very considerably in favour of the landlord' and Sir George Fiddes felt that 'agitators might with some shew of reason maintain that the result is worse than the *thangata* system so far as the freedom of the native is concerned'.[46] The Ordinance became law in September 1917 and in essence forbade the exaction of labour in lieu of money rent – in effect made *thangata* illegal – separating the concept of landlord and tenant from that of employer and employee; but authorized the landlord to charge money rent in exchange for residence, a site and materials for a hut, and sufficient cultivable land for the tenant and his family's sustenance. It provided for six months' notice to quit and summary eviction by the Resident thereafter. It did not alter the Certificate of Claim rights of the original occupants. In practice, by 1917 it had become even more difficult, although not yet impossible, to identify the original occupants, and the onus of proving original occupancy in reality fell upon the occupant himself.

It was soon recognized that the 1917 Ordinance, designed to achieve a system of tenancy based merely on payment of rent, would not work successfully. The Governor realized that the policy that every African 'should be free to offer his labour where he pleases' was being ignored and that:

> certain landlords [had] been endeavouring by indirect means to evade the ... Ordinance. Pressure [was] put on natives residing on private estates designed to compel [them] to work for the landlord and prevent them working for other employers.[47]

Nor were all the means of evasion indirect:

a deputation of planters led by Major Bruce ... threatened to evict all their tenants unless they were given a free hand in enforcing *thangata* ... Horrified by visions that they would have to settle thousands of Africans on Crown Land at six months' notice, the Administration capitulated ... and no tenant was offered the alternative of paying his rent in cash.[48]

Smith, deeply worried, was pressed in mid-1919 by the Chamber of Commerce and Legislative Council to appoint a special commissioner to enquire into 'the position of Africans residing on private estates'. He readily agreed but felt that, with so many officers taking post-war leave and with everyone else very heavily pressed with work, he could not do so for a while.[49] A year later, however, on 19 July 1920, he did set up a Commission of Enquiry to look into the whole question again, and on the same day promoted the Attorney General, E. St. J. Jackson, to be Judge of the High Court and made him Chairman of the Commission.[50] The Commission accepted that, whilst tenancy based simply on rent was 'very desirable', the 1917 Ordinance was not working:

> labour is the only return for which ... estates will accept native tenants. No landlord can be compelled to accept them ... Our problem accordingly is to define terms which are fair to the native and ... such that the European landlord will be prepared to accept and retain native tenants on those terms.[51]

This last point was important because already Crown Land in the Blantyre and Zomba Districts was insufficient to support the African population. Between 1904 and 1920, the population of Blantyre District had risen from 87,000 to 156,000, whilst the density rose from 53.35 per square mile to 95.53; and the population of Zomba District from 46,000 to 102,000, and its density from 24.53 to 51.93. In Zomba, a quarter of the Africans were living on private estates, and in Blantyre half.[52] During the war, the estate population increased considerably because it was easier to avoid military carrier service there than on Crown Land.[53] Furthermore, much Crown Land was leased to Europeans immediately after the war: in March 1919, a total of 13,757 acres had been leased, which had risen to 118,506 acres by March 1921. Over the same period, the number of Europeans engaged in agriculture rose from 124 to 372.[54] By this time, too, the children of the many African immigrant families from Mozambique at the turn of the century were setting up their own families and placing additional pressure on the land.

Jackson was impressed by the persistence of a modern extension of a traditional relationship, *thangata*, despite legislative attempts to abolish it, which he believed showed that it 'has practical convenience for both sides'. He warned that, since the only legal control on the relationship was six months' notice of eviction, 'the absence of stricter regulation leaves numerous dangers'.[55]

The Commission, again ignoring Nunan's *onus probandi* ruling, said that those who could establish non-disturbance clause rights could not be evicted under the 1917 Ordinance.[56] There can be little doubt that if the question had been brought before him in his judicial capacity Jackson would have reached the same decision in favour of the original occupants.

What particularly worried Jackson was that, although evictions were currently rare, conditions existed which could make them frequent – as Bruce and his deputation had threatened in 1917 – and the disturbance of large numbers of tenants 'would obviously produce great hardship, discontent and numerous dangers'.[57] The conditions to which he referred were the recent influx of European settlers which split up the larger estates, introducing many more landlords than formerly, weakening the security which existed through long relationships with well-known estate owners. The 'hardship' referred to was the tenure insecurity of Africans who settled on private land: the possible removal from their homes was 'a source of real anxiety to many'. The 'discontent and numerous dangers' referred to were political threats, of which the Chilembwe Rising had given heightened appreciation. Even if the problem of Africans on private estates had not been clearly viewed in this light before, it was now seen as having marked and worrying political security ramifications.

The Commission recommended that security be enhanced by providing four years as the minimum period of tenure of Africans on private estates, subject to the performance of the terms of the tenancy agreement. To avoid mass eviction for non-performance, which would 'cause serious disturbances', it recommended that eviction should not exceed 10 per thousand acres of individual estates a year and should be subject to six months' notice, failing which a further four years would run. To avoid or reduce exploitation of the tenants, the maximum period of work to which the owner could be entitled was recommended to be two months a year.[58] Jackson also recommended that the government should regain areas of private estates in the Zomba and Blantyre Districts by exchange or purchase.[59] In this, he went a step further than Nunan had in 1903: the latter had recommended that the government be empowered to direct estate owners to create African locations; the former – following (but not acknowledging) Hetherwick's 1910 suggestion, repeated in *Life and Work* in 1916 – now recommended that the government acquire private land, by exchange or purchase, in the two districts containing most European estates and most African tenants.

The government did not act on the Commission's report, probably because the fears created by the Chilembwe Rising subsided and because the current economic depression removed the need to pressurize tenants to work on estates. Also, the greater political strength of the European owners enabled them to resist legislative changes which favoured the less powerful African tenants. The protectorate's annual reports for the next five years said that the proposals were still being considered, no decision having yet been reached, and consequently there was no change in land policy, although they recognized that European settlement, land tenure and African reservations were 'important and pressing problems'.[60] From 1926 onwards, the reports made no reference to the Commission's proposals.

Governor Sir Charles Bowring, appointed in 1924, believed that the protectorate's future depended on developing agriculture by a few European planters, but principally by the Africans with European instructors; that blocks of Crown Land for further European occupation should not be large or numerous; and that the amount of land suitable for that purpose and not required for African use was very limited. Bowring said this notwithstanding the view of the Jackson Commission, which, basing its calculation on the requirements of double the existing African population, felt that 6,000,000 acres, twice the existing amount of alienated land, could be opened up to European agriculture.[61] He expressed these views to the Ormsby-Gore East Africa Commission and, taking Nunan, Hetherwick, *Life and Work*, and Jackson's point about acquisition a stage further, said that in the Shire Highlands:

> the only method of dealing with the problem is to re-acquire from the landowners convenient blocks of sufficient area to

accommodate the natives at present resident on the estates for whom accommodation acceptable to them and to Government cannot be provided elsewhere on Crown Land.[62]

In privately congratulating Ormsby-Gore on his 1924 General Election majority (although 'as a colonial civil servant [he had] no concern with party politics'), Bowring wrote:

> the settlement of that important matter will cost money but there is no point in playing with the problem and . . . it is up to us to pay for the evils of our fathers.[63]

He mooted a graduated land tax – which would hit the larger estates most heavily – to pay for the re-acquired land, and, using arguments similar to those used by Nunan in threatening 'a drastic land tax' in 1903, added that such estates would:

> doubtless under pressure of this form of taxation be either partly released to Government . . . sold, or leased to new settlers or prosperous natives . . . But if the estates are to be freed from the rights of resident natives, they must be prepared to pay an equivalent for these rights in one form or another.[64]

When the Ormsby-Gore Report published and supported Bowring's views, there was an outburst of criticism from the large landowners, and the ALC, A. L. Bruce Estates, B&EA Company and BCA Company produced a memorandum dated 24 May 1925 to voice their protest.[65] They felt particularly offended that the Commission had spent only three days in Nyasaland and had held no formal meeting with the large landowners, who had no idea that the subject of Africans on private estates was being considered, nor that 'drastic' recommendations would be made; they were also annoyed that Ormsby-Gore seemed unaware of the Jackson Report. They believed that the graduated tax would amount to 'confiscation' and 'a predatory measure', and that such 'expropriation' was unnecessary, since there was in fact no shortage of land in the protectorate: 'In our view it is simply a case of confiscation under the guise of purchase.' They hoped that the matter would soon be settled 'once and for all'.

The Report, and the European landowners' sharp reaction to it, led to the whole question of Africans on private estates being re-opened.

THE PROBLEM OF AFRICANS ON PRIVATE ESTATES   33

During 1925 and 1926, the government had discussions with the landowners; the results of these were incorporated in resolutions agreed to at a public meeting in Blantyre[66] and embodied in a skeleton Bill.[67] When he was on leave in the second half of 1926, Bowring had meetings at the Colonial Office and it was 'a very great disappointment' to him not to settle the land problem. He explained to Legislative Council:

> the position of natives on freehold estates ... is one of extreme intricacy and ... negotiations are still proceeding in England between the Secretary of State and the representatives of the landowners.[68]

The Secretary of State directed that a number of modifications should be made to the skeleton Bill, and that it should then be introduced into Legislative Council, discussed, and referred again to the Colonial Office.[69]

In 1927, the government became deeply concerned about the number of evictions, and Bowring brought the modified Bill before Legislative Council as soon as he could 'in order that an attempt to solve one of the outstanding problems of vital importance to the Protectorate may be advanced with the minimum of delay'.[70] In the course of being drafted, the Bill changed its title from 'An Ordinance to secure to natives the use and enjoyment of certain land and of the revenue arising therefrom' to the 'Native Lands Bill', and finally to the 'Native Tenants on Private Estates Bill'.[71] In introducing it, the Acting Chief Secretary, E. F. Colville, explained that:

> Difficulties have repeatedly arisen as the development or break up of estates was interfered with by the presence of native settlements, or as the need for labour forced the landowners to try and make work on the estate a condition of remaining. On the other hand, the native found his liberty to choose his own employment limited, and many of his customs ... seriously interfered with. The difficulty was further accentuated by the absence of suitable Crown Land in the neighbourhood on which the ejected natives could settle.[72]

This last point emphasized a worrying change from the position ten years earlier when the Governor had said 'it is rarely the case that there is not Crown Land in the vicinity on which [evictees] could settle'.[73] Colville partly quantified the problem by saying that there were 115,703 Africans then living on private estates, 63 per cent of them on the land of only five landowners, each having a minimum of 4,000 tenants, and the remaining 37 per cent being distributed among about fifty other landlords. All agreed that a great deal of discussion, resulting in compromise, had taken place: Smith believed the outcome 'fair to the land holders and just to the . . . tenants'; the non-official members acknowledged that the Bill presented 'a fairly satisfactory solution' which 'had been arrived at after a great deal of trouble' taken by the government and landowners;[74] a large landowner later said that 'the 1928 Ordinance was the result of a great many years of consideration and giving way on the part of the landlord on one side and Government and natives on the other'.[75] The Bill was enacted as the Natives on Private Estates Ordinance of 1928, which repealed the Native Locations and the Native Rents Ordinances and replaced them with what a later governor described as 'an elaborate series of provisions to regulate the position of natives residing on private estates'.[76]

Under the 1928 Ordinance,[77] resident Africans were liable to pay rent the equivalent of between two and three months' average agricultural worker's pay. In return they were entitled to a site and materials for a hut, cultivable land sufficient to maintain their families, and compensation for disturbance. They could ask for work or facilities for growing economic crops, the wages or price of which were to be used in remission of rent. If the owner refused labour or facilities for growing economic crops, his rent claim disappeared. Eviction was permitted summarily for rent default or misconduct, and upon six months' notice without cause in the case of not more than 10 per cent of the resident population of each estate on the expiration of a quinquennial period. In every other case, resident Africans who complied with the Ordinance's provisions had security of tenure for a further five years. This quinquennial eviction provision was included at the request of landowners. The Ordinance also obliged the government to find land for evicted Africans,[78] but within a few years district commissioners experienced great difficulty in enforcing legitimate eviction notices because they could not find sufficient land in the vicinity for settling evictees.[79] The Governor was empowered to acquire by compulsion up to 10 per cent of the area of any estate over 10,000 acres for African settlement, by exchanging Crown Land of equal value – not equal area. This last provision was another step along the Nunan-Hetherwick-*Life and Work*-Jackson-Bowring road towards acquisition and dis-alienation of land for permanent African settlement, and, although it might be seen as a sideways step in dealing with exchange rather than purchase, it was the first legislative step: earlier steps had been merely the expression of views or recommendations.

The government had allowed itself to be entrapped by the quinquennial eviction provisions. Landlords had a statutory right to evict 10 per cent of resident Africans each five years. The government had a duty to find land for the evictees. Crown Land nearby was not available and, in order to acquire land nearby, exchanged land had to be of equal value; it was extremely unlikely that such land could be found of value equal to that in the Shire Highlands, except by alienating very large areas indeed in remote parts of the country.

After 1928, the failure to distinguish in practice between Africans protected by non-disturbance clauses and others continued: indeed, a later Governor described this as the distribution of 'the vaguely defined but undoubtedly existing rights of a few natives over a large number who could not claim to have any title to them'.[80] Five years later – against a background in which very large areas of private land were undeveloped and in which economic depression slowed down development on all estates – Governor Young summarized the resulting position:

> The conditions, once universal, under which landowners were more anxious to obtain a supply of labour than to receive rent, do not now prevail ... The result is that a large number of natives who have no claim to special rights under the certificates of claim are enabled to live rent-free upon privately owned land, while the inheritors of the original native rights are in fact being treated in what can only be described as contravention of those rights.[81]

The Blantyre District Commissioner's Annual Report for 1932 criticized the level and different rates of rent being charged; and added that there was insufficient firewood and building material available, that large areas of some private estates were still uncultivated, and that the rent and labour sections of the 1928 Ordinance needed changing.[82] At about the time the Governor was reading this report, he received a copy of a letter to the Colonial Office from one of the large landowners bitterly complaining that, in effect, tenants lived rent-free on the estate. Young quickly concluded, as had most of his predecessors, that:

> the time had arrived for an attempt to be made to place the whole question of the position of natives on alienated land on a final and satisfactory footing.[83]

In his sixteen months in Nyasaland, Young introduced the Native Authority Ordinance and, as he saw it, 'finally disposed' of the question of unalienated land, and now looked for similar action in respect of alienated land.[84] He saw the new native authorities as 'the re-creation of the same kind of Native Authorities as originally parted with the land. These Authorities have replaced the village communities as ... holders of land.'[85] He awaited the end of the quinquennium, 1933, with apprehension, since the eviction of 10 per cent of resident Africans could result in the removal of at least 12,000 people to already congested Crown Land – a formidable and dangerous task. Most large owners refrained from exercising their statutory right to evict because 'it might have proved an embarrassment to Government'. In exchange for this forbearance they hoped that Young would consider favourably representations which they shortly proposed to make.[86] A major reason for not exercising their right of eviction was the current economic depression which lessened their demand for labour and crops.[87] Even so, 781 notices to quit, covering 3,124 people, were served in 1933: 299 in Cholo (of which 150 were enforced), 208 in Zomba, 207 in Chiradzulu, 42 in Mlanje, and 25 in Blantyre. In Cholo, only two of the larger estates – probably both belonging to the BCA Company – insisted on issuing notices to the full 10 per cent of the number of tenants.[88] At this time there were 35,328 families, or 141,312 people, resident on estates in the Shire Highlands.[89]

In 1934, a select committee of the legislature considered what legislation was required to reach a final solution to the problem. The deliberations were carefully guided by Young, whose own view regarding the protection of the Certificates of Claim was:

> every land owner was under an obligation merely to allow ...

the extent of land occupied by resident natives at the date of the grant with provision for normal increase, to be permanently at the disposal of the community concerned. This extent of land could shift from place to place within the boundaries of the estate according to the needs of the community and with their consent and that of the land owner but could not be shifted within these boundaries against the wishes of the community or removal outside them without the written consent of the Commissioner.[90]

Since the rights of the village communities had passed to the new native authorities, Young wanted to be able to answer questions which they might put to him:

> Government should now take the opportunity of the creation of the Native Authorities to . . . reply that the very first opportunity had been taken as soon as there was some organisation . . . to represent the claims of the original holders of rights under the non-disturbance clauses, to regularise the position by coming to some arrangement agreed to by the landowners and the Native Authorities alike by which all such claims would be finally extinguished.[91]

The select committee recommended that a local Commissioner should be appointed to try to identify the original occupants and their direct descendants or, if this was not possible, to take those on the estates at the 1911 census as the original occupants, plus one generation's natural increase. The Commissioner was then to determine the amount of land which it might be possible for owners to hand over to satisfy the needs of those with original rights. He was to attempt an agreement between owners and native authorities to discharge the landlord's obligation by handing over either the determined amount of land or a portion of the rents collected and giving rent-free tenure for life or until the original occupants and their direct descendants moved off the estate. The 1928 Ordinance was to be amended to abolish the quinquennial periods of eviction, and to provide for eviction only if a tenant either failed to pay rent or, having offered to work or grow economic crops, had not been given the opportunity to do so (unless economic conditions prevented it and the tenant was able to earn money to pay rent in some other way).[92] The proposal to hand over to the government a portion of the landowners' estates – to which most landowning witnesses strongly objected – was a further step along the Nunan-Hetherwick-*Life and Work*-Jackson-Bowring-1928 Ordinance road to acquisition of land for the permanent settlement of Africans from private estates.

Young sent these 1934 proposals to the Secretary of State who consulted the large land-holding companies and disagreed that the land question should be re-opened. He argued that the 1928 Ordinance had been reached only after exhaustive enquiries and prolonged negotiations, and although the outcome was a compromise it was regarded at the time as the 'final and best possible solution to a long standing difficulty': the present proposal 'revive[d] a very difficult problem'.[93] Perhaps he realized that the only pressure to revive it came from Young himself and a very few of his district commissioners, and certainly not from the landowners nor, probably, the native authorities, since they had but very recently been appointed and, at this stage, voiced no particular concern to re-open the matter.

In reply, Sir Harold Kittermaster, Young's successor, in December 1934, claimed that the doubts of the non-official members of Legislative Council about re-opening the question had been removed, and that he was not worried about the effects on the native authorities, since they stood to receive funds from the proposals. He suggested that African and European opinion should be gauged by publishing the Select Committee Report, and by appointing the local Commissioner.[94]

The Secretary of State was not moved by Kittermaster's arguments, saying that many landlords – presumably the London head offices of the companies holding land in Nyasaland – were still averse to re-opening the question, and that others had agreed only because Young had suggested that the 1928 settlement might be challenged in the courts. Because of 'public opinion in England' – again presumably the head offices – he preferred, if the matter were to be re-opened, an independent (not local) Land Commissioner. Furthermore, he was much opposed to publishing the Select Committee's Report.[95]

Kittermaster's district commissioners now advised that 'the position was not unsatisfactory and that the 1928 Ordinance was not the cause of any serious complaints'. They felt, however, that this was because the landlords had not exercised their right of quinquennial evictions, and that if they did so in 1938 'a serious situation might result' since it would be extremely difficult to find land on which to resettle the evicted Africans. Kittermaster did not know what to advise: 'abstract justice' required that the original occupants and their direct descendants should have rights of rent-free residence, which could be bought out by the landlord, and that others should pay rent; but this distinction would not be appreciated by those not entitled to non-disturbance under the Certificates of Claim. He felt that a Special Commissioner would give more publicity to the whole question which would run the greater risk of 'upsetting native opinion'.[96]

Although relationships were generally good, there was frequent ill-feeling on the larger estates where supervision was poor, especially on the Bruce Magomero Estate:[97]

> tenants are unable to lay their complaints and troubles before the manager without much difficulty. In consequence, there is bred up a feeling that the landlord cares little for the tenants and, as a corollary, the tenants neglect their obligations.[98]

There were problems too in heavily congested areas: 'the shortage of garden land is also responsible ... for a strong feeling of resentment that unoccupied estates should be allowed to lie fallow and undeveloped, while across the boundary the Trust Land native cannot find room to plant his crops'.[99] The general difficulty was summed up by the Southern Provincial Commissioner in 1936 when he said of the tenants:

> Economically they are not badly off but socially they are not so happily placed. The majority live under "controlled" conditions, opposed to their way of life and irksome to them. They have no real fixity of tenure and their "resident" status conveys few privileges ... and they are not their own masters in any respect.[100]

During 1936, a major reduction was made in the amount of alienated land although this had little effect on land shortage and population pressure. When the Certificates of Claim were issued, the British South Africa Company – who took over the interests of the ALC – were granted 2,731,700 acres, covering practically the whole of the North Nyasa District. An Order-in-Council of 24 July 1936 confirmed the Company's renunciation of its freehold claims in return for its retention of mineral rights.[101] The population of this very large area was only 46,999, with a density of 10.8 to the square mile.[102]

Land congestion and the political security dangers in such congestion were absent, the area was distant from the European settlements of the Shire Highlands, and in practice the renunciation had little effect on the problem of Africans on private estates.

In 1937, Kittermaster discussed Africans on private estates at the Colonial Office, repeating that he was unable to put forward any constructive suggestions; following the view of his advisers, he then suggested waiting to see what the landlords would do at the end of the quinquennium the following year.[103] The Secretary of State in the meantime proposed to await the report of Sir Robert Bell on the finances of the protectorate in the hope, presumably, that Bell could make constructive suggestions.[104] During this year (1937), the Southern Provincial Commissioner reported that 'relationships between landlord and tenant [on the Bruce Magomero Estate had] not been good', and that the BCA Company had applied to evict 1,200 tenants for rent default, but settled for the eviction of 150 of the ringleaders whilst the government decided to 'observe the effect upon the remainder'.[105]

If the Secretary of State had hoped for positive guidance from Bell, he was disappointed. In his report, published in July 1938, he concluded that there were two possible courses of action: either to allow the conditions which had become stabilized over ten years to continue and 'if trouble arises in the future it can be dealt with in the light of the actual circumstances of the time'; or, alternatively, to try to distinguish – he did not suggest how – between original occupants and later tenants, making an equitable distinction between them so as to give the former free rights of occupancy whilst obliging the latter to enter into individual agreements with the landowner. He concluded, however, as had Kittermaster, that there was 'no certainty that such a result, however fair it might be to all the parties, would be accepted by them as satisfactory'. The choice was a matter of policy and Bell's advice – obvious, unhelpful, pragmatic, and very short term – was that:

> the only practical course at the moment is to ascertain the extent to which landowners exercise their right of issuing notices to quit and observe the effects.[106]

Whilst 984 notices to quit were issued (359 from BCA Company land, 289 from B&EA Company land, and 123 from Bruce Estates land), many tenants reached agreement with their landlords that they should stay on the land under special agreements.[107] In the event, no large number of evictions took place in 1938, and consequently no early action was taken, especially since the war intervened and occupied the energies and attention of most people in Nyasaland. Although there were a few evictions for rent default or misconduct, there were no serious problems and the evicted families were accommodated on Trust Land. Even so, Lord Hailey, who visited the country at this time, reported:

> the situation has provided in the past and may again provide incidents which prejudice the generally equable relations existing between Europeans and Africans ... The measures which have been taken towards a solution ... create a relationship which still contains many possibilities of friction ... If a solution is to be found, it is probable that it must be sought on bolder lines than those hitherto followed, and may even involve the acquisition of certain areas in the private estates in order to provide secured holdings for part of the native population now resident on them.[108]

Other signs of concern existed: the Native Welfare Committee in January 1939 said that:

> in some of the very crowded regions of the Southern Province there is a very general and justified complaint by natives that there are large undeveloped areas of land in the hands of owners of freehold estates ... The purchase of freehold land by Government may, in some cases, be necessary to relieve congestion.[109]

1940 was a worrying year. In January there was talk of 'a second rising' on the Chilembwe pattern and the Governor was sufficiently disturbed to remove the Bruce Magomero Estate manager from the protectorate.[110] 2,000 eviction notices for rent default were served in the Blantyre District, although few were enforced because most tenants agreed to undertake work in lieu of rent.[111] Rumours also circulated that the government intended to buy out landlords and abolish *thangata*.[112] The Governor warned Legislative Council at the end of 1940 that 'native land occupation' would have to be tackled as soon as time and staff permitted:

> We cannot settle an inconvenient problem of the first magnitude and importance by simply continuing to ignore it ... we must grasp this nettle, and a very rank and luxuriant weed it is.[113]

At this time, the British government was worried about land questions elsewhere in Africa, and Harold Macmillan, then at the Colonial Office, suggested, in the case of Kenya, the solution of government purchasing private estate land:

> During his brief period at the Colonial Office in 1942, he had suggested that the big, and rich, European farms in Kenya should be bought by the Crown and run as state companies, for the ultimate benefit of both whites and blacks, concluding with ominous prescience ... that "it will be less expensive than a civil war". Macmillan's revolutionary proposal was never taken up.[114]

Acute anxiety returned as the end of the next quinquennium approached in 1943. In 1942 and 1943, several hundreds of tenants in the Blantyre District who were served with orders to quit refused to leave, creating 'serious incidents'. The administration found that, although much of the difficulty stemmed from misunderstanding, there were genuine grievances against the estate owners. Even more disturbingly, agitation among tenants had increased and was now political: 'This appears to have been the first time that agitators had fished in these troubled waters.'[115] Senior administrative officers and leading non-officials now believed that serious trouble would arise if a solution was not soon found, and the Governor asked the Colonial Office to appoint 'an independent commission which could make an exhaustive examination of land questions'.[116]

In 1943, the government took an important, but little publicized, step by purchasing a private estate of 3,200 acres in the Shire Highlands, south of Blantyre, to resettle Africans 'under a controlled settlement scheme ... to demonstrate the best use of land in congested circumstances'.[117] Although the Africans resettled on this estate over the next few years were from Trust Land rather than from private estates, it was felt that the experience would be of value later when more private land was acquired.[118]

Early in 1945, two estate owners in Cholo tried to evict 1,250 rent-defaulting tenants and the government was faced with the daunting prospect of resettling this large number – totalling with their families over 5,000 people – on already congested land. One of these estates was the Mpezo estate from which the owners, the BCA Company, applied for the eviction of over 2,000 people. The District Commissioner, H. V. McDonald, through 'political and tactful handling', succeeded in reducing the evictions to about 120 families and found a number of grievances held strongly by the tenants: the apparent inequity of charging rent on estates but not on Trust Land; the reduction in the size of gardens by owners (which the 1917 and 1928 Ordinances had, by implication, permitted); and the refusal of owners to permit tenants' children to build huts and open gardens.[119]

As a result principally of these worrying portents and of the Governor's representations, the Secretary of State's 1935 suggestion that a Special Commissioner be appointed was revived, and Sir Sidney Abrahams was appointed on 22 July 1946.[120]

Thus, during the period 1900–1945, three general and three specific elements characterized the evolution of the problem of Africans on private estates in Nyasaland and the attempts to solve it. The general elements were: an increasing demand for labour, about which the government was pleased for economic reasons; increasing population pressure, about which the government could do little; and increasing African discontent, about which the government was worried but felt they need do nothing other than 'wait and see' and marginally improve the Africans' lot. The specific elements were: the position of the original occupants; *thangata* (labour tenure); and tenants' rights, in particular security of tenure.

The non-disturbance clause protection of the original occupants was maintained in law throughout the period, but was ignored in practice, and no distinction was made between original occupants and newcomers. Save that this displayed a weakness, a lack of determination on the part of the government to impose its will and ensure protection, no one other than Governor Young and a few of his district commissioners in the early 1930s seemed to be worried by this neglect.

Thangata, the right to demand labour of tenants, very soon became the only reason for owners voluntarily allowing settlers to enter and remain on their land. The B&EA Company's attempts to have this committed to written contracts failed because Nunan ruled it illegal in the case of the original occupants, and placed upon owners the extremely difficult task of proving that settlers were not original occupants. Since the 1904 Ordinance did not mention *thangata*, the 1903 *status quo* remained the legal position. The 1909 Ordinance precluded direct *thangata* but owners achieved it indirectly by paying wages or tax for compulsory labour. The 1917 Ordinance expressly made *thangata* illegal but the owners openly defied it. The Jackson Commission in 1920, without saying whether *thangata* was or was not legal, recommended that it be recognized and confined to two months' labour a year. The 1928 Ordinance made the undertaking of *thangata* voluntary: the tenant could choose to pay money rent or offer to grow crops or to work for the owner. The 1934 Select Committee recommended that it continue to be voluntary, but if undertaken should be the subject of separate written contracts.

With regard to the rights of tenants, throughout the period there was a general acceptance that they were entitled to a site and materials for a hut and sufficient cultivable land to sustain their families (although stipulating an acreage was abandoned in 1917). In respect of security of tenure, subject to the payment of rent if required, the B&EA Company contracts required five months' notice to quit, whilst the 1904 Ordinance provided for perpetual security on locations excised from the estates. The 1914 Bill and the 1917 Ordinance required six months' notice to quit, but the Ordinance, unlike the Bill, did not make it conditional upon alternative accommodation being provided. In 1920, Jackson introduced the notions of security over a four-year period and of evictions limited to 10 per thousand acres. The 1928 Ordinance extended the detail of these notions in favour of the tenants by granting security over a five-year period and by limiting evictions to 10 per cent of the resident population. Since this Ordinance also placed a duty on the government to accommodate evictees on Crown Land, and since there was a severe shortage of such land in the Shire Highlands, the government in practice found it extremely difficult – and in some cases impossible – to enforce any significant number of eviction notices.

During the period up to 1945, the problem evolved of how to balance the rights of freeholders to do as they liked with their land, the need to use as much of the country's land as possible to accommodate a fast increasing population and to grow economic crops, plus the need to facilitate the supply of labour to estates which were the main wealth-creating agencies, against the duty to protect the African people and ensure that they were not exploited.

Whilst doing little to remove the basic problem, the government did take steps, albeit limited ones, to improve the lot of African tenants on estates. It is true that nothing *de facto* was done to protect those who should have benefited from the non-disturbance clauses, but this seemed to worry very few. Labour tenure was made an alternative to money rent at the choice of the tenant, and security was improved by restricting evictions without cause to quinquennial periods and to 10 per cent of the residents.

Why, then, did the government not do more? There were demographic, economic and political factors concerning land which provide an answer to this question. Basically, there was only a given amount of land to support the country's population, and from a narrow point of view the government did not mind whether the Africans lived on Trust Land or on private estates: they were gratified that many lived on private estates and were consequently reluctant to take any steps which would make owners less willing to accept and retain Africans on them. In addition, as an agricultural country, Nyasaland depended economically on its land and the use of its land. So long as estate agriculture contributed so massively to the nation's economic wealth through employment and exports, the government was deeply reluctant to do anything which would decrease the supply of labour upon which that wealth depended. The government wanted Africans to work on private estates.

On the political side, two factors combined to reduce the government's incentive to do more to improve the lot of the Africans on private estates: the considerable political strength of the Europeans, especially the large landowning companies; and the failure of the Africans to highlight and exploit their grievances – in effect their failure to cause sufficient anxiety to the owners and to the government to persuade them to take more positive action. In this latter respect, the existence and predominance of corporate absentee landlords, controlling very large areas of land, was significant, since it was very much more difficult to take effective action locally to influence, persuade, embarrass, even frighten, such landlords than to take similar action against small resident owners. On the whole, relationships with the smaller owners were good and it was the larger, company, estates which presented the greatest difficulties.

3

The Abrahams Commission, 1946, and the Land Planning Committee, 1947

Abrahams spent from 25 July to 4 October collecting evidence and submitted his report on 31 October 1946; it was published early in 1947. He took evidence from 80 individuals, including estate owners, government officers, Africans, and missionaries; and from 37 associations, including 16 of chiefs, 10 of the Nyasaland African Congress, and 3 of missions. He visited every district in the protectorate except Kota Kota, from where he nonetheless met, at Lilongwe, the District Commissioner, the chiefs, and a delegation from the African Congress. J. H. Ingham, Secretary to the Commission, felt that, although Abrahams was a distinguished former colonial Chief Justice, he approached the Nyasaland problem in 'a very unjudicial' fashion, basing his report – which he dictated in a single day – on the 'endless discussions' which he had with Ingham whilst travelling to take evidence.[1]

In his report, he summarized the problems as seen by Africans as: the landlords' concept of land rights being contrary to African ideas; the failure of the law to cater for customary practices; some landlords' infringement of the law and, in other cases, the harsh exercise of their legal rights; and the Africans' inability to understand their rights and obligations under a very complex law. The landlords' complaints were: quinquennial evictions were not politically practicable where large numbers were involved; the 1928 Ordinance did not give what was most wanted (i.e., labour); and the inability in many cases to offer work or facilities for growing crops.[2]

Abrahams found that in every district in which there were estate Africans a number of occurrences had 'excited resentment' or there was apprehension that it was easy for landlords to 'do something at any time to disturb seriously [the] traditional mode of life'.[3] Additionally:

There was not a single district ... with the exception of Fort Johnston, where this grievance ['the possession of large unused areas of land by non-natives'] was not presented ... by deputations of chiefs, by the local branch of the African Congress and by other natives, first in a memorandum and afterwards orally.[4]

Abrahams saw the problem as essentially a conflict between European concepts of freehold land and African concepts of communally held land, and the true difficulty as a failure to appreciate this. The Attorney General had, of course, already stated the conflict of ideas very clearly in 1914, although Abrahams did not acknowledge this.[5] The European estate owner wanted, and believed that he should have the right, to demand rent or (preferably) labour; to select his own tenants and to eject them if they neglected their obligations or became a nuisance; and not to have to cater for burdensome African customary practices despite a general willingness to tolerate those which he considered not to be burdensome. The African tenants wanted, and believed that they should have the right, to live precisely as their fellows on Trust Land, free of rent and obligations in lieu of rent, with security to live in accordance with African law and custom; and to be able to select their own employer or person to whom they sold their crops.[6] Abrahams concluded that reconciliation between the conflicting ideas could not be achieved and – making Bell's point about the choice being a matter of policy – compromise was 'out of the question':

> the only solution is the clear-cut one of getting rid of the status of resident native and leaving him free to quit the estate or stay there on terms satisfactory both to himself and the landlord, substituting contractual for statutory rights.[7]

He referred to this process – which barely differed from the 1917 Ordinance's aims – as 'emancipation', and emphasized that it would be possible only if Trust Land were available to accommodate Africans wishing to leave private land.[8] The word 'emancipation' had connotations of slavery or serfdom and this, coupled with his reference to leaving the resident African free to quit the estate – which gave the false impression that Africans were not free to quit estates – was an unfortunate word to use. Abrahams expressed his solution in disarmingly simple terms:

> There are three problems to be solved, namely the economic problem of the relief of congestion on Native Trust Land, the political problem of satisfying the sense of grievance that Europeans are holding large tracts of undeveloped land while the natives are suffering the acute pangs of land hunger, and the problem of emancipating the resident natives. If the first two problems are settled by the practical method of acquisition of these undeveloped lands, it follows automatically that the ... third problem will be solved since the resident natives are living there. If, on the other hand, the resident natives on undeveloped lands are emancipated by acquisition of the lands, and that is the only practical way in which it can be done, then automatically the other two problems are entirely solved.[9]

In either case, he claimed, acquiring undeveloped private land would solve all three problems. In both cases he relied on sufficient undeveloped land being available to absorb the excess population on Trust Land.

Following, although not acknowledging, the train of thought which had run from Nunan, through Hetherwick, *Life and Work*, Jackson, Bowring, Ormsby-Gore, the 1928 Ordinance, Young, the 1939 Native Welfare Committee, and Hailey, he recommended that private land which was both unoccupied and uncultivated – what Johnston had described as 'waste land' in heavily populated areas half a century earlier – should be acquired to relieve congestion on neighbouring Trust Land or provide space for emancipated families from nearby estates. Land occupied and cultivated by resident Africans should also be acquired 'for the purpose of emancipation if it is situated in congested areas'. With the 'comparative few' (as he saw them) resident Africans living not on undeveloped land but in areas scattered on developed estates, Abrahams advised that the owners should be invited to place all resident Africans on contracts which gave residence rights on condition that they worked for an agreed period – which would have institutionalized *thangata* – and, if the owners agreed, the Africans on Private Estates Ordinance should cease to apply to them.

In their turn, the resident Africans should be invited to opt between entering into the contract or leaving the estate and living on Trust Land (to be enlarged by acquisitions) and being compensated by the government.[10] This was an important recommendation because, by having the tenants leave the unacquired areas, the owners would be left with unoccupied land which they could develop, knowing that the Ordinance no longer applied to them and encroachment could be controlled. The words 'invited to opt' are also important because they do not suggest any government pressure to leave. Where unoccupied and uncultivated land, and land occupied and cultivated by resident Africans, existed on the same estate as land worked by wage labour or visiting cultivators, Abrahams recommended that if the former lands were excisable they should be purchased.[11] He also recommended that estate owners of land which the government wished otherwise to acquire should be allowed to retain 'a reasonable portion of land' for development within a reasonable period of time.[12]

Abrahams was most anxious to test his recommendations on, and secure the support of, both Europeans and Africans. In the case of Europeans, he consulted government officers, estate managers, individual owners including missionaries, the Convention of Associations, and the Cholo Settlers' Association. In the case of Africans, he consulted the African provincial councils, the African Congress, councils of chiefs, and a number of leading African personalities. Only in Port Herald and Mlanje Districts, which he visited first before he had arrived at his solution, was he unable to sound African opinion, but 'in view ... of the unqualified, and I might say almost enthusiastic, approval with which the suggested scheme was met in all the other districts, I find it hard to believe that the reception would have been any different in these two districts'.[13] Abrahams visited Port Herald and Mlanje only a fortnight after his arrival in Nyasaland, so it appears that within two weeks of arriving he had reached a solution and then, possibly, spent the next two months securing support for it, or acquiescence in it.

Abrahams was much gratified by the warmth which his proposals received:

> The results of these consultations both with Europeans and natives were most encouraging. There was no criticism of the scheme from any quarter.[14]

The reception with which the scheme was met by the natives was even more gratifying. Except in one [quickly corrected] instance it was immediately acclaimed with unqualified approval, and in some cases with great enthusiasm.[15]

I think that I am entitled to say that in view of this volume of opinion, European and native, that the scheme has no obvious defect and if there is a latent fault which would seriously affect the success of its operation, I have sinned in good company.[16]

He emphasized the dangers of failing quickly 'to satisfy the political grievances aggravated by land hunger' which were now 'receiving form, direction and force from organised bodies composed of the more intelligent members of [the African] community',[17] and made frequent reference to this:

> It is obvious that a state of affairs which has poisoned the relations between the estate owners and those who work for them, to say nothing of the relations between European and African in general, must contain the seeds of many forms of trouble.[18]

He added that many civil servants, especially administrative officers, and also non-officials, including many estate owners, particularly those of long-standing and considerable experience, 'expressed their view that trouble will arise if a solution is not found'.[19]

He went on to point out that 'if the Government does decide to acquire areas ... on which there is still room for further settlement, it is necessary that these lands should be jealously protected against indiscriminate settlement ... and unsupervised cultivation'. He advocated closely controlled settlement of families from private estates using settlement officers in 'a strong team of Executives'. He thought also that the government should appoint a principal settlement officer: 'an experienced administrative officer with knowledge of the problem, influence with the natives, keenness for the work and proven tact in dealing with Europeans and natives'. He did not think it would be difficult to find such a person: he almost certainly had McDonald in mind.

Abrahams also recommended a Planning Committee of very senior civil servants and disinterested non-officials to consider which land should be acquired, in what order, the method of settlement, the staff required, the cost involved, and the compensation to be paid. Acquisition of private land should be negotiated, including arbitration and umpiring if needed, but if that failed, or if negotiations were refused – 'an extremely improbable event' in Abrahams' view – then compulsory acquisition would be necessary. He could not suggest a means of financing the acquisitions by contributions from either landowners or tenants which would be 'both equitable and practical', but he suggested the Native Development and Welfare Fund – 'designed to promote the welfare or the social or economic development' of the African people. He also recommended that private land might be acquired by exchanging it for a right of occupancy of Trust Land without rent, which 'might be good business for [the estate owners] and of considerable assistance to Government'.[20] This was not a new idea since Executive Council during the 1920s agreed to many such applications, especially from the large land companies.[21]

The government published the Abrahams Report on 15 February 1947,[22] and a few days later it was discussed very briefly in Legislative Council. The Governor, Richards, at the time warmly welcomed it with optimism, regarding it as a:

> most clear sighted and helpful survey of the land question in this country and as the most valuable contribution yet made to the final solution of this serious problem.[23]

Six weeks later, after Richards had left the country on retirement, Brown, the Chief Secretary, in his role of Acting Governor, appointed a Land Planning Committee to obtain the information required to reach decisions on the Report's recommendations. As Abrahams suggested, the membership of the Committee included the Acting Chief Secretary, Talbot Edwards, as Chairman (although he had been in Nyasaland less than six months, having previously served in Nigeria); the Financial Secretary, C. W. F. Footman; the Attorney General, W. J. Lockhart Smith; the Lands Officer, W. G. Alcock; the Cholo District Commissioner, McDonald; and the Acting Director of Agriculture, E. Lawrence. The other members were the Development Secretary, R. H. Keppel Compton, and a Non-official Member of Legislative and Executive Councils, M. P. Barrow. Forestry and

Veterinary Department representatives, although recommended by Abrahams, were not appointed.[24]

The Committee co-opted a dozen European non-officials: Sir William Tait Bowie, manager of the B&EA Company; Kaye Nicol, manager of the BCA Company; Sibbald, manager of the A. L. Bruce Estates; Harris, manager of the Cholo and Michiru Tea and Tobacco Estates; Ferguson of the Zambezi Mission; Fathers Dissard and Hardman of the Montfort Marist Fathers Mission; Raynes of the ALC; Rev. W. H. Watson of the Livingstonia Mission; Rodgers and Borrowman of the Blantyre Mission; and J. Tennett, a Cholo estate owner. They also received evidence from eight African Chiefs, all from the Shire Highlands; Nchema of Chiradzulu; Chimombo and Chimalira of Cholo; Mabuka of Mlanje; Mlumbe and Chikowi of Zomba; and Somba and Machinjiri of Blantyre.[25] In their published report the Committee did not mention the co-opted members or the African Chiefs.[26]

The members, observing that 200,000 Africans were resident on private estates which totalled 1,207,000 acres (5.1 per cent of the protectorate's land area) were deeply conscious of the magnitude and complexity of their task, the amount of detailed planning required, the likely expenditure – probably over a million pounds – and the length of time the operation would take to gather, collate and study information, to agree on the action to be taken on each individual estate, to excise areas, and to employ surveyors. Yet time was not on their side. Abrahams had foreseen that much time would be required but felt that alleviating African discontent provided a pressing reason for an early announcement of the government's intentions. Largely as a result of Abrahams' visit, African interest in solving the land problems had intensified, and this, together with the approach of the quinquennial eviction period in August 1948, persuaded the Committee that more immediate steps than originally contemplated were demanded. Consequently, at the same time as requesting from district commissioners information on the size and degree of development of the estates and the number of tenants in their districts, they also sought recommendations as to which of those estates that were not cultivated under direct supervision should be immediately acquired by the government.[27]

The Committee concluded that in the Shire Highlands districts where the difficulties were most acute, much of the trouble resulted from industrialization, in which term they included intensive agricultural development, and here the heavy concentration of population was on both private and Trust land, making necessary an adjustment from shifting to more settled agriculture. The adjustment was slowly taking place and inevitably involved some friction, to which part of the political problem could be attributed. More clearly evident was the resentment of Africans in the less intensely developed areas when viewing large tracts of unused land held by Europeans. Although there was generally a welcome acceptance of Europeans actively working and developing the estates:

> The growth of racial self-consciousness may perhaps be a contributory cause of the resentment felt by Africans against the holding of tracts of land held by Europeans and at present undeveloped by them.[28]

In turning to which areas the government should acquire, the Committee was guided by the principle that all land should be put to the best use possible in the interests of the protectorate as a whole. These were significantly more economic than political, for they recommended that there should be no wholesale acquisition of undeveloped land suitable for European cultivation when an assurance of development within a reasonable period was given; that estates acquired primarily for African settlement which could be more suitably developed by intensive methods should be granted on long lease to Europeans; that no actively worked estate should be acquired; that when part of an estate was acquired, sufficient land should be left to permit development within a reasonable period; that all estates suitable for African settlement offered to the government should be acquired; and that all fully settled undeveloped estates in congested areas should be acquired.[29]

In considering Abrahams' recommendation that the government should acquire all estates fully occupied by resident Africans, together with those unoccupied and uncultivated if acquisition would relieve congestion on neighbouring Trust Land, and also provide settlement areas for Africans wishing to leave estates, the Committee encountered little difficulty, although they pointed out that in the areas where congestion was most severe, most estates were either already developed or earmarked for early development so that the amount of unoccupied land available for acquisition was negligible. They met considerable difficulty, however, in respect of his recommendation that on estates partially developed and partially occupied by resident Africans, the latter areas should be excised wherever the estate was divisible without being unfair to the owner.[30]

The problem now encountered, a problem unforeseen or insufficiently considered by Abrahams and apparently by members of the Committee itself, was that in the intensely developed areas, where the difficulties were greatest, nearly all the estates were indivisible. This meant that the Committee was faced with reaching a solution without following Abrahams' recommendation of acquiring all the land which the resident Africans then occupied.[31]

Although Abrahams had not foreseen this difficulty, he had been aware of his lack of detailed information, and in his letter to the Governor covering his report he was careful to include reference to this:

> I have been unable to reach completely accurate conclusions on such subjects as congestion of population, cultivability of the soil and European development owing to the absence of a scientific survey of the country and the lack of persons who could give specific evidence of a fully reliable nature in respect to a particular case. In such cases I have had to rely upon general impressions enabling me to reach approximate conclusions, or upon the rule of thumb.[32]

It is puzzling that Abrahams felt that he had to rely so much on general impressions and rule of thumb because, although no scientific survey of the country had been made, there were many administrative and agricultural officers with considerable field experience in the important areas, and there were also many estate owners and their employees with considerable experience who, whilst not perhaps being able to give evidence of a fully reliable nature, should have been able to place Abrahams' understanding well beyond the level of general impressions and rule of thumb. Indeed, in his report he made reference to 'administrative officers, agricultural officers, estate owners, chiefs and headmen intimately acquainted with local conditions'[33] in the congested area of the Shire Highlands, and members of the Land Planning Committee adduced more detailed evidence which cast grave doubts on Abrahams' recommendations within a few months of his report being published. Nonetheless, having expressed himself as being aware of his lack of detailed information, he dismissed its significance by saying, 'I do not think ... that my recommendations need be unduly qualified on this account.'³⁴ Consequently, he recommended that in the case of indivisible estates – which he assumed to be few in number and limited in extent – the Africans should be invited to opt between entering into a contract or leaving the estate. But, as has been mentioned, there was in fact very little undeveloped land sufficiently nearby for the resident Africans to be agreeable to move to it, and it was unlikely that the Africans would readily agree to move to distant areas away from their relatives:

> In short, the recommendations in the report for these partially developed and partially occupied estates were founded on two hypotheses, the first being that a large number of such estates would be found to be readily divisible, and the second being that large scale acquisition of suitable undeveloped land in the same neighbourhood would be practicable. It was the unquestioning acceptance of these hypotheses that secured for Sidney Abrahams the strong support he obtained for his proposals. But after close and detailed examination of the estates involved this committee has been forced to come to the conclusion that the true position is not as it was generally accepted to be, and that it does not lend itself to action on the lines proposed in the Abrahams Report. The problem of the emancipation of natives living on estates under active European development therefore still remains.³⁵

The Committee consequently dealt first with the divisible estates – those which, though partially developed, contained compact (not scattered) areas occupied by Africans – and made specific recommendations. In the highly congested Cholo District, they planned for the concentration of the African population in compact villages in areas to be acquired adjacent to the tea and tung estates so that the Africans, who were in any case fairly recent immigrants, could choose between: living in the villages, with small gardens, and working on the estates; remaining on the estates as contract tenants; or moving some distance elsewhere where larger gardens might be available.³⁶ Their proposals would continue the supply of labour for the estates whilst not allowing that labour to take up too much cultivable land, and at the same time encourage African commercial foodstuffs production albeit at some distance from the estate areas. It was:

no longer possible for a man to work for a few hours as a labourer on an estate and for the remainder of his time to attempt to cultivate his own farm. Apart from the fact that there is not enough land available in the neighbourhood, the ... disappearance of the part-time peasant agriculturalist would not only make much more land available for the genuine farmer but it would provide the latter with an assured and lucrative market in supplying the rest of the urban and rural wage-earners ... there can be no ordered development of this part of Nyasaland unless such differentiation is begun immediately.[37]

They were anxious to emphasize, in their draft report[38] (but not in the published version) that they were not encouraging large numbers to become landless wage-earning labourers – and thus at the mercy of their employers or the vagaries of the economy – since the amount of land used by European estates would continue to be relatively insignificant compared to that available for African agriculture. The Committee foresaw that those who worked on estates with small or no gardens, if they wished, could return from time to time to their more distant and larger village gardens.[39]

In the published report, the Committee simply said 'The land which we have recommended for acquisition in the Cholo District consists of four separate blocks,' but in a draft they went into quite specific details of the areas involved.[40] The north-eastern block of 12,000 acres and the north-western block of 6,000 acres belonged to the BCA Company, and the General Manager personally thought that the Company would be prepared to sell this land to the government 'in view of the serious nature of the political problem', despite the fact that such sale would seriously interfere with the Company's ten-year development plan to grow soya, sisal, tung and tobacco, items 'all urgently needed' by Britain – a point which would not be lost on the British government when mentioned to them by the London directors. Kaye Nicol believed that 'it would be in the best long-term interests of the Protectorate to hand over the land to Government for use by Africans'. This was a view which, even if genuinely held personally by the General Manager, was not necessarily also held by his London directors, and the focus on the long-term enabled the Company, as things turned out, to avoid taking much early action in handing over land to the government. Tait Bowie said that he believed the B&EA Company would probably be prepared to sell the

Ruo Estate of 12,500 acres to the government to form the west-central block. In the east-central block, Harris believed that his company, the Cholo and Michiru Tea and Tobacco Estates, would be prepared to sell the Tuchila Estate of 3,038 acres, and recommended that the government should also buy part of the ALC's Gotha estate which Raynes thought his company would be prepared to sell.[41]

In all, 33,538 acres in the Cholo District were to be purchased: 54 per cent of this belonged to the BCA Company.[42] There appears at this time to have been a considerable willingness on the part of the local managers, representing some of the very largest landowners in the country, to be prepared to sell land to the government. None of these details and none of this willingness was referred to in the published report.

In the published report, no mention was made of the Magomero Estate but the draft report made it clear that the owners, A.L. Bruce Estates, had already offered to sell it to the government, and they recommended that all but 10,000 acres round the factory preparing tobacco for the West Africa trade should be acquired for possible future European development, for settling present resident Africans, for resettling Africans from elsewhere, and for government large-scale 'collectivised' farming.[43]

In the Blantyre District, the Committee recognized a problem different from that found elsewhere. There, in the peri-urban area surrounding the Blantyre and Limbe townships which were expected to expand considerably, they recommended that areas be set aside as accommodation areas for the urban workers. These peri-urban areas would contain only small garden plots and those who wished to farm larger areas would have to move elsewhere.[44]

In all, the Committee recommended the purchase of 545,857 acres of the protectorate's 1,200,000 acres of private land. Of the land recommended for purchase, 80 per cent was in the Shire Highlands Districts – 235,502 in the Zomba District, 103,592 in the Blantyre District, 35,212 in the Mlanje District, 33,538 in the Cholo District – with the remainder scattered throughout other districts. They advised that 453,641 acres, or 83 per cent, of the total should be acquired immediately.[45]

The Committee felt it necessary to make a statement about further acquisition, and in both their draft report and the published version they said that, if their recommendations were adopted, the government should make it 'perfectly' or 'very' clear that 'no further large scale acquisition of freehold land [would] be practicable without seriously prejudicing the European development upon which the prosperity of the [country] so largely depends'.[46] In the draft report, but not in the published version, these words were followed by:

> We emphasise that our recommendations provide a palliative for, not a permanent solution of, an urgent political problem, but it is a palliative which cannot in any circumstances be repeated.

The words which appeared in the published version (and which preceded rather than followed the passage quoted) were:

> We recognise that much of the land acquired by Europeans in the early days has either not been developed or fallen out of use and does not now ... lend itself to European development. To meet an urgent political situation ... such land should now be acquired. Indeed ... the acquisition of land is essential, not only for the solution of the political problem ... but also to prepare for the orderly settlement of Africans working in or near the main industrial areas.

The 'palliative' had become a 'solution': perhaps the Committee reasoned that solutions do not have to 'be repeated' whereas palliatives might have to be repeated. They were also laying down the limits of acquisition: that is, land which did not 'lend itself to European development', but not land capable of 'European development upon which the prosperity of the [country] so largely depends'.

Having dealt with the acquisition of private estate land, members turned their attention to settlement on that land.[47] They expressed the view that the very heavy expenditure involved would be largely wasted unless from the very beginning they ensured controlled settlement. Abrahams had expressed the same point when he said that the acquired land 'should be jealously protected against indiscriminate settlement and unorganised cultivation'. The Committee recognized that the control would also be expensive. They thought that, whilst the broad outline of policy should be laid down by the government at the centre, the settlement of all acquired estates should be the responsibility of the district commissioner in whose district the estates were located.

The Committee was at pains to emphasize its proposals for collective farming:

> The acquisition of large new tracts of land will present Government with an unique opportunity to embark on collective farming schemes on a large scale; indeed it is our considered view that it is only by the introduction of some such methods that the best use can be made of much of this newly acquired land ... By collective farming we mean the farming of small holdings in a single block by large scale farming methods.[48]

Although the Committee did not make it clear, these proposals could be applied only to those areas of private land which had relatively few African residents on them, and which were largely undeveloped – areas such as the Bruce Magomero and BCA Company Chingale estates – and could not be applied to the heavily populated Cholo areas.

They did, however, deal with the view of a number of estate owners: that there were large areas of Trust Land in other parts of Nyasaland which the government should develop and to which the government should compel Africans to move from congested areas.[49] This view was connected with a proposal, made by the Convention of Associations shortly before Abrahams' visit, which advocated a government scheme to settle European ex-soldier farmers.[50] The Committee rejected these ideas on the grounds that such areas were usually far distant from the settled parts, and that compulsory settlement schemes would not be successful and would defeat the object of the Land Commission Report which was to remove discontent: it could not provide an 'immediate solution to the present political problem'.

On the other hand, the Committee believed that where land was sufficient for the immediate and future African needs, or where land was available, unoccupied and unsuitable for African cultivation, alienation should be considered provided: first, that it was in the general interest of the community; second, that the proposed tenant – presumably European – was 'of a type who will be an asset to the country'; and third, that intensive agricultural development would be used and the natural resources conserved. The Committee advocated that the government should make an early policy statement on this proposal, although they did not indicate where such land was to be found: possibly they had in mind some of the Trust Land in the Central Province which was suitable for flue-cured tobacco cultivation.[51]

The Committee members were aware of a number of facts and considerations which they felt the government might, for political reasons, not wish to publish, and which were recorded in a confidential appendix to the draft report.[52] They recalled that Abrahams had formed the very firm impression that the Africans expected their grievances to be remedied and their claims satisfied as a result of his report, and that if this did not happen there might be very serious consequences. The Committee had no doubt that this impression was correct. In his Annual Reports for 1946 and 1947, the Provincial Commissioner of the Southern Province had said that the 'report of Government's policy regarding the acquisition of alienated land for resettlement is eagerly awaited by the chiefs and people', and that his ability to settle individual cases under the Natives on Private Estates Ordinance had 'been maintained [only] in expectation of the radical solution to be found' by the government.[53] They directed their attention to how far the acquisitions recommended in their report would go to satisfy African expectations and concluded that they could be satisfied only if extensive areas of freehold land in the Cholo and Blantyre Districts (which were not in their report) were acquired by the government. Whereas all of the areas recommended in their published report would, they believed, be offered voluntarily for sale – indeed, the general managers of the large estates had led them to believe this – these additional lands could be acquired only through compulsion unless the owners could be persuaded to change their minds. However, they advised against compulsory acquisition on the grounds that:

> Nyasaland has been fortunate hitherto in being comparatively free from racial troubles. To resort to compulsory acquisition at a time when European capital is seeking opportunity in the country and when estate owners are planning to make up for the time lost during the war in long term development of their estates might so alienate European opinion and sympathy as to endanger the happy relations which have so far existed between the majority of European estate owners and their African labour. It might also prevent the further investment of European

capital, without which the prospects of future prosperity would be but slight.[54]

In addition, even if compulsory acquisition were resorted to, the likely result would be only a temporary solution to the problem of congestion, and it might even provide 'an example of the remedy proving worse than the disease'.

The land which the Committee had in mind was land owned by the BCA Company, 'the largest owner of land and the largest owner of undeveloped land in the Protectorate', and the 'target of considerable criticism on general grounds by African opinion' which was particularly sensitive on land issues in the Southern Province. The Company owned large undeveloped estates in Blantyre and Cholo Districts in the most heavily congested areas of the Shire Highlands. That these areas were not a great deal more extensive was the result of the government having redeemed the railway subsidy lands in 1913. As on adjacent Trust Land, where the population density was over 400 to the square mile, these lands were entirely cultivated by tenants on a subsistence basis. In recent years, large numbers of tenants had refused to pay rent and the Committee feared, at the least, embarrassment and political discontent at the end of the quinquennium in 1948 if the Company again applied for mass evictions.

Whilst they believed that the other two major landowners, the B&EA Company and the A. L. Bruce Estates, at least under their current management, would not be the source of serious tenant trouble, the same could not be said of the BCA Company. This was because, in addition to the general grievance against large areas of undeveloped land, the BCA Company was the source of other grievances: compulsory movement of gardens and huts; refusal to permit cash crops in rebate of rent; poor personal relationships and a lack of active interest in tenant welfare; the unfortunate personality of the European estate superintendents and their attitude towards Africans; and the perpetual fear among tenants of the arbitrary eviction of 10 per cent of their number at the end of each quinquennium. The Provincial Commissioner of the Southern Province believed that it was not possible to exaggerate the inherent dangers, and the Committee agreed.[55]

The BCA Company was not prepared to sell these additional undeveloped lands, notwithstanding the political dangers which the General Manager had acknowledged, and notwithstanding the advice

THE ABRAHAMS COMMISSION AND THE LAND PLANNING COMMITTEE 63

of Nunan, which Abrahams had recently repeated, that the landowners should:

> face the matter as businessmen ... They will find that their interests are so bound up with the natives of this country that they will be best served by a prompt, a fair and a reasonable settlement.[56]

The Company claimed that under a fifteen-year development plan the estates would be extensively cultivated and would additionally provide four acres per tenant family, the tenants to be placed on special agreements and restricted to areas near the development areas to provide labour for the expansion of cultivation. The Committee dismissed these plans as 'patently impracticable' and they demonstrated that this was so.[57] They doubted whether the manager's 'emancipation' proposals would improve relationships between the Company and its tenants, and had even graver doubts as to whether he really appreciated the political significance of past troubles and the threat of future troubles:

> He gave the impression that he considered that any unrest among the tenants was entirely the responsibility of Government and that he was unaware of the extent to which the Company's policy in the past was the cause of unrest or how such unrest might involve the whole of the Shire Highlands.[58]

The Committee could conceive of only one way to arrest the growing discontent among the BCA Company tenants: by acquiring those thickly populated blocks of their land which it was clearly impossible for them to develop without wholesale disturbance of tenants. Yet, drawing back from compulsory acquisition, they said it was 'infinitely preferable' that:

> the Company should be brought to realise that it was in their own interests and in the interests of the protectorate as a whole, that such land should be offered to the Government for voluntary sale.[59]

They suggested that, because the matter was so important, this should be done by the government with the London directors, and they felt that if the Board could be made to understand the situation and its implications, they would co-operate. Clearly they had little confidence in the local General Manager – who had prevaricated over the political dangers involved – and were determined to by-pass him.[60]

In summary, then, the Land Planning Committee's enquiries and deliberations led to the recommendations that the shortage of land in the Shire Highlands, and the indivisibility of many partly developed estates there, prevented a solution along Abrahams' lines; that four blocks should be acquired in the Cholo District on which Africans who opted to leave retained land could be accommodated; that suburban residental areas in the Blantyre District should be similarly acquired; that further large-scale acquisition was impracticable and the government should say so; that collective farming should be embarked upon; that acquisition and other plans should include some European development; that compulsory acquisition was undesirable; and that the large blocks of BCA Company land in the Cholo and Blantyre Districts should be acquired by persuading the London directors of the political need to sell them to the government. In respect of relieving congestion on Trust Land, they felt there were no permanent solutions but only palliatives such as acquiring freehold land, developing new areas of African Trust Land, and improving agricultural practices. They felt their recommendations would go a long way to solve the political problem of satisfying the African grievance that Europeans held large tracts of undeveloped land whilst they themselves suffered acute pangs of land hunger. As for the social problem of emancipating Africans resident on estates under active development, however, they felt their recommendations would not contribute much.

These were the recommendations which awaited Sir Geoffrey Colby when he arrived in Nyasaland as Governor late in March 1948.

4
Sir Geoffrey Colby's early reactions, 1948-53

Since Colby was to play a major part in settling the question of Africans on private estates, it is important to give a brief account of his career before becoming Governor and to show what his priorities in Nyasaland were.[1]

Colby was born in 1901, the eldest son of three, and was brought up in Surrey, in a middle class, professional, Church of England, conservative family. On his father's side were three generations of medical practitioners and his mother came from a business family. At the age of seven, he went to preparatory school at Bexhill and stayed there until he was thirteen, in an environment emphasizing 'strict principles and manly games', with a strong cricketing tradition, with Christian influences, and an association with the children of parents in 'the armed or administrative services of the Crown' overseas. In 1914, he went to Charterhouse where he stayed until he was eighteen. This was an important period when significant influences were brought to bear on him. The Carthusian life stressed qualities of leadership, hierarchy, empire, public service, and unruffled reaction to emergencies. He excelled at cricket and played both cricket and football for the School; games were important at Charterhouse, emphasizing competition, leadership and status. From 1919 to 1922, Colby was a scholar at Clare College, Cambridge, where the Charterhouse influences were extended and to them was added the encouragement to make his own decisions as to how he was to arrange his life and life style. After a year back at his old preparatory school as an assistant master, principally so that he could play cricket for the Cryptics, and a sobering year at Galashiels working in a fellmongers' factory, he successfully applied for an appointment in the Colonial Administrative Service and in 1925 was posted to Nigeria.

His career in Nigeria took him from the Northern Provinces as a District Officer, into the Kaduna Secretariat Lands and Mines Department, and back into the districts. Then, in 1939, he was posted to the Lagos Secretariat, first as Assistant Secretary in the Finance Branch, and later as Deputy Director, and subsequently Director, of the Supply Branch. In 1945, he was promoted to be Administrative Secretary – superseding sixty officers – and acted as Chief Secretary and Governor's Deputy. From this position he was promoted to be Governor of Nyasaland.

From the outset in Nyasaland, Colby made rapid and substantial economic development his major, virtually all-consuming, concern. He was an outstanding development governor. The country was, in his own words, 'overdue for a little development' and Lucas Phillips has written:

> Until after the Second World War no development whatever took place in the country, and it had no legs to stand on in the money markets of the world. Sir Geoffrey Colby then came on the scene as Governor and by his drive infused new blood into the torpid body.[2]

The objective of his development strategy was to raise living standards to the extent that the people of Nyasaland might 'live better and happier lives' and to 'bring nearer the day when [they could] enjoy a prosperity and general standard of living far higher' than that which they then enjoyed. He determined to secure this objective through four inter-related means: raising individual incomes; improving social services; extending public utilities; and expanding the supply of consumer goods. Since Nyasaland was overwhelmingly an agricultural country heavily dependent upon land on which to produce crops, individual incomes could be significantly raised only by substantially increasing the quantity and quality of crops from the land. He aimed to improve social services and to extend public utilities, with the proceeds of taxation derived from the increased individual incomes, although in the case of public utilities he also secured support from British government loans and grants. He used his powers of licensing to encourage the supply of consumer goods, but again the supply reacted to the demand based on improved incomes derived from agriculture and the land.

The importance to Colby of an early solution to the question of

Africans on private estates was its effect on his economic development strategy. The European-owned estates contributed significant wealth to the economy, particularly through growing tea and tobacco, but also through commercial activity. Yet African agriculture was potentially even more important, and Colby was determined to increase production by African farmers. He recognized the political dangers of not solving the problem and feared that unrest would divert resources, attention and energy from the prime task of economic development. He clearly saw the inevitability of increasing African political interest and power. In July 1948, only three months after his arrival, Colby used words which bore a remarkable similarity to Macmillan's 1960 'wind of change' speeches (drafted by Sir David Hunt and James Robertson and originally intended to be delivered by R. A. Butler in 1958).[3] Colby had said:

> It is inevitable ... that the very considerable [political] development and awakening that has taken place in ... West Africa will take place here. We ... must be ready to receive the impact that is sweeping Africa ... It must come and ... we cannot expect conditions to remain unchanged.[4]

He was a man in a hurry; initially he was appointed for only five years, although this was subsequently increased to eight; there were many years of neglect to be remedied. He realized, as few others did so clearly, that the rising tide of nationalism was fast and that much needed to be accomplished before it reached full flood so that his successors could build on secure economic foundations. He died only two years after leaving Nyasaland.

On arrival in Nyasaland he quickly turned his attention to the question of Africans on private estates. The essence of the problem, which made it intractable in the hands of Colby's predecessors – although it had been recognized as early as 1914 – was the conflict between the European and the African concepts of land-holding. On the one hand, European land-holders expected to run their estates in accordance with Western ideas of freehold tenure, unencumbered by resident Africans save those of their own choosing who were prepared to work for them. On the other hand, the resident Africans expected to live on estate land in the manner in which their fellows lived on Trust Land in accordance with customary tenure, virtually as of right and without the obligation to work for, or pay rent to, the estate owners.

The ultimate solution to the problem – government acquisition of private land on which to resettle families – had been developed over a long period, successively by Nunan, Hetherwick, *Life and Work*, Jackson, Bowring, the 1928 Ordinance, Young, the 1939 Native Welfare Committee, and Hailey. Their message had become increasingly clear as the years passed, and now Abrahams had repeated it and adopted it enthusiastically as his own, expressing the solution as one of great simplicity. Indeed, so simply was it expressed that it was deeply misleading, as the Chairman of the Land Planning Committee, Edwards, shortly discovered:

> as a newcomer . . . it seemed surprising to me that no one had thought of such a simple answer before.
>
> As the work of the Committee progressed it very soon became clear that the problem was so complex that it would not admit of such a simple solution. Many of the people mentioned [as supporting the proposals] admitted that they had expressed agreement with the proposals without considering their practicability.[5]

He claimed that the landowners believed the scheme to be admirable because it would relieve them of their responsibilities to their tenants, whilst the estate Africans believed that there were to be large areas of land made available to them nearby to which they could move if they wished. The Senior Non-official Member of Legislative Council (Barrow) added:

> Sir Sidney, having made his proposal, sailed away, or flew – I do not remember which – if the latter then I trust that he has now come down to earth. In any case he left this Government "to carry the baby", a baby which he had fed with something which it very much coveted but it will not be possible to give it all it would like. There is therefore danger that this baby will become fractious and it is with this that this Government has to deal.[6]

These views of Abrahams' work, expressed by Edwards and Barrow, were made known to Colby soon after his arrival.

With these factors in mind, Colby moved quickly towards beginning to solve the problem. Although the balance of political power between Europeans and Africans was shifting, the government still very much held the scales; Colby was not reluctant to hold them firmly and, if necessary, to tilt them. Bell and Abrahams had both said that the resolution of the difficulty was a policy question for the government to decide one way or the other: it was a nettle to be grasped, a nettle which, as Colby saw it, was held mainly by Europeans but increasingly by Africans, a nettle with a sting in it which would become much more severe and disabling – possibly even fatal – the longer it was left ungrasped. None of his predecessors – except Johnston (1891–1897) and Thomas (who was not long enough in Nyasaland (1929–1932) to effect any major change) – had been the type of nettle-grasper which Colby now began to show himself to be. The time for dithering was past. One of his earliest tasks was to study the files on the problem, and a month after his arrival, on 28 April, he addressed a long demi-official letter to Andrew Cohen at the Colonial Office, setting out his views.[7] He felt that since the question was new to him, he could regard it objectively. It was an important letter which shows his very early reactions to the problem.

His first point was that since Abrahams' investigations were of a general character, without detailed examination of individual areas, his recommendations were similarly of a general nature, and more detailed investigations would be needed to discover the circumstances on individual estates: hence his recommendation that a Land Planning Committee be set up.[8] Colby fully accepted the principle of Abrahams' recommendations about acquisition, but he and his officials were faced with the difficulty of determining the extent to which they could be implemented and how far they would relieve congestion: both were fundamental points. He accepted the Committee's view that 'the true position is not as it was generally accepted to be and that it does not lend itself to action on the lines proposed in the Abrahams' Report', because it was the 'only authoritative statement of fact available' and one made only after detailed examination of evidence not available to Abrahams. Consequently, they should act on the basis that the statement was correct, and corrective measures could be taken later if it proved to be wrong.

Colby believed that parts of the report over-simplified the problem. He referred to Abrahams' conclusion that there were comparatively few resident Africans on developed estates, whereas the Committee's more detailed investigations – quite quickly carried out, or perhaps they already knew the details – showed that there was actually a very substantial number, which significantly reduced the practicability of Abrahams' solution. He also referred to Abrahams' proposal that parts of estates should be excised and formed into enclaves: in contrast, the Committee believed that in most estates where the problem was most acute, excision would lead to 'a large number of enclaves dotted about over a number of individual estates', and that this was not a practicable solution. Even if it were, it would not be a permanent solution since population increase in the enclaves would lead to further demands on the surrounding areas. The Committee, and Colby, preferred the acquisition and setting aside of blocks – like those which they recommended in the Cholo District – rather than enclaves.

He pointed out that Abrahams' suggestion that land which was unoccupied and uncultivated should not be acquired if it was to be developed within a reasonable period, would seriously reduce the amount of land available for African settlement. Even at this very early stage, Colby seems to have been contemplating the possibility that African interests with their political implications – unrest and security dangers – might become more important than European interests with their economic implications – export crop production. Furthermore, Abrahams assumed that substituting contractual for statutory rights would be a clear-cut solution, but many experienced administrative officers were convinced that to the Africans there would be little difference between contractual and statutory obligations to pay rent; moreover, difficulties arising from natural increase in the family and on the death of the original tenant would crop up under both the contractual and the statutory system.

Like Barrow, who was shortly to express himself so bluntly to Legislative Council, the Governor was worried that Abrahams' fulsomeness in expressing what he saw as wholehearted enthusiasm for his recommendations would raise expectations too high on the part of the Europeans and Africans in Nyasaland and of the Colonial Office in London. He thought Abrahams had significantly overdone it: 'To be quite candid, I can only regret that Abrahams wrote [these particular] paragraphs ... which do little to advance a solution of the problem.'

Colby was convinced that there could never be any clear-cut final solution to the problem: it could only be partially solved and would remain with them indefinitely. He mentioned this because Abrahams' report implied that a clear-cut and final solution could be found. Colby saw the problem as twofold: the political problem of large areas of land in the Southern Province being held by Europeans; and the economic problem of population congestion, also in the Southern Province.

He pointed out that the political problem could be disposed of finally only if the Europeans were completely dispossessed of their land: a 'quite impossible' solution and one not to be contemplated. It was the large areas of undeveloped land and the payment of rents which were the main causes of discontent. He referred to the generally welcome acceptance of Europeans actively developing their estates, but added:

> How long this happy position will remain it is impossible to say, but ... we should not rely on it lasting forever.
>
> So long as Europeans hold large areas of land ... so long will a potential political problem remain.

Clearly, he believed that the amount of land in European hands needed to be reduced, and the amount of undeveloped land very considerably reduced, if the political problem were to be solved, albeit only partially.

With regard to the economic problem, he emphasized that, notwithstanding the government's intention to make more land available for African settlement, the problem of congestion would remain as the population continued to increase and at an accelerated pace. There was the allied economic problem that the big estates were simply hanging on to large areas and taking few steps to develop them. Given the major contribution of European agriculture and the great potential of African agriculture, Colby's development strategy demanded that fuller economic use should be made of all the protectorate's land, including private estates.

Keeping in mind his conviction that only a partial solution was possible, and concentrating on the extent to which such a partial solution could be reached, he felt that the Committee's recommendations to acquire 550,000 acres out of a total of 1,200,000 acres of European estate land would represent a considerable advance, especially since 53,000 of the 74,400 resident African families on estates in the Shire Highlands would be automatically 'emancipated' (a term which Colby considered to be 'unhappy and possibly misleading'). Although the owners of the remaining 650,000 acres not recommended for acquisition had given an assurance that they intended to develop them as soon as machinery and materials were available, Colby was uncertain how much credence could be placed on these assurances. However, he pointed out that in the course of implementing the recommendations the government would find out the true position on each estate: he was not simply going to accept their word for it.

Colby acknowledged the fact that it was not known how much land currently not scheduled for acquisition was developed, and then turned to how he proposed to implement the Land Planning Committee recommendations. Even at this early stage he was displaying a determination to get on and do something positive about the problem in a way which distinguished him from his predecessors. He emphasized that implementation would necessitate a strong team in charge of acquisition and resettlement, and believed his predecessors had not realized what a big job, requiring a substantial staff, this implementation was going to be. He was particularly careful about the need to negotiate with estate owners in a pre-arranged order:

> We should aim at first acquiring areas from estate owners who are really ready to meet us, and it seems reasonable to hope that such estate owners will release their land to us at reasonable prices. By approaching the most reasonable owners first we shall thereby have created some precedents in regard to prices to be paid. These precedents should subsequently be of the greatest use to us when we have to negotiate with owners who are not so well disposed and ... if it comes to a question of compulsory acquisition.

In the event, even the 'reasonable owners' were reluctant to move until the BCA Company had been tackled and the 'going rate' had been fixed. Even at this relatively early stage, the new Governor was not as averse to compulsory acquisition as had been the Land Planning Committee, and also possibly Abrahams.

Colby was keen that the implementation of the Land Planning Committee's recommendations should be based on as much detailed information as possible. On each estate with which negotiations were to be commenced, he proposed that his team should establish with the owner the acreage undeveloped and the acreage required for future development, with a view to acquiring any substantial difference between the two. In examining individual estates, his team would be able to determine the number and location of resident Africans, to prepare areas for resettlement, to conduct an agricultural survey, and to find out how many Africans would wish to remain on the estate on a contractual basis. At this point, he refuted an inference in Abrahams' report: that all tenants on private estates were discontented. Whilst the charging of rent rankled with some, this was not so in the many cases where economic crop growing was permitted, where sufficient land for tenant needs was available, and where relations between landlord and tenant were good. Since these conditions obtained on 'a considerable number of estates', the rent obligation was 'discharged without demur and the tenants are generally content with or acquiesce in their lot'.

He made a particular point of supporting the Land Planning Committee's remarks about the fundamental change needed in securing the disappearance of part-time agriculturalists:

> I am convinced that the objectives to which we should work are, on the one hand, a definite non-farming permanent labour force living either in the residential blocks recommended by the Committee or on European estates in full-time employment by those estates, and, on the other hand, a farming community established on Native Trust Land which will supply not only their own needs but the needs of the labourers on the estates.

In essence, his argument was that if the large and increasing African population was to be accommodated on already congested land, then that population would have to depend upon others, more distant, to produce their foodstuffs. He was mindful also that it would be an uneconomic use of fertile Shire Highlands land to devote it to producing subsistence food crops rather than economic crops.

Allied to this, Colby realized that there was a potential conflict of policies. From a political point of view, there were powerful arguments for acquiring as much private land as possible to hand back to the Africans, but this would conflict with the British Government's economic policy and his own aim to secure the maximum outputs of such estate crops as tung, tea, sisal, soya and flue-cured tobacco. Colby showed that such a reconciliation was possible by pointing out that in paying the estate owners considerable sums for their land – on which Africans would be settled – he would be providing them with capital with which to develop their remaining estates and increase production.

He then turned to the Committee's strong advice that the government should publicly state that no further large-scale acquisition of freehold land would be practicable. Rejecting this advice, he made it clear that he could not rule out further acquisitions and that no matter how unpalatable it might be to the European community, the government would investigate land requirements on individual estates, and if they found that lands not scheduled for acquisition were not to be developed he would consider acquiring them. Furthermore, he would review the position after a reasonable period when development projects had had time to mature and again consider acquisition of areas not developed in the meantime. Once again, he was not inclined simply to accept the estate owners' word for it.

In effect he was dividing private land into two categories: that which was to be developed in a reasonable time, and that which was to be acquired for African settlement. He declined to specify a definite period for development because any such specification might be taken by Africans as an undertaking to acquire European land on a certain date, which in practice the government might not wish to implement for a variety of reasons, including financial costs. He refused to be drawn into estimating how many Africans currently residing on private estates could be accommodated on the half million acres scheduled for early acquisition because this would require a detailed agricultural survey. He did, however, say that by acquiring 46 per cent of the freehold land in the Shire Highlands they would be emancipating 71 per cent of the population resident on it.

He expressed his own views on compulsory acquisition – a question which was to crop up repeatedly in later years – and said that it would be resorted to only if there was no alternative. He was aware from his own experience in the Lands Office in Northern Nigeria and in the Lagos Secretariat, and from the experience of his senior Nyasaland colleagues in Jamaica and Hong Kong, that High Courts often awarded compulsory acquisition compensation 'vastly in excess of the worth of the land'. He thought it advisable to acquire as much as possible by 'voluntary negotiations before [he] proceed[ed] to compulsory acquisition in cases where the landowners [were] not amenable'. The whole tone of this part of his letter was one of a readiness to be tough and to force acquisition if necessary, and he did not conceal this general attitude to the problem with which he was confronted. The difference between Colby and the Colonial Office was that although both felt that compulsory acquisition should be used as a last resort, Colby believed that it might well come to that, whilst the Colonial Office thought or pretended that this would not be the case.

The Governor dealt next with finances. Whilst provisionally accepting that the £300,000 required to purchase lands to be immediately or shortly acquired should be from local sources, he pointed out that this would be a severe drain on protectorate resources and 'may prove to be beyond them if any further acquisition beyond that recommended by the Committee is undertaken'. He was, of course, fully aware that acquisitions beyond those formally recommended by the Land Planning Committee were essential if the political problem was to be seriously tackled, and he did not want this additional burden to fall upon the protectorate's limited finances. He then said:

> As expenditure ... might be considered both of a development and a welfare character, I am wondering whether there would be any chance of seeking your support for obtaining assistance from the general reserve of £12,000,000 under the Colonial Development and Welfare Act.

Colby's view was: 'We are likely to have to spend a very substantial sum of money on unremunerative expenditure in purchasing land from the large land owners.' Frankly, he said, he could not see how they could contemplate spending more than a fraction of that recommended by the Committee since this would, in his view, 'be totally unjustified'. Initially he had assumed that any money spent in purchasing land from companies, such as the BCA Company, would be used in the development of the country, but on reflection he believed that this was a vain hope and saw very little prospect of the monies being invested in Nyasaland, and this was another reason why he could not contemplate heavy expenditure on buying land.

Colby was anxious to get on with the job. He set aside £100,000, a third of the sum required for acquisition, in the 1948 Estimates, his first budget (thereby incurring a deficit), and a further £150,000 in the 1949 Estimates.[9] He asked Cohen to submit the Planning Committee's Report to the Secretary of State and seek his approval for action on the lines which Colby indicated 'as early as possible'. He proposed then to publish the report, and a statement of government policy along the same lines. He was not, however, going to let events overtake him, and concluded his letter to Cohen by saying that it would be necessary to defer action under the next quinquennial eviction period beyond September 1948: the Southern Provincial Commissioner was warning that the approaching end of the quinquennium was bringing 'the problems which exist on many estates into the foreground and a certain disquiet exists among the African tenants'.[10]

It is quite clear from the drafts of this letter to Cohen that Colby personally worked very hard and carefully on it, altering numerous pieces, writing extensive new paragraphs, adding new sections, and rewording several passages so that the final version, whilst containing most of the original points – drafted by Secretariat officers – bore very little resemblance in structure and tone to the original. He took enormous pains over it – even for a newly promoted Governor anxious to make an impressive start – and his redrafting is one of the very few documents on which he worked in black pencil rather than in red ink, possibly because the work was extensive, important, demanded much thought and great care, and because he was drafting for himself rather than minuting to others.[11] These considerations and the very early date of the work indicate that he quickly saw the immediate and great importance of the question of Africans on private estates.

In various ways, Colby communicated his concern and the importance of the question to the public. Only two months after his arrival, he sent a letter to the Tea Association[12] urging them to grow sufficient maize for their labour force, since the shortage of Trust Land made it increasingly difficult for the tea estates to buy enough maize from that land, and their purchases simply reduced the foodstuffs available to the growing urban African population. He reminded them that three years previously the government had asked the industry to produce its own maize and had suggested two suitable blocks of unsettled land for this purpose:

Since then there has been considerable encroachment of native cultivation on both and unless a decision is made quickly it may not be possible to find suitable areas of land.[13]

Colby deliberately did a number of things in this letter. First, he specifically directed his remarks about land shortage and foodstuffs supplies to the tea industry, which was located in the Cholo and Mlanje areas of severe congestion. Second, he urged the industry to develop its lands by growing foodstuffs for its labour force as well as commercial crops. Third, he told them that time had already been lost and urgent action was now vital. Whilst he could be reasonably sure of such tea planters as Barrow and Hadlow, who were members of Executive Council, and also many others, he was far from sure that he could get the larger companies, particularly the BCA Company, to develop their land and furnish their own food supplies. He was trying to use the support of many of the Tea Association members to influence the others.

A few weeks later, the Governor used a Chamber of Commerce luncheon to express his views even more publicly, and particularly to deal with land and accommodation problems in and near the townships from which most of the members came:

The provision of African residential areas on modern lines is obviously a matter of urgency, and the creation of facilities for an African urban population, living in reasonable conditions of comfort will ... do something to resolve the serious land congestion problems ... the present situation where the majority of the wage-earning African population also cultivate small gardens is one which cannot continue. I purposely used the word "cannot". There is just not sufficient land available.[14]

The following week, Colby presided over his first meeting of Legislative Council which debated the report of the Land Planning Committee.[15] It was at this meeting that Edwards and Barrow expressed their reservations about Abrahams' proposals, and Colby used the occasion to seek the support of estate owners as to the price of acquired land and to counter recent local press criticism as to the government's *bona fides* in land acquisition matters. He had already written to Cohen about the severe drain on Nyasaland's resources which land purchase would mean, and had pleaded for British financial support; he now drew the landowners' attention to this drain and appealed to their public spirit:

> It is the earnest hope of the Secretary of State for the Colonies and of this Government that land owners will be willing to meet the Government in this matter in the interests of the Protectorate.
>
> ... any funds that are devoted to purchasing undeveloped land from private ownership will be from the resources of this Protectorate which are provided by the taxpayers of this Protectorate. Thus, those resources, all of which would otherwise be available for development purposes will be depleted by the amount which is used for the purchase of undeveloped land. In other words it would be in the interests of the taxpayers, which include the landowners, that such undeveloped land should be secured at a reasonable price.[16]

Edwards took up this price issue in his speech introducing the report, but rather than appeal to the landowners' public spirit he argued on grounds of market value and also made a scarcely concealed threat. With regard to market value, he argued that much of the land had been so neglected by its owners in terms of soil conservation that it was as bad as areas of Trust Land in the worst congested areas: 'To ask Government to pay one penny for such land would be ludicrous since it would cost Government large sums of money to put it right.' As to the threat, he made the point that some of the areas recommended for acquisition were 'not only valueless but ... if the provisions of the Natural Resources Ordinance were applied to them [they] would cost the owners considerable sums to put in proper condition'.[17]

Barrow also dealt with price and said the current time was an unfortunate one for buying land because of the ruling high prices, and he believed that if the owners demanded their 'last pound of flesh' it would be doubtful whether the government would be justified in spending the money to comply with the Committee's recommendations. He begrudged the money and argued that a 'definite limit' should be placed on the amount to be spent on land acquisition. Clearly, Colby, Edwards and Barrow were much concerned about the probable cost of acquiring private land.[18]

The other matter on which Colby dwelt during this July 1948

Legislative Council meeting was press criticism of the government's intentions in amending the Acquisition of Land for Public Purposes Ordinance. The press statement was to the effect that 'neither a man's home nor his land was safe' from compulsory acquisition. During his period of office, Colby was to suffer numerous press attacks against any step which could be viewed as state intervention in private enterprise. This was the first of such attacks: Colby reacted – maybe over-reacted – quickly. He described the statements as 'unworthy' and said that not only could no country operate without such legal provisions, but also that Nyasaland had had similar provisions for the past forty years. He assured Council that the powers to be given under the Bill would 'be exercised with one object, and one object alone, and that is to benefit the progress and development' of Nyasaland. The powers were needed in order that greater control and strict land use principles could be applied to the acquired land; without them the fertility and carrying capacity of the acquired land would deteriorate, and Abrahams had strongly warned of the dangers of allowing that to happen.[19]

During the following months, Colby continued to study the implications of the Land Planning Committee's report and gave it a great deal of careful thought. He was pleased with the progress in surveying the Cholo accommodation blocks and determining the number of tenants resident on them, but he was unclear – and believed that others were also unclear – as to the precise purpose of purchasing them.[20] He was anxious that his officials should turn their mind to the specific practicalities of what had been proposed in general terms:

> Are we going to stop farming by the Africans who are already settled on these blocks? Do we propose to lay out these blocks to provide housing plots and a small garden ... in order that we can accommodate tenants settled on neighbouring estates, the owners of which want to develop them? It seems to me that we must answer both these questions and have clear-cut ideas of the developments we envisage. It seems to me that it is going to be extremely difficult to take away farming land from people who are already farming in the residential blocks. If, on the other hand, we do not take away such farming land, we shall have some people in these blocks farming and other people precluded from farming. This is likely to cause discontent.[21]

He argued that if the accommodation blocks were capable of absorbing a fairly large number of Africans from neighbouring estates – which in turn would imply the absence of anything other than very small gardens – this absorption would confer a very great benefit on the estate owners.

In exchange for this, Colby thought, they ought to be prepared 'to give a substantial amount of financial assistance to Government in purchasing' the land. So strong did he believe the government's bargaining position to be in such a case that if the owners did not give financial assistance he would threaten to 'drop the whole scheme'.[22] Edwards' response to these views was that the BCA Company would argue that in moving their tenants to released land they would be losing both valuable land and a resident pool of labour, under which circumstances they would not see justice in being asked also to give financial assistance.[23] Colby felt that Edwards had 'rather missed the point' and he held to his view that the estate owners, under these circumstances, ought to be paid little, if anything, for the land released.[24]

In studying the documents, and especially the confidential appendix to the draft report of the Land Planning Committee, Colby quickly realized that he was likely to have the greatest difficulty with the BCA Company because of the size and location of its land-holdings, their undeveloped state, the attitude of its management, and its potential as a source of serious political trouble. In order that he should as fully understand the Company as possible and be adequately briefed in his dealings with them, he followed a practice which he used on major issues, both in Nigeria and in Nyasaland, of seconding an officer for a few months to research the issue thoroughly for him, and he asked McDonald to prepare a history of, and commentary on, the Company and its land-holding activities. He also asked McDonald to report to him personally every month on developments in land matters.[25] From what he was told of the Company's local management, and from the impression which he himself formed, Colby was determined to have no dealings at a policy level with this management, but to have the Colonial Office negotiate with the London directors – advice which the Land Planning Committee had also given. He also wanted to be as well informed as possible about the Company.

McDonald's commentary, sent to the Governor on 12 December 1948, was an extremely well written, clearly expressed document, as closely researched as the material available permitted, and a devastating indictment of the BCA Company.[26]

He showed first how E. C. A. Sharrer, a forceful and shrewd German businessman, between the 1880s and 1902, built up successful interests in trade, transport and agriculture and then turned his attention to railway development. At this stage, he formed the BCA Company which consolidated the interests of the SHR Company, his own estates, and his Zambezi Traffic Company. Having formed this company, he returned to Europe never to revisit Nyasaland, and McDonald concluded that Sharrer had seen the difficult times ahead and had formed the BCA Company as a means of realizing the assets already gained and of distributing among shareholders risks which he knew would be inherent in further development.

The BCA Company started life with an authorized capital of £1,500,000 almost fully subscribed:

> Its history for the next 22 years can only be described as extremely unfortunate; it never declared a dividend; its financial resources dwindled steadily until in 1921 it had to raise £200,000 on first mortgage debentures at the high rate of interest of 8% in order to carry on; and finally in 1924 it went into liquidation and had to be reconstituted.

There were a number of elements in this decline between 1902 and 1924. Initially the Company concentrated on communications – ocean, river and lake by steamers, houseboats and barges; road by ox wagons and a monorail tramway; and rest houses – but these activities were overtaken by the introduction of the railway and the motor vehicle so that the transport activities were closed down after 1922. Similarly, its subsidiary trading company, Kabula Stores, failed to compete with other, more dynamic, trading companies, and after the parent company went into liquidation, Kabula Stores survived for a short time only. Concerning land, the Company started life with 372,500 acres mainly in the Shire Highlands Districts. The principal exports when the Company started were coffee and cotton, and although they spent relatively little on the former they spent lavishly on the latter and lost a good deal of money through extravagance and poor management.

> All those who persisted in the cultivation of coffee and cotton eventually failed, and the British Central Africa Company were perhaps the biggest losers of all.

They also started growing flue-cured tobacco but, although this was a highly profitable crop, especially between 1910 and 1920, they opened up relatively little land and failed to exploit the crop to anything like its full potential, continuing instead to concentrate on cotton. Similarly, their attempts to grow sisal were on a very limited scale. They made two attempts to attract immigrant European planters, in the early 1900s and again in 1919, but both failed and very few who did come stayed long enough to take up land.[27]

In summarizing the Company's history to 1924, McDonald quoted from a recent view expressed by Barrow:

> The truth is that the Company's holding of land always was, and still is, too large for them to control. They have always proved incapable of developing any appreciable proportion of their holdings, denied the opportunity to others to develop the land by demanding high prices in the current market, and were quite incapable of looking after the vast area they owned and of preventing its being ravaged by indiscriminate African settlement.

McDonald's own assessment was equally damning: as a consequence of the Company's inability to control their land, much of it had got into a condition which rendered it useless for future development. One particular aspect he felt would 'always remain unforgivable': they knew from the experience of others that tea was the most stable industry in the country, and knew also that the amount of land suitable for tea growing was strictly limited, and that they themselves owned many thousands of acres of that suitable land, and yet:

> Incredible as it may seem, from 1920 to 1924 they started to allow onto this land uncontrolled immigration of natives from Portuguese East Africa. By doing this they permanently impaired the resources of the Protectorate and at the same time saddled the Government with a grave political problem.

The years mentioned, 1920–1924, were years in which Jackson, Ormsby-Gore and Bowring had been publicly discussing the question of Africans on private estates: it was not a period in which the matter was unimportant and forgotten.

McDonald then turned to deal with the BCA Company from 1924 to 1947, the period of the reconstituted company which started with a reduction of its authorized capital, 'but although . . . reconstructed it was not regenerated':

> Under a joint management with an unenviable reputation for inefficiency it continued to pursue a policy of extravagance, but not in the direction of useful development. And no check whatever was put onto the continued immigration of natives from Portuguese East Africa onto the Company's natural tea lands. In fact the period between the years 1924 and 1930 was as dark as any in the Company's history.

During this period, just as they had earlier concentrated on cotton which was declining, instead of on tobacco which was expanding, they then went on to concentrate on sisal which was declining, instead of on tobacco which was continuing to expand. Of their third of a million acres, they never cultivated more than 1,499 in any one year.

By 1930, the Company was once more in serious financial difficulties, its shares were further written down, and a large overdraft had been incurred. The management was changed and Kaye Nicol was appointed as manager. He put an end to extravagance but did nothing to halt the immigration onto the Company's tea lands despite the fact that they had begun to plant tea, albeit on a very limited scale. The Company's financial position did not improve, and in 1936 there was a further reduction in capital issue:

> Thus in the course of 34 years their original £1 shares had fallen to two shillings and their issued capital of £1,468,000 to £216,000, while the value of their African estates, once standing in their books at £852,000, had been reduced to £107,000.

McDonald then studied in greater detail the last ten years, 1937 to 1947, which he saw as the most interesting part of the Company's history. The management was the same as at the time he was writing; it had adequate capital; it had a planned development programme; the most prosperous agricultural years the protectorate had ever known stretched ahead of it; and it had considerably more land available for development than it had later 'owing to the manner in which continued depredations were made by African immigrants in the years immediately before and during the war'. In April 1937, the Company's chairman had written to the Colonial Office saying that the Company was in a strong financial position and was prepared both to strengthen its old activities and to undertake specified new developments. McDonald examined the developments which actually took place during the decade that followed, and found that the tonnage of sisal produced had fallen from 680 to 192; the production of tobacco had increased only from 221,160 pounds to 306,918 pounds; tea had increased from 414,496 pounds of green leaf – everyone else measured output in terms of manufactured tea – to 3,738,721 pounds, but the company had failed to plant up the full acreage allowed under the international tea restriction scheme, even though they owned land far superior to much of that which they had actually planted; they had grown no groundnuts despite plans to do so; tung nut acreage had increased from 35 to 1,310, which produced 110,216 pounds of nuts (compared with 312,004 pounds on a neighbouring estate of almost exactly the same acreage under tung and at the same stage of development); soya bean acreage had decreased from 3,000 to 1,505, with output static at about 600 tons.

World market prices during the period 1937 to 1947 enabled the Company to make a profit, and for the first time, in 1941, they declared a dividend. Yet, despite this, their assets continued to depreciate steadily, and in 1947 only 6,430 of their 329,354 acres were under cultivation, whilst 11,000 acres were leased to other planters. About 300,000 acres were not being worked, with all the best of this land in the Blantyre and Cholo Districts in the hands of African tenants. Their late attempts to stem the flow of immigration were ineffective and the existing tenants extended their occupation further through the estate lands. McDonald was convinced that:

> extensive development of these areas is now beyond the range of possibility ... the incalculable disservice the Company has done to the Protectorate in the neglect of its lands is beyond all dispute.

He attributed much of this deplorable state of affairs to the Company's parsimony, especially in regard to European staff: the General Manager was a generalist in direct charge of all the Company's activities, and no specialists were employed; the quality of the subordinate supervisory staff was appalling and the personal behaviour of many left much to be desired:

It almost appears as if an unsympathetic and aggressive attitude towards the African is regarded with favour, perhaps because the Company considers such persons are less likely to be imposed upon by their labour.

No other employer of labour in the country engages and retains the services of Europeans who are known to have a provocative and demoralising influence on their labour. The conduct of these men gives rise to numerous incidents, any one of which might provide the occasion for serious political trouble. But the Company is not concerned with such dangers which are regarded as the responsibility of Government; it is only concerned with attempting to develop on cheaper terms than anyone else, and to secure these terms it will continue to sacrifice its own aims and to jeopardise the political safety of the country.

McDonald ended his report by saying that the Company's directors in England had confidence in the current management and did not seem to realize how their affairs were actually conducted in Nyasaland, the golden opportunities that had been lost, and the damage that had been caused to their land. He stated his conviction that:

There seems no hope for improvement until they are brought to realise these things, and to change their entire staff in Africa.

When Colby received what McDonald had written, he was reinforced in his view that the really big nut he had to crack was the BCA Company, and that he should be as ruthless as necessary with them since they had not been, nor did they show any signs of being, reasonable in their use of land, or in their attitudes towards the country's economy and towards the political dangers of land tensions and race relations. They were wasting and destroying the nation's major asset, land, and allowing it to stand idle instead of contributing to the country's wealth, and in doing so were indifferent to the political and security dangers they were causing. Colby would have found the Company's failure to develop the land and their indifference to the political dangers particularly galling, determined as he was to engender substantial economic development based on increased agricultural production taking place in a peaceful political environment.

He found himself very much in sympathy with McDonald's report, especially the point that there was no hope of improvement until the London directors realized the true position and its dangers. He quickly decided that he should now discuss buying the BCA Company blocks with the Colonial Office. He again made it clear that he was 'not prepared to negotiate ... with Mr. Nicol' locally, and he did not want to open up discussions publicly on price at this stage.[28]

So far as price for land in general, and for BCA Company land in particular, was concerned, he pursued his novel but perfectly serious argument that the government was likely to be asked a high price whilst doing the estates a great service in clearing part of their land of tenants and thereby making substantial areas available for further development: 'In other words, the whole operation should be of great financial benefit to the estates who will be relieved of tenants ... the estates will be getting it both ways.' He believed that in view of this argument:

> we have a very strong bargaining card in our hand, and I should have thought that the estates would be prepared to give a substantial amount of financial assistance to Government in purchasing this land in order to obtain relief from their tenants. We might, for example, reach the point where we said that if the estates are not prepared to give financial assistance, then we will drop the whole scheme.[29]

Clearly, even at this early stage he was prepared to be tough with the BCA Company over price but he was also ready to consider softer ways with other landowners: 'Has anyone ever considered the possibility of proceeding on the following lines? Take each estate individually, the owner to provide an area with or without farm land onto which his tenants would be settled, the area to become Native Trust Land and rent to be waived.' On the surface this seems to be a strange question for a well-informed governor to ask, because Abrahams had clearly recommended the acquisition of land upon which could be settled Africans from congested Trust Land and from retained private land.[30] Colby's question may have been based on a number of ideas. He might have had in mind the piecemeal, individual, approach to landowners, and the settlement, at least initially, only of a particular estate's African tenants (and not Africans from Trust Land or other estates) on that estate's released land. His question also implies transfer without payment price, and he might also have had in mind only the smaller owners and the hope of being able to deal with them without waiting for discussions, including price, with the larger owners.

More important is the probability that he was asking the question as a means of solving the crucial difference between Abrahams' recommendation on those indivisible developed estates which contained numerous, scattered African settlements, and the Land Planning Committee's conclusion that the recommended solution was impracticable. Abrahams believed there were comparatively few such areas and that the tenants on them should either enter into a contract to work in exchange for residing on the estate, or move to nearby Trust Land and be compensated by the government for the disturbance. The Committee found that the estates with scattered settlement were numerous and formed the majority, especially in the most congested areas, and that there was scarcely any Trust Land nearby to which tenants could move. It is possible that they were conscious of the cost of compensation and for this reason preferred to avoid Abrahams' solution. As an alternative they had recommended the Cholo accommodation blocks. Colby might have been drawing guidance from the 1904 Ordinance 'locations' idea and have had in mind adapting Abrahams' solution and placing the onus on individual owners to select sufficient land to accommodate their tenants, settling the tenants on that land and then turning it into Trust Land. Which areas were selected would be up to the owner, and the government would not be put to the trouble and expense of buying the land nor of controlling it, as it would have to do if the land became Public Land.

Colby discussed his proposals with the Secretary of State (Creech Jones) during the latter's visit to Nyasaland in April 1949, and he agreed that, if private land were not properly used or developed, the government would be justified in 'exerting considerable pressure on landlords to part with it at reasonable prices'. He also agreed that the best plan was to negotiate with the London boards of the major landowning companies.[31]

Early in June 1949, Colby set up a committee comprised of McDonald, Barrow and Hadlow to advise on the action to be taken in the discussion in London with the BCA Company, the B&EA Company and the A. L. Bruce Estates, specifying the land which the government should acquire and detailing the limits to which Colby should go with the boards of directors. Executive Council felt that since the money for purchase would have to come from protectorate funds, 'even a figure of ten shillings per acre would result in a comparatively heavy outlay which the Protectorate could with difficulty afford'. Ten shillings an acre was the price at which the government had redeemed the BCA Company's railway subsidy land 31 years earlier, and was rather higher than the level to which the Company had written down the value of its estates in its books in 1936.[32]

In July, Executive Council received this committee's report and recommendations.[33] In respect of the BCA Company, their recommendations were based on the Land Planning Committee's understanding given by Kaye Nicol that he would be prepared to recommend his board to surrender land, notwithstanding the fact that he subsequently told the Chairman that he was unable to agree with many of the Committee's findings. Council advised that McDonald should contact each of the three companies individually, emphasizing the serious consequences which would inevitably follow upon ill-considered action by them, and particularly stressing the strong political grounds which made a speedy and reasonable settlement essential. When this had been done, McDonald should report to Colby and a joint meeting should be held with the three companies, the Governor, McDonald, and a Colonial Office representative. In respect of finance, Council advised that since the precise acreage of the estates was not yet known, negotiations should be on the basis of price per acre so that a final adjustment could be made after the estate had been surveyed. The Financial Secretary was asked to examine the payment, especially in respect of whether it could be spread over a period without interest accruing. Colby accepted Executive Council's advice.

In order to exert pressure on the companies, from November 1948 the Governor actively considered imposing a tax on undeveloped land to replace the 1912 land tax which had fallen into abeyance.[34] Creech Jones noted his proposals, but did not pass an opinion on them, and Colby now planned to use them in trying to persuade the companies to sell their land at a reasonable price. Whilst Barrow 'viewed with dislike and misgivings' the idea of this tax, he told Colby that, because of the importance of buying considerable areas of land and the danger of failing to do so, if a price could not be negotiated reasonably within the government's resources he would support the imposition.[35] Colby persisted, again consulted Executive Council on 13 April and 8 June 1949, and was advised not to circulate a memorandum on the tax to the Convention of Associations and the Chamber of Commerce as he had suggested. Instead, during his forthcoming London visit, he should try to persuade the boards of the large companies to part with undeveloped land at a reasonable price because the proposed tax was directed primarily against large landowners who were neglecting to develop their land.[36]

In July and August 1949, Colby and McDonald began discussions in London with the large companies and, by December of that year, the preliminary arrangements were made for purchasing some 200,000 acres of land, over half of which was in the Zomba District and the remainder in the Blantyre, Cholo and Lower River Districts.[37] The discussions were fairly quickly agreed and these significant areas of land were conveyed to the government at a flat rate of twelve shillings and six pence an acre, notwithstanding Executive Council's opinion that Nyasaland could afford ten shillings 'only with difficulty'. At this early stage the companies were fairly co-operative, at least over the particular areas in question. Abrahams had expressed:

> the hope and belief that estate owners, and in particular the great land holders, will not endeavour to drive a hard bargain with Government in respect of the price, nor will endeavour to retain unreasonably large areas of land for future development.[38]

Following another of Abrahams' recommendations, 21,500 acres in the Kasungu District in the Central Province were offered to private planters and syndicates in exchange for land in the Southern Province.[39] During 1950, over half the Africans on the acquired estates were resettled by concentrating them into selected sites so as to provide for the orderly reception of new entrants from congested areas and to make good use of the best agricultural land.[40] The government was able to claim that:

> the response has been excellent and the general rate of progress reflects great credit on the officers responsible.[41]

By the end of 1951, a total of 300,000 acres had been acquired in the Southern Province for resettlement, including 130,000 acres at Chingale from the BCA Company in the Zomba District and 72,000 acres at Magomero from the Bruce Estates in the Zomba, Chiradzulu and Mlanje Districts, and the water supplies and communications had been very considerably improved.[42] These were areas which were not densely populated, were of poor quality, and were not in close proximity to the heavily settled areas on or near the Cholo tea estates:[43] given such improvements, a large increase in settlement was possible. The work continued during 1952 and 1953.[44] At Chingale, the road system was further extended; simple medical, postal and market facilities were provided; the administrative station and agricultural staff housing were built; all leading to a steady and continuing – but not dramatic – flow of settlers into the area. At Magomero, work began on the administrative station, and reconnaissance work was started in the more sparsely populated areas to select residential sites and demarcate agricultural holdings. The owners, Bruce Estates, aware that the government wished to acquire the largely undeveloped Magomero estate, nonetheless offered it for auction in 1947; large blocks were bought by I. Conforzi (40,000 acres) who started to grow coffee and tobacco, Barrow (2,250 acres on behalf of Nyasa Tea Estates) who used it for cattle ranching, and a combine of estates led by Lujeri Tea Estates for growing maize with which to feed their tea estate labour. The auctioneer, Kirkaldy, was paid with 1,000 acres, on which he grew tobacco.[45]

When the Bruce Estates had first put up its Magomero Estate for sale in 1945, Governor Richards had recommended purchase and although he would have been prepared to pay up to ten shillings an acre for the land, the Colonial Office confined him to five shillings, which the Bruce Estates rejected. By the end of 1949, a total of 92,794 acres had been sold to private individuals or companies and only the remainder, and less fertile, 'badly drained and sparsely inhabited' east and overpopulated west sections – 75,000 acres – were left for the government to purchase, and on them they resettled tenants from the privately purchased sections.[46] It had also been intended that the owners should auction the Chingale estate but few potential bidders showed sufficient interest. Between the two world wars, the BCA Company had leased a number of 1,000 acre blocks of the Chingale estate to tobacco farmers but all failed; there was no resident manager and save for two 1,000 acre blocks sold privately –

one to the Montfort Marist Mission and the other to an Italian tobacco farmer – the estate was sold to the government.[47] By the end of 1953, the Chingale and Magomero acquired lands had increased their population from 65,500 to 82,000, but had done little to relieve the congestion in the Cholo tea estate areas. A year later, the population was 111,000, increasing to 122,000 by 1955, most of the newcomers having left congested land in the Zomba and Chiradzulu Districts.[48]

Other, smaller, estates were also purchased during this period from a variety of owners – but not the four important accommodation blocks in the Cholo District. Some transactions were quickly agreed: for example, the handing over of the whole of Likoma Island without charge to the government by the Universities Mission to Central Africa in 1950.[49] Another quickly agreed transaction was the purchase of 1,122 acres in Blantyre from the Church of Scotland Mission; this was valuable land and the price of almost £90,000 was agreed, payable over a ten-year period from 1950.[50]

More often, however, the negotiations took a very long time. The example of the Kuntaja-Kumjowe estate provides an interesting and not untypical case study. This 23,040 acre estate, situated on the fringe of a densely congested peri-urban area near Chileka in the Blantyre District, belonged to the British South Africa Company. Their agents, the ALC, had last inspected it in 1932 since when they had lost the records and consequently had no knowledge of how many tenants there were on the estate. No European had visited the estate since 1941 and in the meantime large numbers of Africans had taken up residence on it for subsistence farming.[51] In October 1947, the Chairman of the Land Planning Committee wrote to the Company's resident director in Salisbury, Southern Rhodesia, told him of Abrahams' recommendation that undeveloped private land should be acquired by the government for resettling Africans in congested areas, and asked if the Company would be prepared to surrender the estate to the government.[52] In November, the resident director replied that he would need to consult his colleagues in London, and a month later said that before he could give a definite answer the land would have to be examined by the Company's technical staff to determine the agricultural and mineral potentialities.[53] A reminder from the government in May 1949[54] prompted the Company to reply that they were having difficulty in releasing a geologist to accompany their agriculturalist, but hoped to examine the property in September.[55] In

August 1949, the resident director advised the government that he had been unable to secure the services of a geologist, and because of the unfavourable weather it would be unwise to release any of his agriculturalists; he asked that the inspection be deferred for a year.[56] In July 1950, the government asked if the Company had reached a decision,[57] and in October McDonald advised Executive Council that:

> The value of this estate for agricultural or accommodation purposes can ... be put down as nothing or next to nothing. The area at stake, however, is considerable and if the British South Africa Company offered the land to Government there would appear to be political justification for acquiring it at a price such as a shilling an acre or the refund of land tax paid.[58]

The following month, the resident director wrote to say that the Company would be prepared to sell the freehold of the estate at ten shillings an acre, but would wish to retain the mineral rights.[59] In December, the government wrote that there was little justification for purchase 'other than that arising from political considerations' and that they would be prepared to pay a sum equal to the land tax paid, amounting to £1,872 or 1.625 shillings an acre, an offer which was quickly declined.[60] In January 1953, the government considered offering 2.5 shillings an acre but did not believe the Company would accept it; nonetheless they went ahead and offered 2.33 shillings an acre,[61] to which the resident director replied that since his Company was 'desirous of meeting the Government in the latter's desire to acquire this land' they would be prepared to accept five shillings an acre.[62] In the meantime, the Provincial Commissioner expressed the view that since the land was of no use for settlement purposes there was no point in purchasing any of it.[63] By February 1955, however, he had changed his mind because Chief Ntaja was now 'very interested in having the land bought as a "pacifier"'.[64] The Chief Secretary then offered three shillings an acre for the surface and mineral rights.[65] The resident director promptly declined this and said that the Company now considered itself free to negotiate a sale elsewhere.[66] A few days later, the Chief Secretary offered five shillings an acre,[67] which the Company accepted.[68] In June 1956, once a clarification had been made over the different names given to the estate, the freehold was conveyed to the government.[69]

So, after nearly nine years, the government acquired 23,040 acres of heavily settled land, devoted entirely to subsistence cultivation at a price five times that which they first offered, half of that which the vendor had first requested, and exactly that requested two years earlier. The purpose of acquisition was a political gesture of goodwill to local African feelings. Political gestures were, however, of very great importance.

Having acquired the 300,000 acres in the Southern Province in 1948–1950, Colby turned his attention to reconsidering the 1928 Africans on Private Estates Ordinance. This Ordinance had been seriously criticized in the early 1930s by Governor Young, but the Colonial Office had then decided against amending it. If he was to tackle the problem of Africans on private estates effectively, Colby needed to ensure that the legislation, enacted over twenty years earlier, was still sound and appropriate for the tasks ahead of him. To do this, he set up a Committee to consider ways, if any, in which the Ordinance should be amended. The Committee was chaired by McDonald and its other members were four Europeans – L. T. Rumsey, A. C. W. Dixon, N. W. Raynor, and R. W. J. Wallace – and three Africans – E. K. Mposa, L. Bandawe, and Chief Chimombo.[70]

The Committee, reporting in April 1951,[71] pointed to the significant changes which had taken place since 1928:

> At that time there were none of the present problems of congestion. There was ample agricultural land for all, not only for those living on private estates, but also for those living on Native Trust Land. The Ordinance was drafted so as to require the landlord to provide for his tenants all the agricultural land they needed for their sustenance which in effect meant all the land they were able to cultivate, and it was also drafted so as to provide for the removal of large numbers of tenants from estates onto adjoining Native Trust Land. In the first years of its life the Ordinance worked smoothly; as the tenant population grew so was more land made available for their use; and those who were required to move onto Native Trust Land could find there adequate areas of agricultural land on which to re-establish themselves. But problems of congestion have supervened, and the stage has now been reached where agricultural land has for all practical purposes been taken up to its limit while the population continues steadily to increase.

Although their view of the position in 1928 and the following years was a somewhat rosy one, the Committee were convinced that it was now no longer possible to provide every tenant on private estates with as much land as they could cultivate, nor was it possible to remove large numbers to Trust Land 'without difficulty and hardship'. They concluded that since much of the Ordinance could not be complied with, either by the landlord or by the government, 'substantial' changes were 'imperative'. Their recommendation focused on three 'main lines of action': first, removing the landlords' obligation to provide sufficient land for the sustenance of every tenant family; second, reducing evictions to the minimum consonant with essential development needs; and third, improving the lot of those necessarily required to leave the estates.

In respect of the first of these 'lines of action', the Committee recommended that each resident African should be entitled to a site for his hut and to the agricultural land which he had under cultivation currently, provided he made efficient use of the land and provided the area involved was not greater than he and his family could cultivate without outside assistance. In addition, firewood and building material should come only from areas allocated by the estate owner. These recommendations were based on the knowledge that there was no longer sufficient land available on estates, nor was there sufficient building material and firewood for the full tenant rights to these items under the 1928 Ordinance unless large numbers of tenants were evicted to enable those remaining to be provided for. The Committee was also concerned to eliminate a growing and worrying practice:

> Africans who set up as farmers on private land, laying claims to excessive acreages which they cultivate with paid labour, thus adding to the problem of congestion and depriving other tenants of a fair share of such land as is available for them.

They aimed to allow the estate owner to settle on his estate 'an indefinite number' of tenants willing to live there in the knowledge that the land available to them was strictly limited and being dependent for their livelihood on working for the estate owner. In effect, they aimed at securing a large resident labour force which did not take up too much land. They saw this as beneficial to both landlord and tenant, as relieving congestion, and also as enabling them to make concessions which would give the daughters of tenants rights to settle on the estate in accordance with African custom, thereby removing a source of considerable dissatisfaction in the past. The second, vital, 'line of action' was to recommend a reduction in evictions by allowing removal only for rent default, misconduct and 'developmental or other essential reasons'. Voluntary agreement to removal should first be sought, and if that failed a specially created Arbitration Board should be used. In short, the Committee proposed to abolish the quinquennial eviction provisions of the 1928 Ordinance, as Young had proposed 17 years earlier. These provisions, they claimed, were created to allow for the development of estates by removing all tenants from them over a period of 50 years, but this did not take into account increases in population – naturally, by immigration, and by trespass – nor did it take into account the landowners' 'neglect or refusal' to exercise their rights of eviction. Because of the great increase in population on the estates, the enormous difficulty of removing tenants to Trust Land (as a result of political objections and congestion), the better standard of tenants' houses (making removal unfair), and the scarcity of building materials, the Committee concluded that clearing all estates of tenants over a 50-year period should be abandoned, and that removal from estates should be confined to rent default, misconduct and 'cases where it is strictly necessary to do so'. By the latter, they principally had in mind cases where economic development – which they saw as 'imperative' – was proposed:

> Nyasaland ... is directly dependent on its exports and without the tea, tung, tobacco and other crops grown on private land ... the whole economic structure of the country would collapse, with ruinous effects on Africans, Asians and Europeans alike.

The Committee's third 'line of action' aimed at helping those evicted from estates by recommending that adequate notice of eviction should be given in every case, whether for rent default, misconduct or the need for development, and that summary evictions should be abolished. In addition, compensation should be paid to those removed for development purposes.

The Committee's report highlights a number of features: the great increase in population and the consequent greater difficulty of solving the problem of Africans on private estates; the recognition of the impossibility of complying with the 1928 Ordinance (the inability of the estate owners to provide the full rights to garden space, firewood and building material, and the inability of the government to provide alternative sites on Trust Land); the potential dangers of enforcing mass evictions; the recognition of the need for economic development and the part played in it by private estates; the need for a large resident labour force which did not make unacceptable demands on space; and a desire or willingness to treat tenants more humanely by abolishing summary evictions, by providing for compensation to those removed for development purposes, and by granting settlement rights to the daughters of tenants.

The Committee's recommendations on the three 'lines of action' were incorporated in the Africans on Private Estates Ordinance of 1952 which replaced the 1928 law.[72]

It is probable that the European members of the Committee – all landowners or managers of land-holding companies – by improving the 1928 Ordinance and, carrying the African members with them, by making it more humane and easier to implement politically, hoped to divert Colby from his chosen path of acquiring very substantial areas of private land. At the very least, they must have hoped that he would halt at the 300,000 acres of land currently acquired without proceeding to the remaining areas, especially those in the Cholo District where two of the members, Dixon of the BCA Company and Raynor of the B&EA Company, managed 80 per cent of the land recommended for acquisition by the Land Planning Committee.

5
The 1953 disturbances and African reaction

The potential for agitation, conflict and civil unrest inherent in the land problem had been long recognized and not infrequently expressed, and despite the considerable steps which Colby had taken to reduce the scope of the problem – by purchasing 300,000 acres of private land and by beginning to settle African families on it – such agitation, conflict and unrest in fact occurred in 1953, coinciding with the imposition of federation. Colby was particularly angered by what he saw as the insensitive, provocative and extremely dangerous action of the BCA Company, with the backing of the Convention of Associations, in issuing eviction notices on their Shire Highlands estates – where little had yet been done to transfer private land and relieve congestion – in the first half of 1953.[1] He said that:

> The question of land was one on which the African felt most strongly. Indeed it was probable that he felt more strongly on this question than on federation and it was doubly unfortunate that he would inevitably link the two in his mind.[2]

The linking of land alienation and federation was remarked on by a visiting journalist who was told at the time: 'Federation is for the Europeans' good only. They will take all our land.'[3] A British Parliamentary Association delegation in 1957 reported that 'the objections to federation among the Africans [include] first ... a fear that land will be taken away from them'.[4] Many Nyasalanders had personal knowledge of racial attitudes and land practices in Southern Rhodesia as emigrant labourers. The Governor considered steps to mobilize public opinion against the BCA Company and to publicly castigate it, but the non-official members of Executive Council advised against this because it might rally support for the Company.[5] The serious disturbances which occurred then, in August and September 1953, were largely confined to the Blantyre, Chiradzulu, and particularly the Cholo Districts in the Shire Highlands. There seemed little doubt that land was a fundamental cause:

> Although the Federation issue had created a tension in the political atmosphere, the disturbances were fundamentally the result of land grievances, among them a dislike of the tenant system at present in force.[6]

Colby, acutely aware of the depth of feeling among African tenants, clearly saw the need for the rapid removal or diminution of this potentially explosive source of unrest. Although by prompt, firm and decisive action, he brought the 1953 disturbances to a fairly quick end, the underlying causes of the troubles – federation and land – had not been tackled. He and Fox Strangways, the Secretary for African Affairs, impressed upon Executive Council that unless the government and everyone else understood the causes – 'fundamentally ... land grievances' – and took early action to deal with them, trouble could result in a form which would be very hard to deal with.[7]

As soon as the disturbances had died down, Colby sharply turned his attention to the land grievances, and on 2 October 1953 he told the Colonial Office that he intended to see individually 'the comparatively small number of landowners who own substantial areas of land occupied by tenants' to try to secure a more reasonable attitude on the part of at least some of them and convince them to 'divest themselves' of those areas in the interests of future harmony.[8] He was not optimistic of success, feeling that the more he had got on top of the problem the harder had become the owners' attitude. He was anxious to have a 'strong card' up his sleeve without which he felt that meeting landowners would serve no useful purpose, and indeed that a further hardening of their attitude might result, together with the adoption of a position from which they might later find it difficult to retreat. He was concerned that although the owners had been badly frightened during the disturbances they had soon forgotten them – as after the 1915 Chilembwe Rising – and by the end their attitude was harder than before. He also believed that federation had hardened attitudes because the Europeans thought it greatly strengthened their

THE 1953 DISTURBANCES AND AFRICAN REACTION   99

position *vis-à-vis* the Africans 'and possibly even solved their problem'.

Consequently, the 'strong card' which he proposed was that if he failed to convince them he would tell them that he intended to revive his 1949 proposal and impose a penal rate of taxation on undeveloped land – perhaps ten shillings an acre – believing that this threat would be sufficient to induce the sale of the land to the government without actually having to impose the tax. He sought the Secretary of State's views on this proposal by cable and asked for an early reply. It was exactly this sort of somewhat extreme proposal and the request for an early reply which Colby knew would concentrate the minds of both the estate owners and the Colonial Office.

Colonial Office officials gave close attention to Colby's cable[9] and Marnham, Assistant Secretary, quickly turned to the first question to be decided – how vital was it that the land in question should pass into the government's possession? – and concluded that 'there is no doubt that this has in one way or another simply got to be done'. His second question regarded the tactics to be employed, and here he disagreed with Colby:

> It is pretty clear that the Governor has given up all hope that anything less than a bludgeon attack will succeed, but even if he is right it is not certain that he has chosen the right bludgeon.

His doubts as to the right bludgeon arose from the view that penal taxation was not only objectionable in principle but on the basis of experience it was unlikely to be effective, and it was politically undesirable because, for example, Dodds Parker, a director of the BCA Company, and Alport, chairman of the East and Central Africa board, both Conservative back-bench members of parliament, were likely to be very critical and to brand any attempt at a constructive solution, as Marnham saw it, 'as appeasement'. Marnham's advice was that the Colonial Office should tell Colby:

> We absolutely agree that something has got to be done to solve this land problem so far as it is still solvable, and therefore that somehow or other considerable areas of undeveloped freehold land occupied by African squatters have got to be acquired by the Nyasaland Government.

He also advised that compulsion should not be resorted to until 'all efforts to achieve a negotiated settlement have been tried and proved fruitless' when, rather than penal taxation, compulsory purchase would be preferable 'even though it costs money'. They should not rule out the possibility of some form of assistance, probably from Colonial Development and Welfare Fund[10] sources, if Nyasaland itself could not afford it. However, Gorell Barnes, Assistant Under-Secretary, aware from experience that Colby rarely missed a chance to press the British government for finance and exploited every opportunity to do so, said that this part should be omitted!

Gorell Barnes waited for the views of Abrahams, who agreed that the problem had to be solved if there was not to be 'perpetual fear of disturbances' and that penal taxation was undesirable;[11] and Bourdillon, Assistant Secretary, who, as always, saw 'great difficulty' in even contemplating funding from CDWF sources, partly because he felt that, if pressed, Nyasaland could find the money itself;[12] and finally the views of the Secretary of State himself. The Secretary of State accepted Marnham's advice,[13] and Gorell Barnes replied to Colby on 24 October:

> The Secretary of State agrees that every effort should be made to tackle the land problem and that one of the first aims should be acquisition by Government of areas of undeveloped freehold land occupied by African squatters ... Secretary of State does not, however, consider that resort should be had to threats or compulsion until all efforts to achieve a negotiated settlement have been tried and proved fruitless ... If negotiations fail and some form of compulsion has to be threatened and if need be applied Secretary of State considers that it would be preferable to resort to compulsory purchase. He does not favour method of penal taxation.[14]

He added that they welcomed Colby's proposal to meet estate owners and said that he hoped Colby would invite members of the BCA Company board to Nyasaland 'to discuss the position on the spot', although he reminded the Governor that in 1949 land negotiations had been carried out successfully in London with Colby's help. His reason for suggesting discussions with board members in Nyasaland (which he did not give to Colby although it had been semi-officially mentioned to him in the past) was that since relations with Dixon, the new General Manager, were 'thoroughly bad' and it was difficult for the Colonial Office to negotiate in London without local knowledge, it would be better for 'some plenipotentiary from the Company to be asked to go to Nyasaland to discuss the matter'.[15] Colby responded that negotiations would not be much quicker in Nyasaland because Brook, the Company's chairman, 'has little appreciation of African political problems and is likely to be unyielding': in any case to negotiate with Brook might well upset Dixon whom – with no great confidence – he hoped to win over to the Nyasaland government's way of thinking.[16] By using the threat of penal taxation, Colby had succeeded in moving the Colonial Office closer to accepting compulsory purchase.

The Colonial Office now turned to how the price of a negotiated – or indeed a compulsory – settlement was to be met. The Governor had said that he had no doubt that a negotiated settlement could be achieved were it not for the cost and that the 300,000 acres to be acquired were likely to require £200,000. In essence, Colby had persuaded the Colonial Office that 'somehow or other considerable areas ... have got to be acquired'[17] and he now said that, although he was sure he could negotiate acquisition, the Nyasaland government could not afford the acquisition price:[18] 'on financial grounds it is impossible to contemplate such a payment'.[19] Without presenting it explicitly, he was repeating his development strategy argument: 'If you want me to get Nyasaland out of this mess, you must pay for it.'

Basically Gorell Barnes and his colleagues felt that 'the Secretary of State would not wish to be faced with a position where nothing can be done about the land problem (apart from the method of imposing penal taxation on undeveloped land which would bring a storm of protest from government back-benchers) because we are short of £200,000'.[20] On the other hand, the Colonial Office Finance Division and the Treasury were adamant that the money could not come from United Kingdom funds and consequently they pressed Colby to find the purchase price from Nyasaland resources. Just as in Colby's view the Africans linked the question of land with federation, so now the British finance officials linked payment for solving the land problem with federation, and, noting Colby's own estimate that, with federal financial support, he should have a surplus of £266,000 on the 1954/5 budget, they wrote to him:

the Secretary of State who is personally most anxious to remedy the present unsatisfactory position ... favours a settlement by negotiation if this is at all possible. He is therefore glad to see that you are confident that a negotiated settlement could be achieved were it not for the difficulties of finding the sum of £200,000 likely to be involved. He agrees that hitherto there would have been very grave difficulties in finding a sum of this order, but now that Federation has come we need not continue to regard it as being completely out of the question, particularly since ... you expect a budget surplus of some £266,000 for 1954-5 which you intend to put to reserve. Nyasaland's reserves are, of course, inadequate and it is very desirable that they should be built up as quickly as possible; but I should have thought that the postponement of this building up process for a year was not too large a price to pay for the final removal of a long standing land grievance and the very considerable contribution which that would make to racial harmony. The Secretary of State hopes therefore that on reconsideration you will be able to agree that the sum of £200,000 likely to be involved in a negotiated settlement should be found from local sources.[21]

Although they did not tell Colby that they had agreed among themselves at the Colonial Office that, if he really could not find the money and if he put up a truly convincing case, the British Government would find it from somewhere, and although they warned the Treasury of this possibility and later that CDWF money might be needed for resettlement purposes,[22] Marnham and Williams would have been prepared to tell him; Gorell Barnes, Melville and Bourdillon were not.[23] Lloyd, the Permanent Secretary, suggested in a minute not sent to Colby that maybe CDWF could find half the money required and Nyasaland could find the other half.[24] There was therefore significant willingness to help; indeed, having 'absolutely agreed' that somehow or other 'considerable areas ... have got to be acquired', the Colonial Office could hardly do otherwise.

In the event, Colby, recognizing the practical force of an argument given in the name of the Secretary of State, accepted the position and on 26 February 1954 wrote to say that he reluctantly agreed 'we' would have to face heavy expenditure although he hoped to keep the figure below £200,000. 'The settlement of this problem is worth a lot of money,'[25] he wrote, to which Marnham, relieved, added in the margin 'Good'. His colleagues read Colby's letter as accepting that

Nyasaland would find the money, whilst other officers 'assumed this to mean that the Governor now accepts full liability for finding the money likely to be needed to effect a negotiated settlement';[26] they had interpreted Colby's 'we' as meaning Nyasaland. In Bowring's terms, Nyasaland was having to pay for the evils of its fathers!

Whilst these financial aspects were being explored, negotiations were continuing with the landowners. Colby had a 'long and agreeable talk' with Dixon,[27] but he found it difficult to assess his personal attitude and believed that Dixon had been unable to convince his board of the need to divest themselves of undeveloped land. Since the problem of large areas of freehold land was restricted, the majority of estates in Nyasaland having little or no undeveloped land, Colby wished to make this clear in any general dealings with landowners in order to counter the 'propaganda that Dixon has been putting about . . . that this is a problem which affects every European estate'. He was keen 'to drive a wedge between the bulk of the estate owners and the comparatively few owners of large areas'. He planned to meet informally with a few landowners within the next ten days to try to convince them that the great majority need not be affected if the BCA Company made 'some gesture' in being prepared to dispose of undeveloped land. Presumably, the 'gesture' he had in mind included both the parting with fairly large areas of land and also a low price, in neither of which respects would smaller owners necessarily be expected to follow suit. He was unable to convince them of this.

Early in December 1953, Gorell Barnes used a social occasion to tackle Alport about unused company land in Southern Nyasaland and made the point that the Colonial Office were looking to him and his board to be rather more helpful and to encourage estate owners to assist in government attempts to deal with 'a most unsatisfactory situation'. Alport took this quite well and, whilst he did not think much progress would be made in discussions between the Governor and the managers in Nyasaland, he believed that if the Secretary of State were ready to discuss the question in a friendly manner with the board some satisfactory solution might easily emerge. Alport added that he would shortly seek an interview between the board and the Secretary of State. The Colonial Office told Colby that they were pinning their main hopes on negotiations in London, using the meeting which Alport proposed as exploratory and working out the details when he came to Britain at the end of April.[28] Direct negotiations with board members in London – now advocated by

Alport – had been the procedure recommended by the Land Planning Committee in 1947 and by Colby in 1948, and had been successfully used in practice in 1949.

On 22 December, Colby wrote that he was optimistic that he could reach a settlement with most landowners although detailed implementation would take some time; he added, however, that there were indications of increasing African impatience and that 'something must clearly be done soon'. He was aware, too, that most owners would not move until a settlement with the BCA Company indicated the level of prices that was to prevail.[29]

When Brook visited Nyasaland in the first few weeks of 1954, Colby met with him and Dixon and made it very plain that he hoped this time there would be a final solution to the problem which was 'not only serious but vitally urgent', and that unless there was at least some indication from the Company of their being ready to do something in the next two or three months 'there would be every possibility that a difficult [security] situation would arise in the coming dry season'. He said it would be useless for the Company to seek to retain considerable areas of undeveloped land since this would only provide a focus for further agitation and he had in any case the Secretary of State's support for acquiring undeveloped land. The problem, therefore, was to determine how much land the Company could develop within, say, the next five years: 'If the BCA Company could reach a position in which they held no undeveloped land, there should be no political problem.' He told the Colonial Office of his view, however, that Brook did not really appreciate the dangers involved and he suggested that – whilst awaiting a letter from Brook indicating what the Company intended to do – Gorell Barnes might see him in London and reinforce the Governor's arguments.[30] No letter had been received by mid-March and Colby again asked Gorell Barnes to see Brook and 'explain that the matter is really extremely urgent and time is not on our side'.[31] The optimism of an early settlement, expressed three months earlier, was now fading fast and Colby was worried.

The Governor felt that he was making no progress with most of the landowners, who were waiting to see and then follow the BCA Company's lead, although the ALC had agreed to release a block of 800 acres in the Cholo District: Colby had originally hoped for 4,400 acres.[32]

Towards the end of March, the Colonial Office sought Colby's views on a proposal that the Secretary of State should announce that he intended to visit Nyasaland early in May in order, *inter alia*, to look personally at the Southern Province land problems, and that he should tell Brook and Alport of this and add that, although he did not wish to decide on a final solution until he returned from Nyasaland, he must do so very soon thereafter. He proposed to tell them that his current view was that an essential part of the solution must be to surrender undeveloped land which would not be developed within the very near future.[33] Colby felt it unwise to announce that the Secretary of State was going to look into land problems because this would intensify African agitation between the time of the announcement and the visit. The announcement would probably be distorted to make it appear that the visit was to dispossess Europeans of their land. He could see no objection to Brook and Alport being told of the visit and its purpose in confidence.[34]

Whilst these various steps were being taken in respect of the European estate owners, Colby was also negotiating with the African leaders.

His anxiety to impress upon the BCA Company the extreme urgency of making progress, and his view that it would be unwise to announce publicly that the Secretary of State's visit was to discuss land issues, were accentuated by the intelligence reports he received during February 1954 of rising agitation and signs of unrest among Africans over the lack of progress in land matters. When these reports were also received at the Colonial Office the officials there received a 'jolt', and they persuaded the Secretary of State to see Brook and Alport and say that some public indication that the problem was being tackled must be given very soon, by announcing either that the BCA Company had agreed in principle to part with a certain amount of undeveloped land, or that, since no such agreement had been reached, the Nyasaland Government proposed to acquire a certain area compulsorily.[35] This the Secretary of State did at a meeting on 14 April, in effect paving the way for his visit to Nyasaland in May.[36]

Even without the grievances, including in particular the land grievances, which erupted in August and September 1953, and the intelligence reports early in 1954, Colby was aware of the deep and growing African resentment over land issues and of the security dangers this posed, because the deliberations of the African Protectorate Council in 1952 and 1953 made the resentment and dangers abundantly clear. During the interview which African representatives had in London at the Federation Conference in April 1952, the Secretary of State had suggested that since the land question was complex it would be helpful if they submitted a memorandum giving their representations in more detail. Gorell Barnes wrote to Colby in July 1952 to follow up this suggestion.[37] In August 1952, the Protectorate Council appointed a sub-committee of moderate and much-respected leading Africans to draft a memorandum on land matters to the Secretary of State, and in late 1952 and early 1953 they worked hard on preparing the memorandum. A draft was discussed in May 1953 with the Secretary for African Affairs, Fox Strangways, and the Secretary for Lands and Mines, Feeny, leading to a number of suggested amendments. A redraft was later translated into Chinyanja and sent to members of the Protectorate Council before being discussed at a meeting of Council on 15 December 1953.[38] In October 1953, Colby asked Fox Strangways to tell the Council that he, the Governor, had sympathy with the African point of view in respect of freehold land covered with tenants and would like to support their submission to the Secretary of State. He added:

> I could not, however, support the memorandum as it now stands and I hope they will alter it to remove all the utter nonsense and political clap trap in it.[39]

Fox Strangways used more diplomatic language in conveying Colby's wishes and asked Council carefully to 'examine the draft to see that there was nothing in it which was either untrue or exaggerated'.[40] It was not simply that Colby wished to support the Protectorate Council, but that he was also looking to them to reinforce his own arguments, and he was aware that inaccuracies and exaggerations would render the Council's memorandum open to attack and thereby weaken the support which it could lend to the Governor's case.

At its meeting of 15 December 1953, the Council discussed the draft at length and decided that it should be looked at again by the sub-committee, with the assistance of Fox Strangways and Feeny. This took place whilst the Council adjourned, and after further discussion Council endorsed the redrafted memorandum.[41] The effect of the redrafting was three-fold. First, it shortened and tightened up the wording of the introduction by major rewriting and, by radically reducing the number of introductory paragraphs, got more quickly to the core of the memorandum. Second, it removed many of the more 'flowery', less meaningful, sections from this introduction. Third, the redraft left virtually untouched, save for a few grammatical improvements, the remainder of the memorandum and the 'requests' (the word substituted for 'demands') which it made. The redrafted memorandum concluded with a statement removed from the introductory paragraphs, a reaffirmation of the Nyasaland African people's 'unwavering loyalty' to the Crown and 'absolute confidence' in Her Majesty's Government.

In the memorandum, the Protectorate Council made a number of requests. First, they asked that 'freehold private land . . . not actively and directly opened up and not . . . under direct use or cultivation by the owner', and 'land on which Africans have lived all their lives', together with land adjacent to congested or fast becoming congested land, and all land owned by missionaries not being used for mission buildings or educational centres, should be purchased by the government at the same price as that for which it was originally acquired, and handed to the Chief-in-Council for African settlement and cultivation. They also asked that 'all land situated in and around all townships' should similarly be purchased and that all forest reserves be examined with a view to opening up some of them for African settlement and cultivation. They concluded their memorandum with what was in effect a warning:

> We believe that in all inter-racial relations in this country, the question of land will stand out as the testing standard and we accordingly urge the Government in the United Kingdom to do the utmost possible to find means by which this most perplexing question may be solved.

6

The policy of progressive abolition of *thangata*, 1954

The Governor forwarded the redrafted memorandum to the Secretary of State on 14 January 1954 as part of the proceedings of the Protectorate Council meeting, and followed it up with his promised comments – which he used to state his views on what government policy should be – on 16 March 1954,[1] when he started his telegram despatch by briefly outlining the steps taken by the government in recent years and added:

> Since 1948 considerable progress has been made, but despite this the basic problem remains and the African's demand for more agricultural land and for "emancipation" still persists; in fact since twelve months ago these feelings have become intensified.

The 'considerable progress' included acquiring 300,000 acres of the 546,000 recommended for purchase by the Land Planning Committee, agreement on purchasing a further 21,000 acres, and current negotiations for an additional 4,000 acres. The intensification of feelings was due in large measure to the imposition of federation and the African's fear of European domination, especially by Southern Rhodesia.

He next expressed his view that although those subscribing to the memorandum were sincere in all that they had written, they had allowed their views to get out of perspective and had overstated their case, giving the impression that 'all tenants on private estates are living in a state of near serfdom', and he tried to put the position in better perspective. Most estate owners, he said, had good relations with their tenants and would deeply resent any suggestion that they treated them in a manner approaching serfdom; and the grievances were mainly confined to the large estate owners, especially the BCA Company; of the 170,000 Africans currently resident on private estates, he estimated that only half were actively concerned to secure a change in their status as tenants. He acknowledged that the remainder, 'notwithstanding the comparative smallness of their number', constituted 'an important and dangerous element'.

Colby then turned to consider how far acquisition would relieve congestion and pointed out that of the 887,000 acres remaining in private hands, 500,000 were already occupied by African tenants; purchasing all this land would remove the troubles between landlord and tenant but would do nothing to alleviate congestion. Of the other 387,000 acres, 100,000 were developed by the owners, and 200,000 were either under indigenous forest or ought not to be cultivated for conservation reasons, leaving less than 100,000 acres available to relieve congestion. He had made this last point – the impossibility of doing much to relieve congestion – to Cohen almost six years earlier, and he now said, 'It would be idle to suppose that acquisition of all of it would give any perceptible or permanent relief to the problem of congestion.' In dealing with the original alienation of land – a matter raised a number of times in the memorandum – Colby said that the Southern Province members of the Protectorate Council felt most strongly and could not be convinced 'that the transactions . . . leading to the issue of Certificates of Claim in the 1890s were recognised at the time and could not now be reopened'. Colby's view was that:

> even supposing African claims to land were deserving of sympathy on ethical grounds, there is no doubt that any claims they might make in a court of law would not invalidate the titles now held by estate owners. Any reopening of the question of freehold titles which were recognised by Sir Harry Johnston in his Certificates of Claim can only lead to profitless acrimony, and cannot be contemplated.

He summarized the early part of his despatch by saying that the problem was essentially political, the Africans directly affected were a comparatively small proportion living in a relatively compact area of the Southern Province, the unoccupied land available for acquisition would have little perceptible effect on congestion, and the present African dissatisfaction contained serious political dangers. He was at pains to explain that 'it is the political aspect of the problem rather than the congestion aspect which is important'. What he was aiming at, in effect, was the full use of the land either for active economic development or for accommodating Africans. As for striking a balance between the two, the political aspects would take precedence over the congestion aspects.

The Governor proceeded to explain his proposed solution to the problem and for the first time clearly introduced a social anthropological dimension to the argument:

> the solution of the problem lies in the gradual adaptation of the use of land in private ownership so as to conform as closely as possible to African usufructual ideas, which are . . . as strong in the mind of the African today as they ever were, and close examination of the African land grievances will reveal that at the base of them there is always the same factor, i.e. that ownership of land can only go with the direct use of it. For this reason they have never disputed the ownership of land in actual cultivation by estate owners. Conversely Africans cannot see that any other person should have any rights to the land which they themselves are cultivating, and it is this belief which is at the bottom of their dislike of the tenant system. Nor can they see that any estate owner has the right to prevent others from cultivating land which he does not require for his own immediate use, dissatisfaction on this last point being particularly dangerous in closely-populated areas.

With this social anthropological dimension to the solution centrally in mind, Colby categorized private land into four groups.

First, there was land in direct use by the estate owner, including land temporarily under fallow; with this he felt there was no political difficulty since it would not be in accordance with usufructual principles to claim it, but it should be fenced to make clear that it was in use. Second, there was private land occupied by African tenants; this he believed should be acquired by the government for African use, priority being given to the areas where dissatisfaction was greatest, thereby removing tenant status and preventing sale to Asians (which was a growing concern expressed in the Protectorate Council memorandum). Third, there was private land under indigenous forest, or incapable of economic development, or which, for other conservation reasons, should not be developed; this he felt should be preserved in its virgin state and, although this would not accord with African usufructual ideas since it would not appear to be used, the government should acquire it because 'any resentment about the preservation of natural resources should be directed against Government'. Fourth, there was land of agricultural value, unoccupied either by the estate owner or by African tenants; this he believed presented the most urgent problem:

> Although the extent of this land is not great, feeling about it is very high, and if serious political trouble is to be avoided all this land should be put fully under development in the course of the next five years, or else surrendered for African use: any such land which cannot be developed during the next five years should be surrendered now.

He made no reference to clearing retained land of tenant occupation.

This categorization of private land and the way in which he believed each category should be handled constituted 'a broad enunciation of the general policy which [he] consider[ed] should be pursued with a view to allaying African misgivings about the ownership of private land and their dislike of the tenant system'. By 'the gradual adaptation of the use of the land in private ownership so as to conform as closely as possible to African usufructual ideas', he was attempting to do what Bell and Abrahams said could not be done: namely, to effect a reconciliation between African and European concepts – or at least practices – of land-holding.

Colby went on to say that he would require the work of resettlement to be done with the full agreement of the local Africans, their village headmen, and native authorities, and in return for the land which they would receive he would require them to sign a document recognizing that the transaction was final so as to strengthen the hand of future administrations and deter 'profitless pursuit' of the way in which the original Certificates of Claim were issued.

Finally, Colby dealt with the requests made in the Protectorate Council memorandum. He believed that his proposals covered all of these save for land near the townships, forest reserves, and land owned by missions. He pointed out that land in and near the townships was controlled under the town planning legislation and, because of the cost involved, acquisition was not justified. In respect of forest reserves, he believed that only education would solve the problem, because although most Africans said that the reserves were necessary, very few really believed it. He felt that mission lands presented no real pressing worries because tenants there lived much as they would on Trust Land and because there was little mission land in the Southern Province where real dissatisfaction existed; nonetheless, he advised that any mission land offered for sale at a reasonable price should be bought by the government.

Colby's concluding paragraph asked for the Secretary of State's early comments on his despatch because he regarded 'African concern over the whole land question as being of great political importance'. Lyttelton replied by cable on the same day as he received Colby's despatch. He generally agreed with the Governor's observations but did not wish to reach a final conclusion on land policy until after his imminent visit to Nyasaland. That he was strongly disposed to accept Colby's proposals is indicated by the fact that he asked for a reply to the Protectorate Council memorandum to be drafted along Colby's lines which could be finalized when he arrived in the protectorate.[2] The resultant reply, sent after the Secretary of State's visit, did in fact follow Colby's reasoning, policy, and often his words, very closely.[3]

The signals which the Governor received from the disturbances, the Protectorate Council, and the early 1954 political intelligence reports[4] persuaded him, or confirmed him in his opinion, that the policy of acquiring private land and resettling African families from congested areas now needed urgent acceleration. He publicly and bluntly expressed his opinion that:

> Africans in parts of the Southern Province live in a state of congestion and that whilst large areas of freehold land, the property of European estate owners, remain undeveloped there will exist a potential danger to the peace and tranquility of the country.[5]

Late in 1953 and early in 1954, he made direct proposals to owners of several of the larger estates that, except for areas already cultivated or to be developed within the next three to five years, all land should be handed to the government for resettling Africans.[6] After the indelicate and boat-rocking issuing of notices to quit by the BCA

Company earlier in 1953, and the serious disturbances in the areas of greatest land alienation, Colby was in no mood to beat around the bush. After decades of gentlemanly negotiation and giving in to landowners – as the Colonial Office had pointed out in 1927 – and after numerous hints that acquisition was the only feasible way forward, Colby had made an early start on settling the problem, but the large acquisitions of 1949 had done little to change conditions in the heavily congested areas of the Shire Highlands, and he was now determined to bring matters to a swift conclusion. Many of the landowners were aghast at these proposals and they immediately formed a Landowners' Association, 'representing the owners of a large proportion of the freehold land' in the country, and whose members controlled over half that land, to resist Colby's proposals.[7]

In a note for the Secretary of State's visit written on 20 April 1954,[8] Colby concluded that 'the only practical means of doing away with the tenant system, since the removal of large numbers of tenants off estates was out of the question, was to buy the lands on which the tenants reside' – a process started in 1949, albeit in respect of land not heavily populated, but which had since come to a virtual halt. He outlined the general plan of acquisition as:

> designed to make as much provision for further European development as the present situation permits. It is not desired to acquire unoccupied land which is capable of and required for European development in the near future, but only to acquire land which cannot be developed by reason of having African settlement on it and other such areas as are unsuitable for utilisation by the owners or are clearly superfluous to their needs. It is intended that the African should also make his contribution to the settlement problem, by confining himself to those parts of estates bought for him, and by withdrawing himself from other parts required by owners for further development.

Colby's reference to European development clearly meant development on existing holdings rather than on new holdings as, in part, envisaged by Abrahams and the Land Planning Committee. The reference to land 'clearly superfluous to needs' was designed to warn landowners not to be ambitious in their claims to retain land on the grounds that it was to be developed: the Land Planning Committee had not been impressed with the BCA Company's 15-year development plan which they saw as being 'patently impracticable'. His reference to the African tenant 'withdrawing himself' from retained land was somewhat firmer and more positive than the earlier references to 'being invited to opt' to move.

He went on to say that for this policy of acquisition to be effectively implemented it would be necessary to start it on the larger estates where tenant problems were most acute. This was a change of mind since April 1948, when Colby's view was that they should 'approach the most reasonable owners first'. Most owners had said that they agreed in principle with his proposals, but in practice, when it came to the point, they were reluctant to part with the land.

In May 1954, the Secretary of State, Lyttelton, visited Nyasaland to discuss land and constitutional reform. He received a long memorandum from the Landowners' Association and the Convention of Associations who joined forces to vilify Colby and attack his land proposals.[9] In their eyes these proposals were the culminating iniquity of a Governor, appointed by a socialist Secretary of State, who had taken systematic steps towards state control and nationalization: the Acquisition of Land for Public Purposes Ordinance; the replacement of private purchasing of crops with statutory marketing boards; the encouragement of Colonial Development Corporation trading stores in competition with private shops in remote areas; the establishment of the African Press publishing company; and now land.[10]

The view expressed in the memorandum – which was given prominence in the local press – was that the claims made during the 1953 disturbances about land were 'made for political purposes and not ... because there is any widespread need for more land'; it was their 'firm conviction that, judged on a territorial basis, congestion [did] not exist'. They were unrestrained in their denunciation of the Governor, accusing him of 'appeasement on a grand scale', of following 'a policy of despair', of being wanting in 'a much more statesman-like attitude', of being 'inflexible', and of working under 'false suppositions'.

Joelson, editor of *East Africa and Rhodesia*, took the opportunity to add that periodical's denigration:

> The general opinion of European non-officials [is] that there has been no firm government of Nyasaland for years, that native agitators now expect to be appeased, that those who incite their

fellows to lawlessness think the risk of punishment slight, and that ... Africans have ceased to look to the government for resolute leadership ... Many Europeans in Nyasaland have been saying for several years that they have no faith in the Governor and no confidence in his ideas.

He compared Colby's government unfavourably with the government of Southern and Northern Rhodesia, which had 'a determination to be firm with the African for the African's own good', adding that 'such a doctrine [was] anathema' to Colby.[11]

The landowners' principal contention was that Colby's proposals would not provide a lasting solution because they were convinced that to hand over private land to African settlement would lead in a few years to further decimation of forest areas and ruination of the soil. Once this had occurred, the demand for more land would resume and pressure would be brought on owners to give up any remaining undeveloped land which in turn would also be ruined. The philosophy behind this fear of the ultimate loss of private land and the destruction of the country's natural resources was clarified in their demands that Colby should recognize:

> that the African through lack of training, has by nature an irresponsible attitude towards the natural resources, and must adopt the policy that the European, by virtue of centuries of civilisation and accumulated scientific knowledge, knows the best way to develop the country and is prepared, unpleasant as it may be, to adopt and enforce a policy best suited to the country as a whole ... that the Africans of Nyasaland cannot be considered at present as being capable of directing the affairs of the country, and this being so the European must continue to govern without fear or favour and irrespective of race.

In this way they linked the question of land to that of constitutional development, the two questions which Lyttelton had come to discuss.

The landowners could not realistically have expected Colby to share their view on the role of Africans, either in agricultural or in administrative, constitutional matters, since improved African agriculture was at the heart of his development strategy and he had given early warnings of the need to be ready for the inevitable political awakenings. They insisted that the African demands for acquisition of freehold land must be resisted, that good race relations with the Africans must not be obtained at the expense of the Europeans, and that a solution to the problem was possible without one section of the community being sacrificed for the benefit of the other. They maintained that, if properly developed, Trust Land could adequately cater for the needs of the African people. In order to deal properly with the Trust Land areas, immediate steps should be taken to increase considerably the staff of European administrative officers and train large numbers of African agricultural instructors. Finally, they said that arriving at a satisfactory solution would require the goodwill and unqualified co-operation of all races and that the Nyasaland Government had special responsibilities in establishing this goodwill and co-operation. They said nothing about their own responsibilities.

This memorandum was sent to the Secretary of State on 1 May by Dixon as Chairman of the European Landowners' Association. Five days later, Lyttelton held a meeting at Government House, Zomba, with landowners nominated by the Convention of Associations. It was a large meeting, with fifteen landowners or their managers, including Brook, Dixon, Barrow and Hadlow. On the government side, the Secretary of State was accompanied by the Governor, Chief Secretary, Director of Agriculture, Provincial Commissioner of the Southern Province, the Land Settlement Officer, the Assistant Under Secretary, and the Lands Adviser to the Colonial Office.[12]

Lyttelton opened this meeting by setting out the policy of Her Majesty's Government. He recognized the contribution of estates to the agricultural development of the protectorate and said that it was 'settled policy' to ensure that owners had security in the possession and management of their developed lands. This point about security was made in response to Alport's view, expressed at a Colonial Office meeting on 14 April to discuss land policy and law and order in Nyasaland: 'The land-owners would hope for some concrete return in the form of increased prospects of future security for any sacrifice they might make.'[13] At his May meeting in Nyasaland, Lyttelton took the opportunity which this view presented to place the land question in a much broader context, and in so doing to take a clear and firm line. He emphasized that the future security sought could be assured only if conditions were created which enabled the estate owners to live in amity with the African population. Without these conditions, the growing unrest and political feeling would make it impossible for the estate owners to carry on; it was not possible to use force to implement a land policy which was not acceptable to the mass of the inhabitants because 'ultimately the necessary force was lacking'. These views on the ultimate impracticability of force were shared by Colby who, four years earlier, had publicly said of agricultural production:

> we must be realistic and recognise that a handful of Europeans can not compel hundreds of thousands of farmers – it just is not possible as there is no effective machinery through which orders on such a vast scale can be enforced.[14]

Lyttelton continued to say: 'Taking into account that there was no ultimate backing of force, the rights of property must be harmonised with the over-riding social contentment of the population.' Few statements could have been clearer in indicating which side the British government would support if the two sides – owners and tenants, Europeans and Africans – did not sort things out amicably among themselves. Lyttelton then went on to say what was to be done:

> Policy would therefore be directed to the progressive abolition of the "tangata" system which would be implemented by purchasing from estate owners all those areas of land which were occupied by tenants or were otherwise unsuitable for estate development or which could not be developed within a reasonable time.

The Secretary of State was anxious to secure the co-operation of landowners and would use compulsory acquisition only as a last resort. Whilst small numbers of tenants could be moved to free some estate land for development, it would be 'completely impossible' to evict large numbers. It would be 'impracticable' for landowners to retain unused and unoccupied land in the congested areas for any length of time. If it were to be retained, it would have to be developed within a reasonable time.

The ultimate aim was that estate owners would have on their estates no Africans with any rights to land, and the substantial labour force required for tea and other estates would be accommodated either in housing built by the estates for permanent labour and 'completely independent of subsistence agriculture', or on neighbouring accommodation blocks. Since executing this policy would be a lengthy process, the government would first direct its attention to those holdings in which discontent and political unrest were growing; thus, early action would be needed only on a small number of estates over the next few years, since relationships on the vast majority of estates were cordial. This last remark was designed to reassure the majority of landowners and to distance them from the larger owners, especially the BCA Company, on whose estates, though relatively small in number but large in area, the problems were much more acute.

In this carefully worded, albeit brief, statement of policy, Lyttelton included all the essential points of the proposals which Colby had put to him seven weeks earlier.[15] The very succinctness of the statement gave it a poignancy which forcefully struck the estate owners present. Lyttelton ended his statement by saying that the existing settlement and development policy would 'be continued and accelerated', and in order to do this, which would be 'subject to the provision of further staff and finance, H.M.G. would be very ready to examine how they could render assistance, possibly through the new Colonial Development and Welfare Allocation'. Later he said that the government would continue its policy 'with help from H.M.G., with staff and C. D. and W grants'.[16] In making these statements, the Secretary of State went further than his briefing notes which simply said 'H.M.G. will examine means of assisting e.g. by the provision of further staff',[17] with no reference to the CDWF. He then asked those estate owners present if they were agreeable to the line of action which he had outlined.

Dixon replied that the Secretary of State's proposals were appeasement, that a 'vigorous attitude' was required of the government, and that 'drastic treatment' was necessary. It was, of course, not the vigour and drastic nature of what was proposed to which Dixon objected, but the pro-tenant direction which the attitudes and treatment were to take. Lyttelton was well aware of the 'hard' line adopted by the BCA Company since, for example, at the Colonial Office meeting on 14 April, Brook had advocated that the external police reinforcements used during the 1953 disturbances should be reimported before trouble broke out again 'to show the flag and forestall any outbreak'.[18] Dixon's own solution to the land problem was that agricultural development on Trust Land would draw Africans away from the estate areas. He was 'certain' that adequate

Trust Land was available but it lacked water supplies and European development: 'An influx of Europeans to the Vipya would be followed by an influx of Africans' presumably – but unrealistically – drawn away from the congested areas of the Shire Highlands hundreds of miles to the south with their different tribes and languages. He was silent on the impact which such a movement of Africans, even if it were remotely likely to happen, would have on labour supplies in the south.

The Secretary of State responded that Dixon's views were 'entirely unsupported by argument' and that many of his statements were 'entirely incorrect'. If a solution were sought along Dixon's lines, he foresaw the ultimate necessity for force – which he had already ruled out:

> absolute control, which would require wholesale evictions, would exacerbate the present tension, and would require the conjuring up of sufficient African Trust Land which was just not available. He was absolutely convinced that a solution on these lines was not possible.

All the estate owners present – save Barrow and Hadlow, who had been closely associated with government policy formation as members of Executive Council – were opposed to the steps proposed by the government to deal with the land problem, but the most vigorously expressed opposition came from Dixon. Part way through the meeting, when it was clear to everyone that Lyttelton was strongly backing the Governor's views and policy, and was having little truck with the views of the large estate owners, Colby asked why the BCA Company wished to retain large areas of tenant-occupied land. It is likely that this simple question was designed to embarrass and expose Dixon who replied by trying to 'duck' it, saying that it was incorrect that his Company wished to retain such land since in February – presumably when Colby had approached the large landowners – they had offered 60,000 acres to the government. Colby taunted him a little more, saying he did not recollect this offer, whereupon Brook came to his General Manager's aid, explaining that Dixon had mentioned the 60,000 acres to him and that he had felt prepared to discuss it subject to the government making clear what would happen to the land and also agreeing to 'undesirables' being kept off the land retained. Colby pushed a little further, saying that it had not been

THE POLICY OF PROGRESSIVE ABOLITION OF *THANGATA* 121

made clear to him by Brook that he had made a firm offer. Brook quickly said that he had not made a firm offer, but, in order to get out of what was becoming too detailed and confining a discussion, especially in the presence of other landowners, he suggested that the government should now get in touch with Dixon to discuss with him what land it required.

Brook's suggestion was potentially such a major shift in attitude that Lyttelton was quick to secure the ground which Colby's simple-sounding question had made available; he did not want Dixon to be able to wriggle out of this opportunity as Kaye Nicol had wriggled out of recommending to the Company the release of land following the deliberations of the Land Planning Committee in 1947. Lyttelton closed the nut-crackers around Dixon, and immediately after Brook had made his suggestion about further discussion on what land the government required, he said:

> that was what was wanted but he had gathered that Mr. Dixon found such a solution distasteful. He was very glad to hear that Mr. Brook was prepared to discuss the sale of land ... He felt that 60,000 acres would be a notable contribution. Mr. Dixon had however led him to believe that both he and the meeting were opposed to acquisition of land by Government.

Colby was equally keen to secure the ground presented and possibly to secure even more, and – pushing the wedge between Dixon and Brook a little further than the Secretary of State had just driven it – he said that the impression he had gained from the Landowners' Association memorandum and from Dixon was that Dixon was opposed to handing over tenant-occupied land. He was surprised that Brook now said the Company had been prepared to discuss the sale of 60,000 acres and enquired whether they were prepared to negotiate the disposal of all tenant-occupied land. Brook, however, was not going to yield more in this discussion and said he was not prepared to dispose of all such land, as they wished to retain some because of the value of tenants as labour. Clearly, he had not grasped, or had not accepted the significance of, Lyttelton's statement that 'all those areas of land which were occupied by tenants' would be purchased – but he did say that the government should suggest what areas it required so that the Company might consider them.

Nonetheless, Colby was well pleased: he had got the BCA Company chairman to say that he was prepared to consider sales of land and to agree, in front of the Secretary of State and many others, that the government should suggest to Dixon what areas it required so that the Company could consider the requirements. This was a considerable piercing of Brook's otherwise implacable opposition to government acquisition of tenant-occupied land.

For whatever reason, the BCA Company appears to have become somewhat more amenable to the government's wishes after the May 1954 meeting,[19] although the transformation was not sudden: rather, Colby, having pierced the Company's opposition, was determined to exploit his advantage by isolating the Company from the other landowners and pushing it hard. From the very beginning, he had seen that the BCA Company would be the biggest nut to crack: over the years they had become more, rather than less, entrenched, and he had been dissuaded by Barrow in 1953 from exposing them in order to get public support on his side. He, and Hadlow, believed that African grievances over *thangata* arose from the 'situation prevailing on only four or five of the European estates ... primarily from that prevailing on the British Central Africa Company land'.[20] Apart from this company's recalcitrance, all was going fairly well, and in pursuing Brook and Dixon he did not wish to hinder or retard that other progress. He was, however, now faced with a further difficulty: the publication of a document setting out the government's land policy in Nyasaland.

Less than a week after Lyttelton's visit – a success from Colby's point of view because the Secretary of State had not only accepted the Governor's proposed policy but also firmly announced it to the landowners – Colby went on leave to Britain, leaving Footman as Acting Governor.[21]

In the summer of 1954, Colonial Office officials, after 'months of cogitation', embodied their provisional conclusions in a draft despatch showing the way in which it was intended to implement the policy of progressive abolition of *thangata*. The draft despatch contained a good deal of historical background material, but the essence of it was an amplification of what was meant by 'progressive abolition of tangata', some of the measures to be taken, and the time in which they were to be taken. Private land occupied by few Africans but otherwise capable of development should be freed of Africans so that development could take place, by moving the Africans either on to neighbouring

THE POLICY OF PROGRESSIVE ABOLITION OF *THANGATA* 123

land acquired by the government or on to other parts of the estate. Private land which was heavily occupied and undeveloped, and which was not required for early development, should be acquired. Estate owners should as soon as possible make their development plans known to the government 'so that Government could judge in estate-by-estate discussion with them what course would be in the interests of all concerned'. The aim should be to complete the whole exercise in four years, which Colby had said was achievable 'given the necessary co-operation' from landowners. As each estate became cleared of tenants, the Africans on Private Estates Ordinance would cease to apply. On 16 August, the Colonial Office sent the draft despatch to Footman who agreed with it and hoped very much that it would be published.[22]

Colby's opinion was also sought,[23] and, at a meeting which he and Hadlow had with the Secretary of State on 12 and 13 October,[24] he also agreed. He wished, though, to qualify his agreement on the question of the rent payable under the Africans on Private Estates Ordinance; he had in mind that a severe reduction in rent payable might so reduce the value of the land that the owners would be more ready to sell to the government. He emphasized his strong view, however, that the despatch should not be published unless it had been discussed among Africans and had gained at least a degree of acceptance.[25] Whilst he could see that publication might reassure interested parties in Britain that the policy of abolishing *thangata* would proceed, he believed that publication in Nyasaland 'would simply stir up feelings which were now quiescent'. If his government could make some positive progress in acquiring estate land heavily occupied by tenants, that would be received by Africans as much better proof of the government's intentions than the despatch.

Marnham accepted the Governor's views, saying that if his advice was not to publish then they should follow it, since the only reason for publication in the United Kingdom was to demonstrate to both sides of the House of Commons 'that something was being done', and this could just as well be achieved in reply to a Parliamentary Question (to which Colby objected less, although he still preferred the Colonial Office not to instigate one).[26] When this advice reached Gorell Barnes, though, he took a very different view:

Publication, which is also favoured by Mr Footman, seems to me to be essential, not so much in order to satisfy public opinion here that it is really our intention to implement the policy, but rather to make it quite clear to all concerned in Nyasaland what the Government's policy is.[27]

He must have been aware that the policy was well known in Nyasaland since the Secretary of State's visit, but felt that, if this were not done, those landlords who had been difficult in the past would continue to attempt to 'avoid facing the needs of the situation'. Three views therefore existed: Marnham's, which focused on reaction in the House of Commons; Gorell Barnes', which focused on European landowners in Nyasaland; and Colby's, which focused on African reactions in Nyasaland. Colby agreed to look closely at the question of publication on his return to Nyasaland and to give his considered opinion as soon as possible.[28]

There were probably three influences which made Colby reluctant to publish the despatch: the introduction of what may have seemed to him an academic debate at a very late stage into a matter which had deeply worrying practical implications and which he had always treated in a pragmatic way; the changed circumstances in Nyasaland; and his wish to have room to manoeuvre in his dealings with the BCA Company.

During his visit to Nyasaland in the first week of May 1954, Lyttelton had been accompanied by S. R. Simpson, Lands Adviser to the Colonial Office. On his return to London, Simpson took it upon himself to write a report on the *thangata* system which Gorell Barnes sent to Nyasaland on 27 May: it was possible, therefore, that it was a rather hastily compiled report.[29] On reading it, one senses a somewhat snide, highly critical, superior, academic attitude in the writer. In his first line, he referred to the 'so-called' *thangata* system and said that, notwithstanding the fact that the Secretary of State had recently announced that the system was to be progressively abolished, he wished to draw attention to certain points and to make some suggestions. In his view, the Nyasaland Government, unlike Abrahams, had 'underrated' the significance of *thangata* and its implications for land policy and development. The Land Planning Committee had not realized its significance and had 'completely reversed the fundamental basis of Abrahams' whole report' by recommending that 'far from abolishing tangata, the Natives On Private Estates Ordinance should be revised in such a way as to retain it'. The Ordinance of 1952 was 'reactionary and non-aggressive' and

THE POLICY OF PROGRESSIVE ABOLITION OF *THANGATA* 125

the extent of this had not been appreciated in Nyasaland; the retention of *thangata* in that Ordinance was 'indefensible'. He felt that 'a good deal of time and energy [had] been spent on asserting that unoccupied land is a national asset at the disposition of the State' and that it was 'revealing and shaming' that the Natives on Private Estates Ordinance of 1928 should have been enacted 'for the benefit of the estate owners'. When Young and Kittermaster had tried to get the 1928 Ordinance altered in the 1930s it was, of course, the Colonial Office which refused to re-open the question. He then turned to the rights of Africans under the non-disturbance clauses in the original Certificates of Claim and said – almost certainly incorrectly – that these had been swept aside by the 1928 and 1952 ordinances, adding:

> I am not greatly impressed by the argument that discrimination between residents, immigrants and migrant labour is impossible. If 'peaceable, public and uninterrupted possession' for a prescribed period conferred title ... much apparent – and actual – injustice would be avoided.

Simpson agreed with the payment of rent: 'The days are past when each African should be considered as entitled as of right to the occupation of a piece of Africa.' He thought that the word 'rent' in the 1952 Ordinance was 'strange' and a 'misnomer' and more like 'an extremely heavy poll tax'. With regard to administrative officers being required by law to evict rent defaulters, he said that he found it 'particularly repugnant ... that the prestige and good offices of British District Commissioners should be used in such a cause'. He hinted that the estate system in Nyasaland was akin to the former 'Kaffir farming' in Southern Rhodesia.

He then came to the core of his argument: that the policy of acquiring estate land would not in itself offer a complete solution, and that only by acquiring all tenant-occupied land could this method bring *thangata* to an end. In order to reduce the incidence of *thangata*, estate owners had to give up land and 'they do not like doing this'. He insisted that the government had lost all the advantages and immense bargaining power which outright abolition would give them, and that gradual decrease in the incidence of *thangata* by the slow process of acquisition could have none of the effect on public confidence which its outright abolition would have. He did not say which 'public',

European or African, he had in mind, nor did he explain why he used 'gradual decrease' rather than 'progressive abolition', or why this should necessarily be a 'slow process'. He believed that to retain *thangata* even if its incidence were much reduced 'constitutes a very real danger. It is an easy and fair target for the agitator or even the mere reformer.' He then delivered his supreme insult:

> It can only have survived so long because Nyasaland, as a queer little appendage hanging from the side of British Africa, is so much off the beaten track.

What he feared was not that acquisition by the government might lead to further demands later – as the Landowners' Association had claimed – but rather that a fair attack on *thangata*, which was inherently bad, might readily spread to a general and unjustifiable attack on all European land-holding. 'We must put our own house in order before we can defend it.'

Pointing out that 'reduction' was not the same as 'extinction', and ignoring the fact that the policy was one of 'progressive abolition' (which is logically at least as close to extinction as it is to reduction), Simpson urged that rent should be reduced to a nominal sum, perhaps a shilling a year, and that the provisions as to labour in lieu should be cancelled: 'This very simply finally abolishes tangata.' He seems not to have recalled that the 1917 Ordinance, if enforced, would have prohibited labour as payment for residence rights: that is, it would have abolished *thangata* without doing away with rent. Nor did he deal with the political repercussions of the inevitable European reaction to his proposals. His view was that there was a 'fundamental distinction' between *thangata* and the question of tenant-congested estates; the former should be 'abolished out of hand', but the latter would 'continue to require much sympathetic and patient cooperation between the Government, the landowners and the tenants'.

When Footman, in Colby's absence, received Simpson's report he asked Executive Council to consider it, and this they did on 9 June 1954.[30] The Acting Governor opened the meeting by outlining what he saw as 'the crux of the problem' – Simpson's view that *thangata* was undesirable and should be abolished immediately – and concluded that the rent charged was excessive and ought to be reduced to a few shillings: 'If it was equitable to reduce the rent, *thangata* must go automatically because the equivalent amount of work in lieu would be so small as to be useless.'

McDonald, who was invited to the meeting, was worried by Simpson's proposal that *thangata* be abolished immediately, since that would affect the negotiations for acquisition of land – acquisition which was essential if the political problem were to be solved. The proposal ran counter to the Secretary of State's announcement that the course to be taken was progressive abolition by negotiated purchase:

> Immediate abolition would render Government's task in removing tenants very difficult since they would have no inducement to move and the negotiations with landowners would be greatly prejudiced.

Whilst he said that he believed Footman's arguments to be 'logical', their implementation would not be feasible and would have adverse repercussions. Barnes, Provincial Commissioner of the Southern Province, who was also present, agreed that the rent was grossly excessive but felt that its reduction 'required very careful timing'.

Council, whilst agreeing that the rent was excessive, found it difficult to reconcile Simpson's proposals with the Secretary of State's statement that *thangata* would be progressively abolished, preferably with the landowners' co-operation. Immediate abolition would run counter to this, would lack the landowners' consent, and would prejudice the chances of co-operation and negotiation. Youens, Acting Chief Secretary, said that it was not possible to disagree with Footman's arguments on the rights of the matter, but he did not believe that the matter was so simple that it could be solved by the stroke of a pen. He did not agree with Simpson that the proposal was supplemental to what had been agreed by the Secretary of State. To reduce the rent to a shilling would amount to virtual expropriation of estate land and would remove any incentive to Africans to move. Simmonds, Financial Secretary, also agreed that the *thangata* system was indefensible but he was uncertain whether *thangata* could be divorced from rent. If rent were reduced and *thangata* abolished, a degree of semi-permanency for tenant holdings would be created while the landowner would receive no advantage, which would be tantamount to expropriation.

This, in many ways, was the most perceptive of all views expressed.

If residents on private land were not obliged to pay rent, or work, or grow crops, they lived there without conditions and without any obligation or inducement to move, either to a different part of the estate or to new land. How, under these circumstances, was the estate owner to exercise any control over settlement or encroachment and be able to develop his estate, and what would freehold title mean in Nyasaland?

Hadlow, pointing to the Secretary of State's statement that abolition of *thangata* would be progressive, felt that any 'panic legislation' would have a bad effect on the Africans, who would not be slow to realize the absurdity of the position. In his view, the rent should be reduced from fifty to thirty shillings. Rumsey, the other non-official member, agreed that thirty shillings seemed a reasonable rent. The suggestion that rent should be somewhat, rather than radically, reduced was a political and equitable gesture which really had little to do with Simpson's suggestions, save that if the reduced rent were at a level which residents could readily afford they would have a genuine choice between paying rent and working in lieu, rather than being virtually forced to work because the prevailing rates of rent were higher than they could reasonably afford. This was not a point expressed in Executive Council, although members probably had it in mind.

Kettlewell supported this proposal to reduce rent to thirty shillings, and added that the Africans should be told that the government expected them to observe their rent obligations and that any failure to do so, or opposition, would interrupt progress in acquiring land. To some extent this would be bluff, but he felt it might work, as did McDonald. King, the Acting Attorney-General, Youens, Simmonds, Hadlow and Rumsey agreed with Kettlewell, and Council advised that the Secretary of State should have put to him the proposal that the Africans on Private Estates Ordinance be amended so that a standard rent of thirty shillings or, at the tenant's option, a period of work not exceeding three months in lieu of rent should be imposed. Footman, faced with this unanimous advice, 'did not feel able to dissent from the advice given and ordered that the whole position be reported to the Secretary of State'.

Thus Footman, in Colby's absence, had been willing, possibly keen, to go along with Simpson's proposals, but his advisers had dissuaded him, countering his arguments of logic and principle with arguments of practicalities, and had steered the ship of policy back to the course on which Colby had set it: progressive abolition of *thangata* by purchasing undeveloped private land, preferably by negotiation, and resettling tenants and others from congested areas – and from areas soon to be developed – on the purchased lands. As a token of the government's intentions, however, and as a means of facilitating or accelerating the progressive abolition of *thangata*, rent was to be reduced by two-fifths to thirty shillings a year.

Other attempts to introduce what Colby may well have felt were academic arguments were made by the Nyasaland government's Lands Adviser, Winnington-Ingram, when he was appointed to Nyasaland in January 1955, from Tanganyika – having recently been seconded for two years to the African Studies branch of the Colonial Office.[31] Like Simpson, but in a lesser way, he was a specialist in African land tenure; neither had first-hand personal experience of circumstances similar to the situation in Nyasaland. On a number of Winnington-Ingram's early papers in Nyasaland, Colby minuted such remarks as 'He misunderstands the whole exercise', 'This is all based on a fallacy', 'They are not', 'I don't think so!', or simply 'No'.[32] Later, Winnington-Ingram suggested to Williams at the Colonial Office that the 'Africans should be encouraged to raise funds to buy back land from the estates'. Williams' view was that this was not a 'likely starter as the Africans would not be likely to put their hands in their pockets to buy land from Europeans when they disputed the Europeans' right to it'.[33] It was a naive suggestion with which Colby, had he known, would have had little patience.

Colby must have felt that Simpson's arguments were unhelpful and clouded the issue. His line of advance, though not easy, was clear and simple, and he would not have taken kindly to arguments – especially from outside – which made it less clear and less simple. On his return in November, he found that Footman had already advised the Secretary of State that the draft despatch on land policy, when finalized, should be published, and he set about trying to reverse this advice. Winnington-Ingram's input to the finalizing of the draft, and his failure in Colby's eyes to understand the exercise, added to the Governor's increasing reluctance to have the despatch published. Indeed, Simpson's suggestion, coming from the Colonial Office, served only to throw doubt on the firmness of the policy decided by Colby and endorsed by Lyttelton. Simpson fundamentally disagreed with the policy of progressive abolition of *thangata* and until this difference of opinion was cleared up policy was unclear; it would have been very unwise to publish the draft statement during such a period of uncertainty.

Another reason for his reluctance was given to Executive Council on 10 December 1954, and later to the Colonial Office, using language very similar to that used by the Secretary of State almost exactly twenty years earlier in restraining Young from then re-opening the issue of Africans on private estates:

> His Excellency considered that publication would only serve to revive interest in a subject which Government felt could be solved in the very near future by land acquisition and resettlement. He felt that the work on the ground would do far more to convince the public of Government's intention of solving the land problem than the mere publication of documents such as the despatch from the Secretary of State. He also felt that publication of the despatch might stir up trouble unnecessarily with the African Congress and might also upset European opinion both within Nyasaland and in Southern Rhodesia where a wrong interpretation might be placed on the terms of the despatch.[34]

Colby believed that publication could do no good and might well do considerable harm; and his reference to work on the ground doing far more good than would publication reflected a view which he had expressed from his earliest days in Nyasaland: 'I am convinced that a pound of examples is worth a ton of precept.'[35]

In order to help Executive Council to reverse its earlier advice, however, he did accept Council's compromise, initiated by Rumsey, that the despatch should be shown to the Convention of Associations and the Landowners' Association, with the request that they deal with it in committee.[36] The circumstances in Nyasaland had changed with Lyttelton's visit. Things were going quite well for Colby. The Secretary of State had publicly endorsed his policy and he had weathered the storm of abuse from the European landowners and the press. He was gradually forcing open the wound caused by piercing Dixon's opposition and was turning it into a fatal injury; and other landowners were awaiting the outcome of the negotiations with the BCA Company. Also, security threats had decreased somewhat since the Secretary of State's visit, but Colby would not have wished to emphasize this, in order to keep up the pressure on the Colonial Office. Furthermore – a factor not yet widely known – constitutional amendments were soon to be made which would increase African representation in the legislature and these, when announced, would both indicate to Africans the government's intentions in their favour and help assuage their fears of European domination; it would also attract further criticism from Europeans. Why risk raising the land issue again by publishing a major policy document when the policy was already well known?

Unfortunately, the Secretary of State was by now much in favour of publication – and in fact had formally agreed to the draft[37] – presumably because the idea had originated in the Colonial Office and because Footman, with Executive Council's approval, had initially advocated publication. Also, although this was not stated, Simpson's diverting proposal had been disposed of, having been rejected primarily on the grounds that: first, it would be heavily criticized and opposed by landowners in Nyasaland and by government backbenchers in Britain, because it would deprive the owners of a fair rent and render much of the land valueless to the owner; and second, it would make the task of resettlement much more difficult because it would take away any incentive for the tenants to move and leave land free for development.[38] The Secretary of State was particularly doubtful about showing the despatch to the Convention of Associations and the Landowners' Association because they probably would not respect its confidentiality. Parliament in Britain would hardly be satisfied with a simple ministerial statement in the House when others in Nyasaland had been given much fuller information, but would insist instead on publication, and conceding this would be much more embarrassing than voluntary publication.[39]

The Secretary of State was puzzled by Colby's strong opposition to publication, and both Gorell Barnes and Williams doubted whether the policy set out in the draft enjoyed the Governor's wholehearted support.[40] Although the Colonial Office was firm in its view and kept up the pressure on Colby to agree to publication, they were prepared to go to considerable pains to understand his concerns and to win him over to their view.

It is not surprising that the Secretary of State should be puzzled by Colby's reluctance, because the statement made by Lyttelton during his May 1954 visit was of a policy designed by Colby himself, communicated to the Colonial Office both in his despatch accompanying the Protectorate Council Memorandum and in his note prepared for the Secretary of State's visit: progressive abolition of *thangata* by purchasing private land occupied by tenants or otherwise unsuitable for development or not to be developed in a reasonable time; withdrawing of tenants from developable retained land to acquired land; the process to start where the problems were most acute and to be on the basis of negotiated acquisition and voluntary resettlement. Few statements of policy could have been clearer; they emanated from Colby who must have agreed with them.

The first disruption of the clarity of policy was made by Simpson only two to three weeks after Lyttelton had stated it in Nyasaland. Simpson argued not for progressive abolition, but for immediate abolition of *thangata* by reducing rent to a nominal figure and abolishing the obligation to work in lieu. This was a fundamental attack on the policy, not merely supplemental as he claimed. Footman, in Colby's absence, was prepared to go along with Simpson's ideas but Executive Council dissuaded him.

Colby, like Executive Council, saw that Simpson's proposal would alienate European opinion and make estate owners very reluctant to sell – even if under these conditions there was any point in the government buying the land – and would remove from the African tenants a major inducement to vacate estate land, or move to different parts of the estate, which in turn would make the economic development of the estate very much more difficult. He much preferred, therefore, to adhere to the policy of progressive abolition of *thangata* through negotiated acquisition and voluntary resettlement which, if accomplished, would retain the goodwill of both European owners and African tenants and lead to the fuller development of estate land.

What the Governor feared, however, was that this – or the important parts of it – would take too long to accomplish. He was deeply aware of the profound and growing African feelings of opposition and the political, security, dangers involved, and he knew both how much these feelings were focused on BCA Company land and how recalcitrant, dilatory and unhelpful that Company could be. He knew also that the BCA Company was the key which he must first turn because others would wait for a lead from that Company to set an example and to establish the general price level. He believed that Nyasaland had little more time left in which to solve the problem if political catastrophe were to be avoided, and he knew that he

THE POLICY OF PROGRESSIVE ABOLITION OF *THANGATA* 133

personally had little time – not much more than a year before he was due to retire.

Whilst agreeing with the main policy of progressive abolition of *thangata* through negotiated acquisition and voluntary resettlement, Colby wanted other levers which he could use either as alternatives to the main policy or as threats to secure compliance with it. The main policy would work with other landowners but he feared it would not work with the BCA Company. Furthermore, if the main policy were to be implemented it would require very substantial financing and it was unlikely that Nyasaland could provide this by itself or that the British government would readily grant the additional funds needed. Consequently, Colby did not wish to be tied down exclusively to the main policy in dealing with the BCA Company but wanted room to manoeuvre, and it was for this reason that, at the 12 and 13 October 1954 meeting with the Secretary of State, he qualified his agreement to the policy on the question of the rent which should be charged. In effect he was saying, 'Let me think about this because Simpson's idea may have some merit in it, not necessarily in itself but as a lever or threat to gain the BCA Company's compliance with the main policy.' As other alternatives or levers, he also sought the Secretary of State's support for compulsory acquisition and for arbitration.

It was these considerations – which Colby unfortunately did not make entirely clear to the Colonial Office – which brought about the drawn-out argument over whether or not to publish the despatch. Numerous telegrams – described by Williams as 'not happy'[41] – passed back and forth between Colby and Gorell Barnes, on behalf of the Secretary of State, throughout March and early April 1955, the Secretary of State increasing his pressure to publish, Colby resisting the pressure to publish.[42] By this time, too, officials in the Colonial Office were beginning to lose patience: Williams found the Governor's arguments 'incomprehensible' and advocated that they should 'bring further pressure on Sir G. Colby to agree', and Gorell Barnes agreed to 'a rather fierce draft' reply to what he saw as 'one of the most inconsistent and incomprehensible performances I have witnessed for some time'.[43]

Finally, the Secretary of State seized on Colby's agreement to a fairly full Parliamentary statement and suggested that the despatch should be published in Britain as a Colonial Paper, 'which would not necessarily attract any more attention than a Parliamentary statement'. If this were so, Colby said on 6 April, then he 'could raise no objection to such publication in the United Kingdom', although he continued to make it clear that it was the publication in Nyasaland against which he advised:

> because there is a malicious European minority combined with a young editor of the local newspaper who will I think lose no opportunity to discredit the territorial government and the Colonial Office.[44]

With this issue out of the way, even if it was not solved entirely to the Governor's satisfaction, and even though he continued to advise against too much public discussion whilst things were going well,[45] Colby was able to continue his efforts to secure the acquisition of tenant-occupied tracts of BCA Company land.

7
Negotiations with the BCA Company, 1954–5

Immediately following Lyttelton's May 1954 visit, 'the Governor had a private talk with Brook before he left which obviously much impressed' the BCA Company Chairman. It must have been a very forthright talk because Footman (Colby now having gone on leave) immediately found Dixon 'very much more cooperative than he [had] ever been'. On 22 May, Footman reported recent progress to Gorell Barnes:[1] when he had seen Dixon three days previously, the latter had indicated that, in addition to the 20,000 acres immediately offered, he was urgently sorting out what he could offer in northern Cholo and was putting to his board specific proposals which he felt they would accept. He was also examining the southern sector to make early proposals. McDonald and Barnes felt that Dixon's proposals 'would make a considerable contribution' to solving the problem, particularly in the worst areas. Dixon was anxious that the full co-operation of the Company should be made publicly known to the Africans, presumably for both political and public relations reasons. Footman was also pleased with the response he had received from the General Manager of the B&EA Company, and with Tennett's agreement — but no more – that McDonald should discuss with him details of development and acquisition of his 8,000 acre estate with 980 families on it in the Cholo District.[2] Footman concluded that most estate owners 'have in fact seen the red light and are now prepared to cooperate'.

Footman's optimism over the BCA Company's 'conversion', like Colby's a few months earlier, was in the event premature. Whilst Dixon himself may have been willing to progress, Brook, once out of the country, continued to drag his feet. Sometime after the Secretary of State's visit, the Company 'voluntarily suggested three areas of land totalling about 20,000 acres which might be purchased' by the government, but Brook, by no means fully won over, told his shareholders that the government's policy would not result in any lasting solution of the land problem and that the whole question of land tenure and African immigration needed revision. 'Why', he asked, 'cannot Nyasaland re-organize itself on a realistic basis?', although he did not say what he considered to be a realistic basis.[3]

At Colby's request, the Secretary of State wrote to Brook early in August urging progress, but by the middle of the month the former told Colby that 'no (repeat no) meeting with BCA Company has been held recently or is at present proposed'.[4]

On 12 and 13 October, Colby, accompanied by Hadlow, discussed the abolition of *thangata* at the Colonial Office with Marnham and Robertson.[5] He was disturbed that since leaving Nyasaland nearly five months previously he had not heard of any progress towards acquiring heavily occupied BCA Company land, particularly since the core of the problem would be removed if progress could be made there, and other estate owners would quickly fall into line with the government's wishes. He impressed upon Marnham and Robertson his firm conviction that the most important step was to acquire a substantial block of BCA Company land, and that once this was done 'the back of the whole problem [would] be broken and a lot of other Europeans in Nyasaland would applaud in private if not in public'. Colby asked for a meeting with Company representatives before he returned to Nyasaland, but feared that the board of directors would remain no less unco-operative than in the past, so he asked if, in that event, the Secretary of State would be willing to support him in compulsory acquisition:

> If the Secretary of State's support for compulsory acquisition were forthcoming the Governor believed that it would be possible quite soon to ease the dangerous political situation which had arisen out of African grievances over the tangata system.

Colby concluded by saying that negotiations in Nyasaland itself would get nowhere – both he and Marnham were convinced that the Company were 'out to stall as long as they can'. Consequently, Colby felt he must see the Company while he was still in Britain, and he hoped that the Secretary of State would authorize him, if negotiations failed, to make it clear that compulsory purchase would be resorted to

– a solution towards which he had gradually been moving the Colonial Office over a period of time. He added that he thought it best if the Secretary of State and he met the BCA Company representatives together, to show that the latter could not drive a wedge between the Governor and the Colonial Office on this issue; and that, if this were not possible, a member of the Colonial Office should be present so that the Company could not later misrepresent what he had said. He still deeply mistrusted the Company.

Gorell Barnes supported Colby's request that the Secretary of State join the Governor in seeing the BCA Company representatives because this would show them that Lennox-Boyd – the new Secretary of State – fully supported Lyttelton's policy. Gorell Barnes also believed that:

> whilst this interview will require firm handling, it will also require rather more tactful handling than it will receive if it is handled by Sir G. Colby alone.[6]

In this connection, Lennox-Boyd a little later had to 'confess to some uneasiness at the number of complaints [he got] (and not only from difficult types) about the approach of the Governor on land and kindred issues'.[7] Gorell Barnes advised that 'if nothing else will bring the BCA Company to their senses, then the threat of compulsory acquisition will in the ultimate resort have to be used and, if necessary, applied', although he believed that they should avoid using this weapon.[8]

Footman reported at this time that he had made no recent progress with Dixon, who still did not have his board's authority to negotiate, although he personally appeared willing to part with 'a considerable amount of land'. The main difficulty seemed to be the price and whether a flat rate per acre should be agreed irrespective of location, state and value of the land.[9]

Colby had a preliminary meeting with the Secretary of State on 4 November 1954, and fuller discussions took place the next day at the Colonial Office between Lennox-Boyd, Colby, Brook, Sir John Huggins (a new BCA Company director), Gorell Barnes, Marnham and Williams.[10] This was an important meeting and most of the talking was done by Brook and Colby.

Brook was interested in two points: the price to be paid for land sold, and the freeing of retained land from Africans. In his turn,

Colby wanted to know how much land was to be developed so that he could acquire the remainder. The discussion moved back and forth between these points, Brook trying to take them in his chosen direction, and Colby trying to bring them back his way.

In respect of price, Brook said that he had to have constant regard to the strong views of his shareholders and that any sale should be on the basis of an independent valuation so that he could assure his shareholders that a fair price had been received: 'He had no interest in the price to be paid by the Government so long as it was a reasonable one.' 'Each piece of land should be examined separately and a price worked out,' he went on. He did not like the flat rate approach of 1948, particularly the rate of twelve shillings and sixpence an acre which was paid then.

With regard to the freeing of retained land from African occupation, Brook's basic point was that his Company had sold to the government 186,000 acres, about half their holding, in 1948, and that 'they did have a good deal of land that could be handed over to Government . . . but he could not let further land go without the most stringent safeguards being given of the Company's position to avoid encroachment'. He did not mind having the occasional African village on his land, but he did object of having 'islands of African Trust Land in the heart of the Company's tea growing area'. Huggins asked if the government could undertake to stop Africans going back onto the retained land since it was crucial that the Company be left in peaceful possession of that land. Colby said he would look into this and the Secretary of State added that it was clearly the government's duty 'to do its utmost to keep Africans off Company land'.

Although he did not say so, Colby was prepared to use considerable pressure to have Africans removed from retained land, but he knew that legally and politically he had to tread very carefully, and that removal would have to be, or appear to be, voluntary. Abrahams had used the expression in 1946 that Africans should be 'invited to opt' to leave retained land; this wording had also been used by the Land Planning Committee in 1947. In preparing a briefing note for the Secretary of State's visit of May 1954, Colby had referred to the tenant 'withdrawing himself' from the retained land. The Colonial Office draft despatch, prepared after the May visit, included the phrase 'moving the African' from the retained land.[11] So, a number of different expressions, hinting at varying degrees of pressure, had been used up to this point, and Colby continued to use different expressions, striking a balance between letting the Company know that he would see that the job was done and the retained land was freed, but at the same time saying that it would be voluntary:

> The idea was that the Government would clear all Africans from land immediately surrounding the present developed land.[12]
>
> Africans would be asked to move from [retained] areas of Company land to areas which were to be acquired.[13]
>
> [We would be] arranging to evacuate these people voluntarily from your land.[14]
>
> Government would assist to the best of its ability in securing the voluntary transfer of African tenants living on potential tea land ... to land acquired.[15]

Colby insisted that the meeting should continually re-focus on what he saw as the really essential issue: which land was to be developed – to assist the economy – and therefore which land should be acquired – to assist political stability. The price to be paid and the freeing of retained land, important as they might be, especially to the Company, were secondary issues for him. On the question of preventing encroachment, they discussed the practicability and expense of fencing the retained land – a point made by the Governor eight months earlier – but Colby eventually intervened to say that this also was a secondary issue, the main point being the government's anxiety to reach a settlement agreed by all parties which would result in there being no squatters left on the Company's land.

When they seemed to be spending too long on price, Colby intervened to say that the question of price was not of prime importance; the real question was rather that the Company should have a plan so that the government could know what land they were prepared to hand over. He asked if Dixon could be authorized to work out a plan for acquisition in co-operation with the government but Brook refused: 'He did not want another deal like the previous one which had been a little unorthodox.' When pressed to return to the question of how much land was, or was soon to be, developed, Brook replied that 15,000 acres were currently developed, 'including fallow'. In the Cholo District, there were another 25,000 acres suitable for tea and although only 10 per cent of these were currently planted, the remainder would be required for planting tea at the rate of 500 acres a year. Colby quickly pointed out that this would take 40 years 'and that was too long'. Furthermore:

> The Government wanted to see as much tea in Nyasaland as was possible provided it was practical politics, but if Government had to move 10,000 Africans to release the area wanted by BCA for tea it was not a practical proposition.

He pressed Brook again to allow Dixon to negotiate with the government, but Brook made it clear that the government had to deal with him, as chairman, and not with Dixon. It is likely that he felt he had been rash during the May 1954 meeting when, under pressure from both Lyttelton and Colby, he had agreed to Dixon discussing with the government its requirements for BCA Company land. Brook added that he was not prepared to give up all the Company's land 'at one bite' but he was prepared to discuss the Cholo land. This was important, since it was the acquisition of the Cholo land which the Land Planning Committee, in 1947, had distinguished as vital for political security reasons. It was in Cholo, too, that the 1953 disturbances had occurred.

The Secretary of State concluded the meeting by saying that if the position at Cholo were settled it would be a very big step and – somewhat pushing his luck – he added that discussions need not stop there but could go on to other areas:

> All were agreed that Mr Brook and Sir G. Colby should continue their discussions in Nyasaland, with particular reference to the BCA Company's land in the Cholo area. He emphasised that the Government attached the greatest importance to reaching a friendly settlement and he would watch the progress of the negotiations with the liveliest interest.

His reference to 'a friendly settlement' indicated that he had taken to heart Alport's advice to his predecessor that if the Secretary of State were ready to discuss the question 'in a friendly manner', a satisfactory solution might well emerge.

An extraneous factor now unexpectedly and briefly entered into the dealings with the BCA Company. Brook became aware that a 'group of unnamed Jewish speculators' were about to try and take over the Company.[16] Colby told the Colonial Office of this 'rather alarming' development and suggested that they and the Nyasaland government should combat it by going into the market immediately and buying all the shares they could at seven shillings and sixpence, 'or even more if necessary', in order to discourage or preferably prevent the takeover. If successful they would have a good investment; the government proxies would strengthen Brook's hand in dealing with his shareholders; and they would secure a stake in the Company which would give them some influence, especially if they eventually had a seat on the board. At the very least, there would be an 'identity of interest' between the Company and the government. Colby mentioned this idea to Brook on a strictly personal basis and the latter welcomed it.[17]

The Colonial Office predictably found these proposals open to a number of 'serious objections'. First, there were objections in principle to the government putting money into one of several competing concerns; Colby accepted this. Second, the BCA Company had a bad reputation with Africans and it might be politically unwise for the government to be identified with it; Colby agreed, but felt it just possible that the Africans might believe that they would get a better deal if the government were associated with the Company. Third, in the short term, far from exercising influence, the government might be required to fall in with Brook's wishes; Colby thought that this was a mistaken view. Fourth, the Colonial Office argued that any price over six shillings a share would be 'a doubtful investment. There are obvious objections to the use of Government money for a speculation of this type'; to which Colby replied, 'This is clearly a matter of opinion and I suggest we might resolve it in twelve months time by looking at the Stock Exchange quotations together! . . . I suppose the obvious objections to the use of Government money for a speculation of this type would fall away if the speculation was successful!' He concluded by outlining the dangers of an outside takeover and said that if the danger had receded then the proposal could be dropped, but if there was a risk of it becoming a reality perhaps they should talk it over with Brook.[18] The danger did in fact recede and the proposal was dropped. In the meantime, Colby had shown a helpful friendliness to Brook and had enjoyed twisting the Colonial Office tail.

Brook visited Nyasaland and had meetings with Colby on 19 and 26 November, which the latter found, at least in part, to be constructive. Colby felt that the talks had started encouragingly, since Brook had put forward proposals which would go some way towards accomplishing what the government wanted in Cholo but 'the snag, of course, is the price and it will undoubtedly be heavy, though possibly not prohibitive'. Brook said that although his shareholders had been readily persuaded in 1948 to agree to part with land at the price then offered, the position was now very different and his shareholders would take a lot of persuasion and could only be persuaded if the price was reasonable. Colby accepted this point.[19]

It is clear that, at least on the surface, Colby and Brook were beginning to see eye to eye and the gap between them was narrowing. Between their two meetings Colby wrote to Brook, explaining:

> My sole concern in this matter is to reach agreement with you on the basis of equity and true value and to be in a position to justify that value to the Legislative Council: I believe that your concern is identical except that you will wish to justify that value to the shareholders of your Company. We must therefore proceed in the closest consultation with the object of drafting a joint memorandum which will serve both our purposes.[20]

Even so, Colby's proposals were tough. Stopping just short of his 1948 idea that owners should pay the government to take the land off their hands, he asked if the government succeeded 'in arranging to evacuate [tenants] voluntarily' from retained areas, ought not the Company to hand over an equivalent area without payment? Ought not areas occupied or cultivated by tenants to be handed over without payment because 'such land is worthless ... since statutory rights exist over it': a site for a dwelling, cultivable land, timber, firewood, brushwood, thatch grass and compensation for disturbance? In all other cases of the land under negotiation, ought not the Tea Association to be asked to categorize it in two ways: that suitable for tea growing and that not suitable, and the government and the Company to agree to accept their valuation in both categories? Colby realized that these proposals were over-simplifications but he was concerned at this stage to establish a logical method of approaching the problem.

In reply,[21] Brook produced figures of acreages offered and a valuation prepared by land valuers in Salisbury, Southern Rhodesia, and argued that the valuation should be increased by way of compensation for loss of profits: 61,295 acres priced on this basis at £250,185 (or an average of over £4 an acre), together with an area of land adjacent to the Chisunga tea area, suitable also for tea, to be compensated at £562,500 (or £182 an acre) – 'a conservative figure under today's conditions', as Brook saw it. In reporting this, Colby said the Colonial Office would 'immediately see that Brook is opening his mouth much too wide . . . I found it necessary to explain to Brook that this was just "not on" and that we could not possibly contemplate a figure of such magnitude.'[22]

Their conversations nonetheless continued to be friendly and the Governor returned to his formula of 22 November, but it became quite clear that they were not going to find an agreed basis for negotiations – primarily because Brook refused to accept that the rights of tenants had any bearing on negotiations for compensation, or that the land they occupied 'was sterilised for development and that no development could take place unless the Africans were removed'. After several hours discussing these points and concluding that no agreement on price was to be reached, they provisionally agreed to proceed under the Acquisition of Land For Public Purposes Ordinance but to use the procedure only to arrive at a price rather than formally and actually to acquire the land compulsorily. The Governor asked for the Secretary of State's approval of this proposal and for quick action:

> it is only by making a move that we can quiet the fears and anxieties of the Africans in the area and unless we do something soon it will be inevitable that there will be, if not a recurrence of agitation, at any rate a considerable exacerbation of feeling.[23]

Although the provisional agreement between them had been recorded in a note,[24] Brook changed his mind soon after leaving Nyasaland and sent a letter to the Governor from Nairobi on 29 November,[25] reviving a suggestion which Colby had made earlier but which had then not found favour with Brook: that the Tea Association should value the land. Brook proposed that the two nominees from the Association appointed by the Company should view their task of valuation on the assumption that the land was completely free of African tenants. Rather than argue this point, the Nyasaland government included in the terms of reference of their two nominees the obligation to have particular regard to the statutory rights of tenants and the extent of land covered by those rights.[26]

The four nominees wrote to the two parties expressing their concern over the differences in their terms of reference, especially since they were anxious to produce a single report and valuation.[27] In reply, the Chief Secretary quickly – on 31 December – said that they were keen to reach a price which was fair to the BCA Company and which would protect the interests of the Nyasaland tax payer who would have to pay the bill. They were content for the nominees to draw up their own terms of reference, to include a request for a firm valuation of the land, and, if the BCA Company did the same, to accept the valuation as an award binding on both parties.[28] Colby's anxiety continued and he told the Colonial Office that:

> Matters are becoming increasingly urgent as signs of unrest are apparent among the local community who attribute delay entirely to the Government. BCA Company's lands are the focal point and early action to demonstrate the Government's intention to acquire the land therefore is essential.[29]

Brook, who thought that the Nyasaland government was being 'tiresome',[30] was rather slower in responding and did not do so until 7 February 1955,[31] by which time the nominees were becoming worried and considered asking to be absolved of their responsibilities.[32] Brook now told Colby that he had intended his reference to valuation on the assumption that the land was free of tenants to apply only to the potential tea land leaving the remainder free, in theory, for resiting huts, gardens and fuel plantations. He hoped that this explanation would enable the nominees to proceed with their task. He found the government's suggestion that the nominees should form their own terms of reference and that their award should be binding unacceptable, as going 'far beyond what was originally contemplated'. He would agree to being bound only if the question of statutory rights were treated as a separate issue, largely because the nominees were not legally expert in this field.

In respect of non-tea land – approximately 56,000 acres – he felt that the only basis of valuation should be the value of rents which the Company should receive for the huts on the land; he already had a valuation from the Salisbury firm on this basis. The Land Planning

Committee in the confidential appendix to their draft report had dismissed this basis of valuation seven years earlier, because it would mean that estates heavily populated with tenants would be more valuable than those which had succeeded in excluding tenants.[33] If agreement could not be reached, Brook suggested that private arbitrators should decide the matter on the lines recommended in the Abrahams Report.[34]

In consequence of this, and on Colby's instructions, Footman told the nominees that, since Brook would not accept the revised terms of reference, the Governor, 'with great regret', had concluded that it was difficult to see how they could usefully pursue their task.[35]

In replying[36] to Brook's letter, Colby challenged the rationality of basing a valuation on the assumption that the potential tea land was free of tenants. Such a valuation, he said, would bear no relation to reality because the land was not free of tenants and, if it were, the government would not be negotiating for its acquisition. The tea land should be valued according to what it would fetch on the open market as it stood, and this is what he had asked the nominees to do. Colby could also not accept Brook's proposals in respect of the non-tea land, because the income actually received from rents was reduced from its full potential by relief from payment obtainable by a period of work, and because where large numbers of defaulters existed, evictions were impracticable unless the Company employed a very large and costly staff to effect them. He doubted if the Salisbury valuers had any real appreciation of the situation which actually prevailed.

Confessing to being somewhat at a loss as to how to proceed, Colby now offered twelve shillings and sixpence an acre for the whole 60,000 acres, together with the tea land, and added that he would do his best to secure the voluntary transfer of African tenants from the retained potential tea land to the government-acquired land. If this was not acceptable to Brook, he made it clear that he would ask the Secretary of State to proceed under the Acquisition Of Land For Public Purposes Ordinance, 'with all the disadvantages and expense which that entails'.

When Colby reported the current position to the Colonial Office on 27 February 1955,[37] he admitted that he and Brook were 'poles apart regarding an agreed basis of assessment of compensation for the land he offers', and that unless Brook was bluffing he did not think that there was any point in his coming out to Nyasaland as he had suggested because he would only insist on consulting shareholders in Britain and this would cause further delay. Colby asked Gorell Barnes to see Brook and seek to persuade him to accept that the four nominees should draw up their own terms of reference, including a firm valuation, and that this award should be binding on both parties so that they could make a start on the tea land and negotiate for the remaining 56,000 acres; or to accept an overall figure of twelve shillings and sixpence an acre for the lot; or proceed to compulsory acquisition. Colby preferred the flat rate of twelve shillings and sixpence an acre, arguing that this was not ungenerous since this was the figure paid in 1949 for land which was much less densely occupied.

Early in March 1955, the nominees, having in the meantime got on with their task, reported on the value of the BCA Company land. On three estates, they recommended that: 500 acres were useless and not valued; 800 acres, suitable for tea, were valued at £5 an acre; 1,790 acres were 'fair', and valued at seventeen shillings and sixpence an acre; and 1,276 acres were badly eroded and valued at ten shillings an acre. The average price was, therefore, a fraction under thirty shillings an acre.[38]

Brook and John Huggins – upon whom the Colonial Office thought the Chairman was 'leaning' and who they felt was being 'less than helpful'[39] – continued to negotiate strongly over price and preferred arbitration if agreement was not possible.[40] By early April, Brook was offering the 60,000 acres at a flat rate of thirty three shillings and sixpence an acre; Colby was able to beat him down to twenty three shillings but no lower. The Governor was worried that such a figure, 'which would undoubtedly set the tone for all subsequent purchases', was too high. Even so, he told the Secretary of State that a week earlier he would have accepted this offer.

In the meantime, however, he had been told what Nyasaland's CDWF allocation for the coming year was to be, and, since it was 'so unexpectedly small' and would necessitate scrapping territorial development plans, he could not contemplate spending the quarter to half a million pounds required to acquire the 500,000 acres necessary to abolish *thangata*. Consequently, he reluctantly returned to the earlier idea that it might be better to abolish *thangata* by reducing rent to a nominal figure and removing the obligation to work. It would, as he was aware, bring strong protest from the Europeans,[41] incur all the disadvantages which Executive Council had outlined the previous year in considering Simpson's advocacy of a similar solution, and be contrary to the policy of progressive abolition of *thangata*.

In replying, the Secretary of State said that twenty-three shillings an acre was too much and would create an embarrassing precedent for the future, as well as cause resentment among those who had already parted with their land for less.[42] He thought that fifteen to sixteen shillings an acre 'is about as far as you should go. But of course I must leave this to your own judgement.' If the Company were unable to accept what Colby believed to be a fair price, he should consider arbitration. As to the effect of the CDWF allocation of £1m, he 'thought that expenditure on land acquisition should be accorded as high a priority as all but the most urgent development projects'.

A week after receiving the Secretary of State's letter indicating that fifteen to sixteen shillings would be nearer the mark, Colby offered fifteen shillings an acre but Brook would not go lower than £1 and the discussions ended in deadlock. Colby told the Secretary of State of this and added that he was opposed to arbitration because the arbitrated price would be likely to exceed £1 and they would be entering into an unlimited liability. He was now worried by sales of land by the BCA Company to Indians:

> Whilst [the] great bulk of land cannot be developed the fact remains that tenant-infested land has attractions to certain types of buyer (notably Indians) in view of prospective revenue from rents. Moreover, landlords can purchase produce from tenants particularly maize at sub-economic prices and, if dishonest, can use freehold land as a base from which to pirate produce from trust land.[43]

He instanced two recent cases where land under offer to the government had been withdrawn during negotiations and sold to Indians, totalling 6,035 acres and with 2,010 tenants: 'I do not know the price for these blocks but it is clearly higher than anything we can pay.' He also said that, during this visit, Brook had purchased an estate of thousands of acres adjoining BCA Company property, free from tenants, containing 100 acres of immature tea, 'for an allegedly high figure'.[44]

Since it seemed to Colby that the government could not buy any worthwhile amount of congested land at a price they could afford, they should seriously consider compulsory purchase.[45] The Colonial Office were disappointed at the deadlock and decided that they should take advantage of Colby's imminent visit to London to re-examine their land policy and agree a course of action.[46] Although neither side mentioned it, this was really a vindication of Colby's reluctance to have the draft despatch on policy published because, as it now transpired, to have done so would have been premature. Gorell Barnes was recommending to the Secretary of State that rent should be reduced to one shilling and the obligation to work in lieu should be removed, despite the well rehearsed arguments against such a course of action.[47] Williams believed that they had 'not got a policy' but Morgan disagreed: 'To go on buying tenant-infested land as and when we can, and as and when it can be afforded, does constitute a policy.'[48]

When he arrived in Britain, Colby had a meeting at the Colonial Office with the Secretary of State, Gorell Barnes, Morgan, Simpson and Williams.[49] They first considered Simpson's suggestion – to which Colby and Gorell Barnes had recently returned – that rent should be radically reduced and the obligation to work in lieu should be removed. When Footman had responded to this suggestion, he had assumed that if rent were reduced to a shilling a year there would be no further acquisition of land, but, whilst this would remove the worst evils of *thangata*, the political problem of large undeveloped areas of alienated land would persist since the Africans resented the landlord-tenant relationships altogether. The meeting discussed the possibility of the BCA Company lowering the price demanded in the face of a threat to seriously reduce rents, and agreed that this 'would be taken as sharp practice', and that it was a course they should not take. Colby made the point that it was very likely that the price which the BCA Company, and others, would ask would go up as land became more and more difficult to buy: consequently the policy of acquisition would probably prove too expensive. In addition, he thought that going to arbitration would be unwise as it would probably also be too expensive.

The Secretary of State and Colby then concluded that the deadlock at £1 an acre was unlikely to be broken by Brook reducing the price still further, and they agreed that they should settle at this level which was well below the average price recommended by the four nominees. They felt that the BCA Company held all the cards and that there was no alternative but to pay the price. Colby's view was that £1 an acre should be the average price paid. The Secretary of State agreed and himself telephoned Brook on 4 May to put this decision to him; Brook agreed subject to his Board's acceptance.⁵⁰ Colby confirmed the offer in a letter of 11 May and was at pains to spell out what was meant by an average of £1 an acre:

> to average the price over blocks of different quality for which we would pay prices above and below £1 as the case may be. The total price received by your company would, of course, be the equivalent of £1 per acre for all the land involved.⁵¹

There was no real need for Colby to spell it out in detail and it is most likely that, since he knew he was on the verge of succeeding, he wanted to be quite sure that Brook could not escape an apparent agreement by saying he did not understand what the offer was. He asked that once Brook's board had agreed, Dixon should be authorized to complete the details of negotiations in Nyasaland and he concluded, 'I am anxious to announce locally as early as possible that these negotiations have been completed.' Colby's wish to make an early announcement was designed to reassure Africans that a major step forward had been agreed and – with Dixon's local detailed help – was about to be implemented, and also to encourage other landowners to come forward and offer their land for sale. Brook's board agreed at some time before 20 June 1955, by which date local discussions had started in Nyasaland to finalize the details.⁵²

Brook had become worried that rents might be reduced to a nominal sum and the obligation to work removed, and, realizing that he was not going to win the battle no matter what delaying tactics he adopted, and that he should get the best deal he could, had agreed on an average price of £1 an acre. His view as reported to the shareholders was:

> We consider this arrangement satisfactory and in the best interests of the Company, as we shall still have all the land we require for our immediate needs and for development. Furthermore, if, as we hope, Government is correct as to the effect of adopting this policy, the Company should be better off by reason of an atmosphere of greater contentment among the population in the vicinity of our estates, from which our labour is to a large extent drawn.⁵³

In August 1955, the government announced that the purchase of the area negotiated with the BCA Company had been agreed – now re-assessed at 48,750 acres.[54] Brook, who visited the country at that time, found that the removal of tenants from Company land to newly acquired government land was proceeding 'smoothly and satisfactorily'. In some cases, removal was preceded by organized visits of tenants to the acquired land, so that they could assure themselves that the land to which they were being moved was at least as good as the land retained by the Company.[55] In other cases, small parcels of unoccupied land sold by the Company to the government in 1949 were returned to the Company in order to secure larger occupied areas under new agreements.[56] On his return to Britain, Brook sent a letter to his shareholders, dated 21 September 1955, saying:

> My colleagues and I would like to pay tribute both to the Government Officers and to the members of our own Staff concerned for the excellent manner in which they are carrying out this most delicate operation. Government has given an undertaking that, as and when our estates are cleared, the Africans On Private Estates Ordinance will cease to apply to the land in question. This means that any encroachment can be dealt with and that, in future, our land can be kept clear.[57]

Colby took very swift action to remove Africans from the land retained by the BCA Company in the Cholo District and to resettle them on purchased land. Before the sale on 8 August 1955, the Company owned 74,622 acres with 36,400 residents; the government purchased 36,470 of these acres and automatically emancipated 24,600 residents. They then moved 3,240 of the remaining 11,800 residents onto acquired land, so that, by 30 September 1955, the BCA Company retained 38,143 acres (compared with 74,622 two months earlier) with 8,560 residents (compared with 36,400 two months earlier).[58] This process, taking place as it did in the very area where the 1953 disturbances had occurred and at a time when many of those convicted for their part in the disturbances were being released from prison, brought with it security worries. The Political Intelligence Reports for August 1955 and for several months thereafter[59] included sections on African discontent and on the agitation of local Congress leaders who were influencing a number of others, although there was 'much evidence of the enthusiastic agreement of the great majority of the people to move onto land which [had] been acquired'. The discontent was centred on a belief of some that the land to which Africans were being removed was less fertile than that from which they were being moved, and this without compensation.

The resettlement nonetheless proceeded smoothly and without untoward incident, save in the Bvumbwe area where the 'hard core of Congress agitators' was to be found. In December, dealing with the Bvumbwe situation, the Report said:

A generally hostile attitude is noted in the area towards Europeans and Government and any evictions on a large scale for failure to pay rent might cause a local security situation.

This was particularly true in that the chairman of the Bvumbwe branch of Congress was served with an eviction notice in November for seven years' rent default. Tension continued to grow in January 1956 as 'a number of European settlers in the area [were] becoming increasingly apprehensive of possible disturbances in the not too distant future'. There were worries also in February and March with 'the marked hostility on the part of Africans affected by the scheme and threats of forceful resistance to any attempts ... to move them from their present sites'. However, in April it was reported that the situation had recently shown signs of easing, and this more favourable atmosphere persisted until the land was cleared, so that Colby's successor, Armitage, was able to report on the Bvumbwe area to the Secretary of State in September 1956 that 'only 35 families now remain and they are all making preparations to move. The leading personalities [who threatened forceful resistance and upon whom eviction notices had been served] have all moved without forceful eviction'; (indeed they had all moved before the expiry of the notices).[60] The Secretary of State, much relieved, cabled back: 'This is good news and reflects great credit on the persuasive powers of the officers concerned.'[61]

8
Land acquisition and resettlement, 1955–64

The 1955 agreement with the BCA Company to sell almost 50,000 acres at £1 an acre, following the Secretary of State's endorsement of Colby's policy proposals and 15 months of hard negotiation thereafter, was a major step forward and removed a log jam which had held up other progress in the abolition of *thangata*. By October 1955, Colby believed that there was 'a reasonable prospect of reducing the problem of resident Africans on private estates to very small proportions within the next four or five years ... and prospects of a permanent and satisfactory solution are now in sight'. The landowners generally were much more ready to sell. The tenants generally were more willing to move off estate land now that they received reassuring reports from those who had already moved, although the delay in paying them compensation tended, naturally, to hold some of them back.[1]

The attitude of most estate owners changed quite quickly. Impressed with the ease with which government officers moved large numbers of families in 1956 without disrupting the supply of labour and without the petty sabotage by former tenants which some had feared, several landowners in the Cholo and Blantyre Districts sought government help in freeing their retained land of tenants. In 1957, a total of 23 estates were completely cleared, leaving the retained land in a much more readily developable condition. In principle, most owners were unwilling to sell their land to the government, but in practice the benefits were being appreciated and many saw the wisdom, or the necessity, of selling part of their land to raise sufficient capital to develop the remainder. The government was gratified by the ready co-operation of the owners in clearing their land – generally they gave re-settlement officers a free hand – but were surprised by how little the owners knew about the number and location of their tenants. There was an increasing awareness that undeveloped land – whether now free of tenants, like the BCA Company's Cholo estates, or still 'over-run by tenants', like the B&EA Company's Zomba estate and Conforzi's Magomero estate – was a liability of which it would be wise to divest themselves.[2]

The attitudes of the tenants varied. There was a general resignation to the inevitability of the situation: 'We've got to move sometime, let's get it over.' There was also, however, a general resentment which smouldered beneath the surface and which the government recognized could be sparked off, either by natural hardships such as drought and famine, or deliberately by political activists. The volume of families moving off private estates caused nervousness and unrest among those remaining who had lived on the estates, undisturbed, for many years, and also among squatters who had entered illegally in recent years.[3]

The general acceptance of the accelerated progress in abolishing *thangata*, by both Europeans and Africans, lasted from the peak year of 1956 into 1957, but thereafter dwindled.

On the European side, some estate owners with large numbers of tenants continued to refuse to sell their land to the government. Armitage privately recorded:

> This is an annoying sword hanging over the heads of many landowners, some of whom refuse to treat with the Government for the solution of the problem.
>
> The short point is that the land with resident Africans on it, or vacant land, is a political liability and will not be solved until the problem has been further reduced.[4]

In his Report on Land Acquisition and Resettlement for 1956–7, Armitage commented on the intransigence of Conforzi and Tennent in refusing to sell their estates in Cholo and Blantyre Districts – the former held 58,000 acres with 4,850 tenant families, and the latter held 14,000 acres with 980 tenant families. A number of other, small, landowners also continued to refuse to release their undeveloped land.[5] Although Conforzi showed signs of belatedly changing his mind, the position in regard to these estates remained unchanged in 1958, which persuaded the government to amend the Africans on

Private Estates Ordinance. They were worried by the slow-down in acquisitions and the increase in cost per family emancipated: 17,949 families averaging £7 each in 1956; 5,516 averaging £13 in 1957; and 3,227 averaging £29 in 1958.

They were also much concerned about the outstanding 1,000 applications for eviction and the impracticability of enforcing them.[6] The law was changed so as to make compensation payable in suitable cases for eviction on grounds of rent default. In this way they hoped that there would be less resentment among rent defaulters ordered to leave private land, that the number of applications for eviction would drastically decline, that the price of land heavily occupied by tenants would also decline, and that there would be:

> an appreciation on the part of those owners who so far have been reluctant to cooperate that it is in their best interests to dispose of land [heavily] occupied at [a realistic] figure.[7]

In addition to some owners refusing to sell their tenant-occupied land, others hardened their position and considered sale only at inflated prices. In this latter category were a number of well-developed large estates, and a number, in or near the Blantyre-Limbe urban areas, about to be developed for residential purposes without regard for the African occupants who had spent all their lives on the land, generally without disturbance and without rent being demanded of them:

> The Government is now, therefore, being offered large tracts of land, which are at present politically unimportant and which it has not at present sufficient cash to acquire while, at the same time, the Government is being asked to evict as rent defaulters without payment of compensation families from land which the owners refuse to sell or will sell only at unreasonable prices.[8]

It was this latter land, the urban residential land, which the government felt formed 'the present political trouble centres', and at which was aimed the amendment to the law to require compensation even in some cases of rent default. The refusal of a few landowners to consider selling their land and the willingness of others to do so only at high prices was accompanied by a general disquiet among

Europeans. Armitage first noticed this feeling very late in 1956 and reported it more fully to the Colonial Office in April 1957:

> estate owners and the non-African public generally are becoming restive and are enquiring when the process of acquisition is going to cease; this attitude has become more noticeable during the past few months.[9]

The Governor thought that it would help if, in his reports and in the government's publicity generally, instead of focusing on the amount of land which had been, was being and would be acquired – which might be too much for the Europeans, and too little for the Africans, readily to accept – he should emphasize the reduction in the number of Africans subject to *thangata*.[10] There was not always a direct relationship between the acreage acquired and the number of families emancipated; indeed, the early, very large acquisitions at Chingale and Magomero had been in non-congested areas and resulted in relatively few tenants being freed from *thangata*. The landowners' restiveness later turned to anxiety over the security of tenure in any constitutional changes which might increase African representation in the legislature, an anxiety which Chief Mwase stimulated in 1957 by agreeing that the Africans would take away freehold land when they got a chance to do so.[11]

On the African side, as the number of tenants decreased, their influence as a group declined but the potential influence of ex-tenants correspondingly increased; many of these would have liked to return to their former homes on private estates and the government was aware that they were an easy target for political activists:

> those who have moved far away, especially those who have returned to their ancestral lands, are likely soon to forget, but those who can see regularly their former gardens, especially if they have cultivated them all their lives and now see them unused, could form fertile crowds for agitators. There is evidence that in a few cases agitation is already [in 1958] beginning to take its effect.[12]

The Nyasaland Situation Report for October 1958 took up the point expressly in relation to the removal of tenants from estates: 'No one enjoys being moved and . . . although extreme care has been taken to reduce hardship to a minimum, a further tool is being placed in the hands of political agitators.'[13]

African political pressure on the government increased considerably after 1956 when African representation in Legislative Council was increased to five elected members, as against six non-African elected members and eleven officials.[14] During the Secretary of State's visit to Nyasaland in January 1957, representatives of the African Associations claimed that freehold title was not valid and – in terms similar to those used in the African Protectorate Council memorandum three years earlier – they strongly urged that 'all land not in occupation and use by the owners should be acquired by the Government'.[15] Lennox-Boyd quickly reaffirmed the validity of freehold title and added:

> The question of further acquisition of unoccupied or unused land by Government was related to the 'tangata' problem and it was not agreed that it would be wise to acquire more land than was needed to carry out the declared policy of progressively abolishing "tangata." ... The policy ... was in the best interest of the country as a whole.[16]

He also said that acquired land automatically became Public Land, under the African Trust Land Order in Council, but that when arrangements had been made for settling Africans on it on 'sound land use principles', and they had 'received secure title to holdings', then the land would be declared African Trust Land. This response did not satisfy the African representatives, and at the February 1957 meeting of Legislative Council[17] a concerted attack was made on *thangata* by the African members who proposed that:

> all land occupied by Africans, and all land used by Africans on private estates [should] be taken over by Government and be proclaimed Trust Land by law. That the estate-owners whose land [was] taken over by Government [should] be compensated at a normal minimum rate of costs per acre.

They attacked the validity of title based on Certificates of Claim and felt that the pace of abolition of *thangata* was 'slow ... mighty slow'. They spoke of the tenants being 'pushed like a ball', of bitterness and of 'a sort of slavery' resulting from the removal of tenants from estates. They referred pointedly to the 1915 Chilembwe Rising and the 1953 riots, both of which resulted from land grievances, and to the 'mistakes and blunders in the handling of land problems in Kenya' which precipitated a rebellion in the form of Mau Mau 'aiming at the expulsion of the Europeans from the surface of Africa'.

This last point would not have been lost on Armitage, whose early service from 1929 to 1948 had been in Kenya and whose brother-in-law still lived there,[18] nor on Ingham who had also served in Kenya, from 1947 to 1954.[19] It was particularly to the removal of tenants from their homes on estates that they objected and which they felt created most distress, especially when compensation was low or absent, and it was for this reason that they advocated that the government acquire all the land occupied by Africans on private estates. It was not the progressive abolition of *thangata* which they wished for, but its immediate abolition by virtually expropriating the land and declaring it African Trust Land.

The Secretary for African Affairs pointed to the loss of confidence in the security of tenure and the fragmentation of holdings and of Trust Land in 'which the motion, if carried, would result'. He pointed to the way in which the current policy of progressive abolition of *thangata* was avoiding these two evils – bearing in mind European disquiet over security of tenure – and he particularly regretted that African leaders should introduce a motion 'which strikes at the very root of security of rights in private property and also at the sanctity of contractual relations'. Although the motion was defeated by eighteen votes to four, the speeches in its favour significantly contributed to the growing unease among Europeans, and the reluctance of estate owners to develop retained land when selling off other parts to the government.

This failure to develop the retained freehold land was a source of considerable worry to the government and to the Colonial Office. Many of the reasons for the failure were valid – lack of capital; low primary product prices; the considerable increase in cleared, developable, land; and the need for a fallow period – but these did 'not lessen the dangers of deliberate mass trespass' and of political agitation and violence.[20]

Armitage's Report on Land Acquisition and Resettlement for 1957–8 was received at the Colonial Office early in March 1959 at the very time that he declared a State of Emergency in Nyasaland to control the widespread rioting and other disturbances which had been building up during the second half of 1958 and the early part of 1959.[21] Colonial Office officials, naturally, were particularly sensitive to political dangers which might stem from the land issue, being mindful of the Mau Mau troubles in Kenya and the part which land grievances had played in the 1953 disturbances in Nyasaland. They were especially worried about the failure of landowners to develop retained land and of the Nyasaland government to fully control, from a land use point of view, settlement on the acquired areas, a matter about which they had been at least mildly concerned, for agronomic rather than for political reasons, in the past.

Colonial Office views on the failure of the Nyasaland government to use the acquired land properly were significantly moulded by representations made to them by the chairman of the Nchima Tea and Tung Estates Company and the Michiru Company, Rolf Gardiner, who had frequent personal meetings with, and wrote frequent personal letters to, Lennox-Boyd.[22] Gardiner's basic stance was indicated in a letter written to Lennox-Boyd in October 1955:

> I think we are entitled to know ... what Government intends to do to improve [acquired] land and prevent its becoming a desiccated wilderness, and to be assured that steps will be taken without intolerable delays ... I would consider that I was betraying an obligation if I enabled Government to take over any land and allowed it to become a rural slum. Rather than do that I would prefer to retain the land and improve it at my Company's expense ... provided some compensation was paid when the land was eventually handed over ... [we must] save the country from developing its, we hope much milder, version of Mau Mau. Here is a danger which must be met by foresight and not when the situation has drifted from bad to worse and from worse to tragic. I implore you to take this plea most seriously.[23]

Colby's relationship with Gardiner was not always of the best, and although they were usually civil to each other,[24] Gardiner was 'dismayed by the adamant position of [the Governor's] mind: it seemed impervious to fresh ideas';[25] while Colby felt that 'Gardiner's main trouble is that he seems quite unable to appreciate that the problem which faces us is ... one of formidable proportions which will never be solved by the expression of pious generalities ... He is

... quite unrealistic – to use a mild word.'[26] On Colby's behalf, Footman requested Gorell Barnes to ask 'that Gardiner's prolixity may be discouraged; it causes much waste of time to already overworked officers. We are fully alive to all these problems and within the limits of staff and finances they are being tackled with great determination.'[27] Although the Colonial Office thought Gardiner was an idealist, they were significantly influenced by his views – indeed they adopted some of his expressions in writing to the Governor – and they thought that Colby ought to have done more to handle the acquired land in accordance with sound land use principles. They hoped that Armitage might react more positively.[28]

Armitage had himself warned the Colonial Office of the dangers a year earlier when, on 10 February 1958, he had pointed out that the great strides made over the previous two years in resettlement work had increased population pressure on Trust Land at the same time as neighbouring areas of undeveloped, cultivable, private land were being enlarged.[29] He regarded 'this problem of undeveloped freehold land as very serious and one which cannot fail to cause political unrest'. He also felt that the aggravation of the political problem of undeveloped land caused by resettling Africans – as opposed to simply buying the land on which they were already settled – could undo the political advantage gained by emancipating them from *thangata*. Regarding development on acquired land, he said that a good deal of it had been so filled with families resettled from retained estates that 'for the time being it is impracticable to do anything' much about strict land use planning.

Policy, however, remained to keep all acquired land as Public Land until it had been conserved and reorganized and the people had accepted the idea of individual title, thereby reducing the likelihood of large-scale continued objection to freehold land in principle. Armitage was aware of the growing feelings of insecurity among European landowners and believed that their only safeguard once eventual self-government was granted was 'to give more and more Africans a stake as freeholders in the maintenance of freehold tenure'.[30] The point about the dangers of not developing retained and acquired land was also made in the Situation Report for October 1958:

> If the present fairly extensive areas of land in private ownership remain unoccupied and undeveloped while population pressure on African Trust Land and in the acquired resettled areas

develops, the inevitable result is a miniature Kikuyu Kenya highland problem in embryo.[31]

The Colonial Office had not really pursued the early worries about the failure of private owners to develop retained land and the inability of the government to resettle acquired land on good land use principles, but Armitage's Report for 1957–8, arriving at the time it did, and following the Kenya references in the October Report, highlighted the problem, and Gorell Barnes wrote to the Governor on 17 March 1959 saying that he found these two factors 'extremely worrying' and their combination potentially 'quite fatal':

> The first is the failure of the landowners to develop land from which tenants have been moved. The second is the inability of Government to develop properly much of the land which has been acquired. If my memory serves me aright the original conception was that large acreages of land occupied by African tenants under the tangata system would be acquired with the dual purpose of freeing the Africans from tangata and redeveloping the land in such a way that its carrying capacity would be increased. This in turn would enable the Government to move from land which landowners wished to develop tenants for whom there would then be plenty of room on the land acquired by the Government. It seems that this conception is not being fulfilled in two respects and there is therefore the danger of the land acquired by Government developing into a rural slum whilst land from which some of the people on it have been moved is not being used by the landowners ... it seems to me most urgent that something should be done very quickly to alter it.[32]

Gorell Barnes failed to adjust the original concept to the fact that in the most seriously congested areas of the Shire Highlands there was not 'plenty of room' on which to resettle Africans from retained private estate land, no matter how well the acquired land was developed. He concluded by asking the Governor to let him know what plans he had to deal with these worries.

Armitage, inevitably much occupied in handling the State of Emergency, replied a month later and said that, whilst the Colonial Office fears were 'substantially accurate', a great deal of soil conservation had taken place, tree planting was proceeding well, and 'substantial blocks' of land had been closed completely to settlement in order to declare them as forest reserves:

> Apart from one or two areas in Cholo and North Blantyre it has not – as yet – proved possible to conduct resettlement on the basis of a satisfactory detailed land use plan. All that we have been able to do is ensure that houses are situated in areas which enable the maximum amount of agricultural land to be made available and to close to cultivation those areas which, in the interest of soil conservation, should in no circumstances be cultivated.[33]

He went on to explain that there were two main reasons for this. First, insistence on resettlement on a planned layout – which would have been costly in staff training and mapping terms – would have been received by the Africans as a degree of control at least as great as, and probably greater than, that which they had so deeply resented on private land, and would have reduced the incentive to voluntary movement. To have insisted would have made it doubtful whether any progress in moving people could have been made: as he had told the Colonial Office two and a half years earlier, 'regimented settlement would have meant much slower progress and considerable immediate discontent, which could have led to a complete breakdown'.[34] Second, since most of the resettlement land already had 'a fair measure of African settlement on it' those already there would have resented reorganization even more strongly than any newcomer:

> The necessity for removing the basic grievance of Resident Africans was considered to be so urgent that the slow process of obtaining acceptance to reorganisation could not be adopted. This was the reason which finally decided for us that resettlement on a properly planned basis was not possible.

Armitage also explained that he was using his limited resources and expertise to effect agricultural improvement, including land reorganization, in the most promising areas of the country and this included many areas of Trust Land, for example at Ntaja's, and excluded many areas of acquired land, for example in the peri-urban areas which were used as dormitories rather than as agricultural holdings. 'The need for reorganisation of holdings is certainly as great on African Trust Land as it is on ex-private estate land,' he stressed. He was also doubtful whether it was still prudent to keep acquired land as Public Land on which to force through reorganization which was likely to create 'considerable antagonism'. He thought it might be better to convert acquired land into Trust Land (which might result in increased confidence and co-operation from the African people) and seek to secure the support and assistance of traditional leaders and 'African settlers of long standing' in land reorganization. In his 1957–8 Report, Armitage had explained that the feeling of Africans on Public Land was that they had little, if any, more security than they had when resident on private estates, and the chiefs, similarly, felt that they had little control over their people.[35] Consequently, there was less development of the acquired land than there might otherwise have been, and it was these factors which the Governor had in mind in suggesting that acquired land might be better converted to Trust Land than remaining Public Land.

Concerning the failure of estate owners to develop retained land, Armitage felt that the current disturbed political conditions made them reluctant to invest further capital in their estates, and he could not blame them for this attitude.

He summed up by saying that given three factors – reducing the number of tenants on private estates still further; settling the major political problems and thereby restoring confidence to both Africans and Europeans; and making 'finance ... available not only on a considerable scale but on terms which will not greatly add to our recurrent expenditure budget' – he was confident that 'substantial and rapid headway' with land reform could be made, irrespective of the status of the land.

The Colonial Office, alarmed by what they saw as an extremely explosive situation, were not reassured by Armitage's arguments and explanations. At a meeting in London on 17 April 1958,[36] Simpson and Hall again raised the issue with Armitage, who explained that in respect of not developing retained land:

> this danger was fully appreciated and ... the British Central Africa Company, as the main culprit, had been made aware of this and was being urged to remedy the position in the case of its own estates.

Indeed, he was already discussing with Brook the possibility of

164   SEEDS OF TROUBLE

African tenants growing tea on the Company's undeveloped land.[37] In respect of the failure to resettle Africans on acquired land in accordance with good land use principles, he said that although this had been the case, the situation was improved now that tenants were leaving the estates in smaller numbers, which enabled the government to exercise better control over their resettlement.

Simpson, in particular, found these explanations unsatisfactory and revived a proposal which he had made in 1954: an ordinance should be made requiring landowners to develop their undeveloped land or dispose of it.[38] Gorell Barnes also continued to be worried and felt that the Nyasaland government was 'not handling this matter with the energy and imagination required and that their failure to do so [was] capable of having serious consequences'.[39] He felt that they should not leave the Governor 'unprodded' for very long, and consequently Morgan wrote to Armitage in September 1959 and suggested:

> Ought we not ... to consider ... bringing in an ordinance to compel land owners to develop their property within a short time or else surrender it to Government on valuation? Should this measure of compulsion be accompanied with arrangements for granting of loans to landowners for development purposes ...?[40]

Morgan's suggestion was not adopted, and the difficulties over the failure to develop retained land and properly resettle Africans on acquired land were tackled, first, by the government continuing to persuade estate owners of the political dangers involved and encouraging them to develop their estates with the proceeds of sale. The large estate owners, particularly the BCA Company, the B&EA Company and, belatedly, Conforzi responded well to this encouragement to invest the income from sale of land in their other property in Nyasaland.[41] Second, the government maintained the staffing levels in the Land Settlement Section of the Provincial and District Administration.[42] Maintaining these levels despite the very considerable fall in the acreage of land acquired in 1959 and 1960 enabled the Section to devote its resources to ensuring better land usage of the acquired areas.

Despite – and to some extent because of – increased African political pressure, which received considerable additional impetus after Dr Banda's return to Nyasaland in 1958, and notwithstanding the failure to develop retained land and properly to resettle acquired land, the work of progressively abolishing *thangata*, of acquiring land and resettling Africans on it, continued both in respect of BCA Company land and in respect of other land.

By the end of 1956, all the BCA Company estates in the tea growing area of the Shire Highlands had been freed of tenants. In all, 3,240 families had been resettled from the Company's Cholo estates 'without incident of any description'. A further 850 tenants remained to be removed, mainly from their tobacco estates in the Blantyre District, and the Company were prepared for the government to acquire further land to accomplish this. Whilst the Company had feared a severe shortage of labour on the tea estates, they were pleased that these fears turned out not to be justified, and although there was some decline in labour supplies, they were building houses in compounds, together with some garden space, for their labour – as Colby had advocated much earlier – which was proving successful in attracting workers. The Company also was pleased that the money received from acquisitions had enabled them to build 'the fine new Chisunga factory' and to open up new tea gardens at Cholo:[43] again, Colby had argued from a very early date that such development would be made possible through sales of other land. The government recognized that the ease of resettlement was in large measure due to the 'extreme cooperation' given by the Company:

> They have been generous in the provision of transport, timber and other facilities, and they have no doubt taken the attitude that the sooner the tenants are resettled on Government land the better, from their point of view.[44]

In 1957, the government asked to purchase more land to complete resettling Africans from the Company's estates; they had in mind 7,457 acres of tobacco land – which the Company proposed to close down – in the Lunzu area of the Blantyre District. Brook and Dixon saw this as an excellent solution to their difficulties because no alternative profitable crop was available, and the government agreed on a price of £5 an acre on the understanding that the sum received would be re-invested in other BCA Company estates. Brook was sure that this arrangement was in the Company's best interests since it allowed them to dispose of an area which had produced disappointing tobacco crops and at the same time to proceed more quickly with tea development.⁴⁵ In Colby's words of almost a decade earlier, the Company was 'getting it both ways' but, as he had also pointed out, government expenditure in purchasing private land would be very much more justifiable if the proceeds were invested in Nyasaland so as to further its economic development.

In 1960, the government told the Company that they wished to purchase another 4,980 acres adjacent to the land purchased at Lunzu. This land also had proved uneconomic for tobacco growing, was somewhat isolated from the Company's other estates, and was already partly occupied by squatters, so agreement was not difficult to reach and the government bought the land for £15,700. The Company paid this sum into the capital reserve and from it was able to build a third tea factory – another step in the right direction in accordance with the government's 'reinvestment in Nyasaland' wishes – and to recommend a capital distribution to its members.⁴⁶ By the end of 1958, no tenants remained on the Company's land in the Cholo District, and the only tenants – 480 families – were in the Chikwawa District. Between 1954, when Dixon first mentioned the 60,000 acres which might be offered to the government, and the early 1960s, the government purchased 61,210 acres of BCA Company land.⁴⁷

The BCA Company's conversion to the government's policy was indicated in the chairman's statement to the shareholders in 1963, the year in which the Company was taken over by Lonrho. Colby might have drafted the statement himself:

> In my view it would be entirely unrealistic today to envisage that the Company can retain large tracts of land which are surplus to its requirements ... there is an ever growing hunger for land ... and in these circumstances we may expect to be approached by Government with a view to the acquisition of all land at present owned by the Company and not required for its tea and sisal operations. The extension of Government areas may be expected to help in the very pressing problem of encroachment on the Company's existing plantations.⁴⁸

Whilst the BCA Company land was being dealt with, work continued on acquiring other estate land. Between 1946 and 1955, the government acquired 296,977 acres and emancipated 20,158 families. In 1956, following Colby's breakthrough with the BCA

Company, a further 155,622 acres were acquired, emancipating 17,943 families. In 1957, the figures were 23,317 acres and 5,516 families, and in 1958, they were 31,157 acres and 3,227 families.[49]

At the end of 1958, only 20,460 families remained on estate land as tenants. Of these, 6,700 were in the Magomero share-cropping tenant tobacco area, and 3,500 were in the Mlanje tea estate area. Only 3,100 remained in Cholo.[50] Armitage had decided in 1956 that it would be unwise to purchase the Magomero lands because the share-cropping system was not unpopular and the tobacco crops contributed 'considerably ... to the economic benefit of the country as a whole ... The acquisition of further freehold land in this area ... is hard to justify, particularly when the financial cost to Government is also taken into consideration.'[51] In practical terms, therefore, only 13,760 families remained under the *thangata* system.

As the retained parts of the estates were cleared of tenants, they were individually certified as free of resident Africans and the Africans on Private Estates Ordinance ceased to apply to them. By the end of 1958, a total of 38 estates, covering 61,956 acres, was certified. On these estates African residents had no statutory rights, only those entered into by contract; and encroachment could be dealt with as trespass and the land kept clear for development.[52]

At the end of 1958, after detailed enquiry, the government had calculated that only 20,460 families remained on private estates. It is probable that the number of families emancipated since 1946 was greater than the 46,856 claimed by the government because it is likely that they underestimated the number of families on private estates in 1946 by taking into consideration only those in the Shire Highlands. The 1945 census report gives the number of Africans living on private estates in the protectorate as 211,394 or (by assuming an average family size of four) 52,848 families, as opposed to the figure of 49,600 used by the government. At an annual rate of natural increase of 3 per cent, and ignoring the continued, if small, immigration onto private estates, the 1958 figures would have been 310,428 people or 77,607 families (as against the government figures of 269,200 and 67,305). Using the 1945 census figures, an annual rate of increase of 3 per cent and an average family size of four, by 1960, had it not been for the policy of land acquisition and tenant resettlement, there would have been 328,932 people, or 82,233 families, resident on private estates; the policy had by this time resulted in there being only about 80,000 people, or 20,000 families.[53] Almost a quarter of a million

Africans had been emancipated and 467,073 acres of private land had been acquired in the 14 years following the Abrahams Report, or, more importantly, the 12 years following Colby's appointment as Governor.

After 1958, the disturbed political situation, the civil unrest and the State of Emergency effectively put a stop to the policy of progressive abolition of *thangata*, and in neither 1959 nor 1960 were any further private estates acquired or African tenants resettled: the owners were deeply reluctant to sell, the tenants refused to move voluntarily, and the government, under the circumstances prevailing, did not feel able to compel them.[54]

These unsettled conditions continued into 1961, and then abated somewhat with the General Election of 15 August 1961, which produced an overwhelming majority for the Malawi Congress Party under Dr Banda. In September, the new Legislative Council was appointed with 23 Malawi Congress Party members, five other – European – members, and five official members. Executive Council now had the Governor as President, five official members, and five Malawi Congress Party members, all of them ministers.[55]

The government – now essentially an African government – was concerned about the lack of progress over the past three years, not so much because of the potential for political violence and civil disturbance, since this had already been minimized by the earlier acquisitions and resettlement, especially in the period 1954–8, but because *thangata* still existed as a system and because there was still a good deal of alienated land not fully developed. *Thangata* was an irritant which earlier steps had not yet fully abolished. Consequently, the government introduced a new Africans on Private Estates Bill in June 1962.[56]

In the debate on the Bill, there was inevitably a good deal of rhetoric and verbal abuse of *thangata*, reminiscent of the 1957 debate but without the innuendos of violence. The greatest worry was that of 'certain evil practices by estate owners and these practices are the eviction of children or dependants of resident Africans who become of age'. This had been a long-standing grievance not tackled by earlier legislation. The offspring of resident Africans were not entitled to their parents' status and rights once they reached 18 years of age, which was a particular and acute hardship in the Southern Province where uxorilocal residence after marriage prevailed among the matrilocal peoples; on reaching the age of 18 years, offspring and the husbands of female offspring could be, and often were, treated as trespassers and were liable to eviction. Whereas the 1952 Ordinance – in order to lessen the increase in Africans on private estates – had confined the status of resident African to those then on the estates, the 1962 Bill now gave the status to all those on estates on 1 January 1962, and entitled all children and dependants of resident Africans to register as residents as of right. In moving the second reading, Dr Banda explained:

> In the past it was the habit and practice of at least some if not all of the estate owners to evict anyone that they did not like or thought was troublesome and who was not on that estate in 1952 by simply declaring him a trespasser . . . There will be no trespassers of this class now. It is my intention to have as few trespassers as possible. In the past it was the practice of many estate owners to declare children and dependants of resident Africans when they became of age trespassers, or else force them to pay rent or work on their estates as labourers. I am putting a stop to that.

Additionally, the 1952 restrictions were removed or eased concerning: first, the right only to a site for a dwelling and the amount of agricultural land which was then under cultivation, efficiently used and cultivable by a family without assistance; and second, the right to take building material and firewood only from areas allocated by the landowner. The 1962 Bill restored the rights of residents, including children and dependants, to cut building materials and firewood, apparently without restraint as to where it came from on the estate except from areas protected under natural resources legislation.

The 1962 Bill reduced the rent payable by each family to £1 a year and exempted from payment a significant number of residents: unmarried women; wives of resident Africans; those exempted from paying tax; those without the means of paying because of sickness, age, infirmity or preoccupation with the care of infants; and all those who were resident Africans under the 1928 Ordinance on 30 June 1942. This last category finally recognized that some Africans still held rights of non-disturbance under the Certificates of Claim and should not be liable to pay rent. There was also to be a period of six months, July–December 1962, during which rent was not to be payable.

The object of the Bill was the abolition of *thangata* but it did not do this directly because it retained the right of residents to 'elect to work for wages' with which, presumably, they could pay their rent. The owner could no longer reject requests for work outside the rainy season or at any other time, for sufficient wages at normal rates to pay the rent, save by providing facilities for growing economic crops or by forgoing the rent. Rather, the Bill aimed to abolish *thangata* by putting considerable pressure on estate owners to sell their land to the government for resettling African families.

This pressure was to be exercised through a number of elements in the Bill: reducing the rent; declaring a six months' rent holiday; protecting those who between 1952 and 1962 could have been treated as trespassers; introducing extensive categories of exemption from paying rent; adding children, dependants and spouses to those entitled to resident status; lifting the restrictions on the cutting of building materials and firewood; obliging owners to provide work at normal wages, or facilities for crop growing if asked, or else to forgo the rent. No longer would it be worthwhile for estate owners to hold on to land unless it was sufficiently well worked and profitable to pay proper wages and to put up with the pressures applied by the 1962 Bill. As Dr Banda said at the close of the debate:

> I have drafted this Bill to meet estate owners, the Europeans in this country, half way. My intention is to abolish *thangata* altogether but I have drafted this Bill to give [them] a chance ... to sell their land wherever there are Africans on it, to Government ... any clause in this Bill which seems not so good for the estate owners is giving them a warning. Sell the land. Not that I don't want private land in this country, not at all. I want private owners ... to employ direct labour and pay wages rather than this vested system ... If they have not enough money to pay labourers, they must disgorge those estates ... I won't prevent [them] from making money if [they] employ labour and pay ... people a living wage on these farms.

That the warning was heeded and the chance taken is indicated by the fact that to the 600,490 acres of freehold land acquired by the government up to the end of 1962, a further 102,272 acres were acquired in 1963, and 12,203 in 1964, the year of independence.

Shortly after this, the government announced that no new resettlement acquisitions were to be undertaken.

By this time 714,965 acres had been acquired since 1946, leaving only 431,770 acres in private hands, and the application of the Africans on Private Estates Ordinance had been withdrawn from 47 estates, totalling 72,780 acres, in the Southern Province, with 40 of these estates, totalling 64,721 acres, being in the Cholo District.[57] Although no details were then given of the number of Africans remaining on private estates still subject to the Ordinance, it is likely that, other than the Magomero tobacco share-croppers, those still there were either employees or, in a few cases, illegal squatters.

9
Conclusion

Two political issues increasingly became important through Nyasaland's colonial history: closer association with Southern Rhodesia, and land. Constitutional advancement, from the Africans' point of view, became an active issue only very late in colonial times, but land and closer association were fears which troubled them for decades, and ever more acutely as time passed. From the Europeans' point of view, constitutional advancement was intimately connected with the quest for closer association which they pursued over a long period and which many of them believed would consolidate their dominant position both politically and – including questions of land alienation and use – economically.

In the Africans' mind these two issues – closer association and land – were closely linked: the fear of Southern Rhodesians depriving them of their land and subjugating them both politically and economically. The fears were long-standing and were well known, as the following examples show. At the time of the Native Reserves Commission in 1929, 'One Chief did not object to Europeans coming but wanted to know what kind of Europeans they would be. "Will they be Europeans of Nyasaland or of British South Africa?" he asked.'[1] Politically the Africans feared the removal of British protection, a halt to their own political advancement, and, particularly, white domination. Welensky, who, in the late 1940s and early 1950s, urged widespread immigration of Europeans into Central Africa,[2] was nonetheless aware that the Nyasaland Africans:

> were afraid that if there were any closer links with Southern Rhodesia – which was their big bogey – they would lose their land. They were afraid that political progress would be

curtailed. They were afraid that there would be an extension to their territories of what they regarded as Southern Rhodesia's rigid and reactionary pass laws. Finally they feared that there would be social and educational discrimination against them.[3]

In 1954, in Colby's view, 'European landowners are already beginning to hope for amalgamation rather than federation with the Rhodesias and the day when they imagine that they will be able to turn their African tenants off their land at will.'[4] In a letter written to his imminent successor only a week before he left Nyasaland in March 1956, Colby wrote to Armitage and said that he did not want to inflict a lot of handing-over notes on him but after eight years it would be unusual if he had not formed very strong views on certain subjects: he devoted his letter to two subjects only – federation and land.[5] Very soon after his arrival, Armitage recorded that the Africans were 'fearful of losing their land to European occupation'[6] and he told Lennox-Boyd:

> The underlying tone of the utterances of the new African Members of the Nyasaland legislature has consistently indicated their fear of an extension of a South African form of apartheid to the Federation and the possibility of land alienation.[7]

Indeed Armitage believed that it was the 'feared threat to their land [which contributed] largely to their insistent emphasis on attaining African self-government'.[8] A senior Nyasaland civil servant many years later said:

> the implied threat of deprivation of land was at the very taproot of the nation-wide opposition to federation in 1953 – much more so than any other single factor. It should have surprised no experienced administrator ... when the 1953 eruptions in Cholo and Blantyre occurred. What is more to the point, perhaps, is that in my view similar eruptions were inevitable, even with no federal issue, if any attempt were made at large-scale evictions of tangata tenants.[9]

In addition to these political and social fears, there were deep economic concerns. The Africans resented the holding of large undeveloped areas in the hands of Europeans whilst neighbouring African Trust Land was heavily populated. Those living on private estates additionally resented having to work for the owner or pay him rent, and the poor treatment meted out by some owners. They feared that these matters – all of which restricted their ability or incentive to increase their economic productivity – would become more oppressive with closer association.

The resentment was intensified by the frustration arising from African political impotence, since for most of the colonial era the Europeans were much more powerful. The Europeans had seats in Legislative Council from 1907, but there were no African seats until 1948. The European non-officials outnumbered the Africans on Legislative Council until 1959. There were European non-official members of Executive Council from 1940, but no Africans until 1959. The Europeans had strong and influential contacts in London, through members of parliament, ministers and leading Conservative Party figures, and through the directors of large companies with headquarters in Great Britain. In contrast, the African contacts were few, late in being developed, and much less effective.

European political organization was also much stronger: the Chamber of Commerce was formed in 1895 from associations which had started in 1892;[10] the Convention of Associations was founded in 1928 from an amalgamation of seven existing bodies;[11] and the Landowners' Association was created in 1954. All of these, and the non-official elements of Legislative Council, had interlocking membership. Whilst there were a number of African Associations dating from the first in 1912, they did not become numerous until the 1920s, their influence on the government was small, and the African National Congress was not formed until 1944.

The Europeans also commanded support from the press; the *Central African Planter* was first published in 1895 and its successors, the *Central African Times* and the *Nyasaland Times*, were the only regular newspapers in Nyasaland, being published eventually twice a week: the publishers were European and the editorial stance was strongly pro-European. In contrast, *Msimbi*, the government vernacular newspaper, was not regularly published until 1949 and was both small in size and limited in circulation. Attempts by the government to establish a commercial African newspaper in 1950 were soundly defeated by the powerful objections of the *Nyasaland Times*, the

Convention of Associations, the Chamber of Commerce, and non-official members of Legislative Council.[12]

In respect of land, what the European estate owners wanted was, first, to enjoy undisturbed possession of their private land to develop it immediately or in the future, or simply to hold on to it for sale later as its value increased; and second, an adequate and readily available, preferably exclusive, source of labour with which to develop the land. What the African tenants wanted was a site and materials for a dwelling, garden space (and time to cultivate it during the rainy season), access to firewood and water, and, in particular, freedom to live undisturbed in their traditional fashion. They also wanted work in order to earn money for consumer goods and to pay taxes and rent; to this extent there was a common interest in labour between landlord and tenant save that, especially as employment opportunities increased, the Africans did not want to be bound to work only for the owner of the land on which they lived but wanted freedom to choose their own employer and whether and when they would work. There was also a common interest between the government and both the European owners and the African tenants in respect of labour, because by working on the estates the tenants earned the money with which to pay their tax: indeed, in many cases the owners paid the tax instead of wages. Government revenue was more assured and much more easily collected in this way.

Because of the Europeans' greater political strength, the major contribution which the European estates made to the protectorate's economy, and the tax-earning aspects of estate employment, the British government – and, at its behest, the Nyasaland government – for most of the time favoured the estate owners, especially in respect of labour. They did nothing *de facto* about the rights of African original occupants under the non-disturbance clauses whilst acknowledging them *de jure*; they persistently declined to remove the obligation or pressure on tenants to work for the owners during the rainy season; and they long ignored the advice that the government should acquire private land for settling African tenants: even when the British government accepted this advice they consistently avoided providing the funds with which to implement it until the last moment. This general stance of favouring European interests began to change only when the political dangers became really pressing after the disturbances of the early 1940s, and especially of 1953; and when the contribution of African agriculture to the protectorate's economy

CONCLUSION 177

began significantly to increase – and that of Europeans proportionally to decline – after Colby's arrival in 1948 as his development strategy began to take effect.

In times of political unrest – especially during the later years of colonial rule, when nationalist aspirations and government resistance to them led almost always to conflict and often to violence – land grievances could be a very dangerous issue. In an agrarian society such as Nyasaland, land directly and intimately affected everyone: it was the source, and generally the only source, of their livelihood, essential to life, and had a direct and vital effect on the national economy and on individual welfare. Land was also a highly emotive issue: it was understood by all, it was tangible, and could lead to eruptions of conflict at any time, whether as the result of a natural catastrophe, or of deliberate agitation, or of isolated provocative incidents. Furthermore, in Nyasaland, land ownership was race-based: private estates were almost exclusively owned by Europeans – only one Certificate of Claim was issued to a non-European[13] – and tenants were Africans; indeed, the legislation governing the relationships in 1904, 1917, 1928, 1952 and 1962 consistently included the word 'Natives' or 'Africans' in the title. Racial conflicts, of all conflicts, are particularly dangerous.

The need, from the government's point of view, to settle the problem of Africans on private estates became a good deal more urgent after the Second World War as it became clearer that the colonial territories would move to self-government more quickly than had previously been assumed – the result of the eclipse of the imperial will in British society and politics, the opposition to colonialism of the United States and the United Nations, the increase in African political organization and power, the granting of independence to India, Pakistan, Ceylon, Burma and Palestine, often accompanied by violence – and the emerging view in British political circles that continued colonial rule against the wishes and active opposition of the colonial peoples could be maintained only by significant force, which Britain was not prepared to use, certainly not in too many places at once.[14]

Long before Macmillan's wind of change speeches in Accra and Cape Town in January and February 1960, presaged a dozen years earlier by Colby's own speeches, there was a zephyr of change: the wind was undoubtedly blowing where it listed. There would be enough difficulties, enough sticks with which the African politicians and people could beat the Nyasaland government, without the unresolved land grievances of Africans on private estates being left as a hefty and readily available cudgel.

For years the government had vacillated and inconclusively investigated the problem, committee after committee had looked into it and made recommendations, legislation had been changed on numerous occasions, and yet the problem – which became progressively more acute with population increase and with greater African political awareness over the years – was very little nearer being solved than at any other time since Johnston's original, and in many ways sound and farseeing, settlement in 1892. As Marnham of the Colonial Office said: 'It is a problem as intractable as it is of long standing. It has baffled generations of Governors and Secretaries of State since the beginning of the century.'[15]

Successive governors knew where their duty ultimately rested – with the Africans, since Nyasaland was a protectorate and the Royal Instructions from 1907 required that:

> The Governor ... is especially to take care to protect [the African inhabitants] in their persons and in the full enjoyment of their possessions, and by all lawful means to prevent and restrain all ... injustices which may in any manner be practised or attempted against them.[16]

Yet the Europeans were politically far better organized and it was they who had played the dominant role, both in economic development, upon which the country's wealth and the government's revenue significantly depended, and in maintaining the *status quo* in respect of Africans on private estates.

Impatient to begin work after a long leave in Britain since leaving Nigeria, with little time at his disposal and deeply conscious of the rising tide of African nationalism, Colby, who arrived as Governor early in 1948, was influenced by three important factors. First, he was abundantly aware that the balance of political power between Europeans and Africans was changing. Although the 1915 Chilembwe foretaste of African power had been forgotten or ignored, a reminder had been given in Blantyre in 1942 and 1943, and the Nyasaland African Congress, formed in 1944, had been sufficiently well organized to make a significant impression on Abrahams in 1946. Additionally, there was the growing, if still limited, influence of communism on the African population, of which Colby was acutely aware. Second, he recognized that the greatly increased economic power which would accompany the marked upswing in African agricultural production, which he was determined his policies should bring, would further increase Africans' political power as the economic balance moved in their favour. Third, as a result of these other two factors, Colby was determined that, so far as he was able, political activity should not hamper the rapid increase in agricultural production and economic development which he saw as essential to the protectorate's future.

Bearing these factors in mind, Colby moved quickly towards beginning to solve the problem. His starting point in 1948 was the Abrahams Report, the significance of which lies not in the quality of its recommendations, since it expressed few, if any, significant new ideas and grossly glossed over details crucial to the success of implementing the recommendations. Rather, its significance lay elsewhere. First, the Report raised African expectations of the problems soon being seriously tackled and solved to such an extent as to make it difficult for the government to continue to avoid reaching solutions and making decisions — especially under a governor like Colby, who was not in the habit of avoiding making decisions:

> A Governor's task is not difficult provided he is prepared to make decisions because nothing happens until a decision is made.[17]

As Dr Banda was later to say, 'Sidney Abrahams' report pricked and has pricked ever since the conscience of the Government of this country, in London and Zomba.'[18] Second, since Abrahams was the first outsider to consider formally the question of Africans on private estates and since he was currently, and for several years continued to be, the Colonial Office's adviser on land tenure, the British government could scarcely ignore or underplay his recommendations as they had those of earlier enquiries, or so easily yield to the large land-owning companies' opposition. Third, the Report provided the new Governor with the platform from which to launch his attack on the *thangata* system.

In this attack, Colby quickly recognized that successfully tackling the BCA Company was the key which he must turn if the remainder of the problem was to be solved, and this for a number of reasons.

African criticism of the Company was severe because they owned huge areas of land, much of it in some of the most densely populated and politically sensitive parts of the protectorate; the treatment of tenants by the estate managers left much to be desired; 205,000 acres of the 546,000 acres publicly recommended by the Land Planning Committee for acquisition belonged to them; through its General Manager, the Company exercised much influence over the opinions and activities of the Chamber of Commerce and the Convention of Associations; and other estate owners looked to the Company for leadership.

Colby niggled away at them and, after 1953, persistently hammered away at them. He was quick to acquire their Chingale Estate in 1949, and although this did little immediately to relieve congestion or increase emancipation, it was a large area purchased at a reasonable price; his successor found the land settlement scheme there, with its poor soils, 'depressing', but it was nonetheless an early, politically important purchase.[19] Colby skilfully turned the Landowners, Association meeting with the Secretary of State in 1954 against the Company and was able to exploit the falterings in their arguments and the concessions which they then made. Thereafter he persuaded the Colonial Office and the Secretary of State to intervene directly with Brook and Huggins and to support him much more actively and positively than in the past.

Colby employed a number of methods to attack the *thangata* system. He used the Abrahams Report as a platform for launching his attack. He made two extremely large early purchases – Chingale and Magomero – which very substantially reduced the acreage in private hands. He made a number of early speeches warning of the rising tide of nationalism and the need to be ready for it. He used the 1953 disturbances to remind Europeans of the dangers of land grievances, and he was severe with the African activists to keep them quiet for a while, although he immediately took up the issue with renewed vigour and used the African Protectorate Council memorandum to express his views and plans in an accompanying despatch. He secured additional African seats in Legislative Council to indicate to both Africans and Europeans that the former's interests would become paramount. He frequently warned of the political and security dangers, and played on Colonial Office and local European fears of 'another Mau Mau', goading the Colonial Office into a more positive response after the 1953 disturbances.

He used a battery of levers, or the threat of them, in dealing with the BCA Company: negotiated purchase, compulsory acquisition, arbitration, undeveloped land tax, reduction in rents, and the removal of the labour requirement. He engaged in personal and direct confrontation with the prominent landowners, particularly Brook and Dixon. He deployed a number of very able officers to deal with the Africans on private estates problem: McDonald, who was on good terms with the Cholo planters; Ingham, who had been Secretary to the Abrahams Commission; Reeve, as successor to McDonald; and – admired by the Colonial Office, if not by Colby himself – Winnington-Ingram. He used the easing of the BCA Company logjam to win over other landowners. Having secured the Secretary of State's agreement to policy which he himself had designed, Colby used the occasion of the Secretary of State's visit and announcement of the policy to tease out the BCA Company. He pushed the estate owners between the 1953 disturbances and the 1954 Secretary of State's visit, by attempting direct and individual negotiations with them, thereby provoking them into first forming the Landowners' Association, which provided him with an audience before which to tackle the BCA Company, and afterwards petitioning the Secretary of State who then had to make up his mind one way or the other whether to support fully the Governor's policy proposals.

He made very clear to the British government the cost of containing the 1953 disturbances and thereby made them still further aware of the impracticability of imposing by force a land policy, or any other major policy, against the wishes of the majority of the people. Finally, he made Dixon a member of Executive Council,[20] thereby virtually forcing him to take a more favourable view of the government's actions and wishes. Dixon may well have been conscious of the fact that both previous senior non-official members of Executive Council had been owners or managers of large estates and both had been knighted.

Even with these various methods of tackling the general problem, and particularly that of the BCA Company, the important and worrying question existed throughout of how the solution was to be financed.

Of those who over the years had suggested that private land should be acquired for African settlement, none until 1946 had specifically turned their mind to how the land was to be paid for. The 1904 Native Locations Ordinance would have recompensed the land owners for setting aside locations with the payment of rent by those residing on the perpetually leased land. Hetherwick was silent on funding the acquisitions which he advocated. Bowring in 1925 simply warned that acquisition would 'cost money', and his comment that the evils of their fathers had to be paid for implied that the government would have to pay for it. Since, however, he was already relying upon British grants-in-aid to balance his budget, the chances of either the Nyasaland government finding the money or the British government increasing its grant were extremely slight. The 1928 Natives on Private Estates Ordinance provided that the payment for land compulsorily acquired by the government should be in the form of an exchange of land 'of equivalent total value'. The Legislative Council's proposals in 1934 did not envisage that land surrendered to the native authorities should be paid for because they saw it more a matter of handing over land equivalent to that to which the original occupants were entitled under the non-disturbance clauses; in effect, the owners would be buying out and extinguishing the rights of original occupants. Hailey in 1939 did not mention the financial aspects of acquiring land.

In his Report, Abrahams felt it:

> incumbent upon [him] to consider whether any contribution towards the expenses of [acquisition] could be fairly exacted from both or either of the [European landlords or African tenants] and in that event whether it would be practicable to do so.

He briefly examined the possibility of estate owners compensating Africans leaving their land, in which case some 'landowner[s] might be mulcted a heavy sum', and he concluded, 'It would be hopeless to try to propound a scheme for contributing which would be both equitable and practicable.' He then turned to the possibility of African contributions and dismissed the suggestion that for a number of years the former tenants should continue to pay rent, but now to the government, as also being 'neither fair nor practicable'. He did, however, have two positive suggestions. First, the expense could be lessened if owners of acquired land were offered 'a piece of reserved land or . . . a right of occupancy of native trust land without rent', and, second, he suggested obtaining money from the Native Development and Welfare Fund (NDWF).[21]

CONCLUSION 183

Although the Land Planning Committee in 1947 estimated the cost of purchase – £328,149 – they made no recommendations as to the source of funding, so the new Governor received no guidance from that quarter, notwithstanding the fact that the Financial Secretary was a member of the Committee.

Colby had always been concerned about the cost of acquisition. He had three main views. One was that, since the land in question was generally incapable of being developed because it was heavily congested with squatters, it had but little market value and consequently only a nominal sum should be paid; he had even argued that the owners should pay the government to relieve them of the burden. The second view was that he did not want funds which could be used for other, economic, development to be diverted to acquisition of land for basically political, security, purposes, and he made this point in his very first address to Legislative Council. The third view was that the British government should be prepared to pay for, or at least make a major contribution towards, these purchases. When, at the end of 1949, he had asked Cohen if there was any chance of getting support from the general reserve in the CDWF, he added:

> The fact is that unless a great deal more money than is now envisaged is spent on the development of the Protectorate, there will be little chance of our making any real progress within a reasonable time and our resources as they now stand when compared with our commitments are unlikely to be able to contribute very much ... the problems with which we are confronted and which Abrahams tried to solve, arise from past policy and it seems very hard, at a time when we are striving to set the Protectorate more firmly on its feet, that we should be faced with expenditure of this nature ... I very much fear that, without considerable further financial assistance, there is little prospect of this territory, potentially so prosperous, being put on a sound footing.[22]

Colby was, of course, aiming his remarks only partly at the acquisition of private land – and was really introducing the thin end of a wedge of an argument which he was to pursue repeatedly later for general development purposes. This was, in essence, 'The British Government has neglected Nyasaland far too long. It's now in a mess and if you want me to get the country out of it, you ought to pay for it.' In the event, it was to be several years before the British government did use the CDWF to support Colby's land acquisition policy.

In the period after 1946, three sources of financing were used. First, during the late 1940s and very early 1950s, central government revenue account funds were used to purchase land. In 1946, the Ntonda estate price of £3,781 was met from this source. In 1948, Colby allocated £100,000 for land purchase from the revenue account – and incurred a deficit in doing so – and in 1949 a further £150,000: sums which were used to make the early purchases of the large Chingale and Magomero estates.

From about late 1952, the government found their finances becoming more restricted and, instead of using central government funds, they used NDWF monies – as Abrahams had suggested – although scarcely any land was bought at this time and any drain on the Fund could have been only slight since the Fund increased at a steady rate, and indeed doubled, from £655,000 in 1952 to £1,244,000 five years later.[23] In March 1954, McDonald's view on whether they should use NDWF sources was quite clear:

> Government should have no hesitation in continuing to draw on NDW funds for the purpose of resettlement of land if it suits it to do so. I cannot think of any better way of providing for the welfare of the African than buying land for him and in his eagerness to acquire the land he is not likely to worry about the source from where the money comes to pay for it.[24]

Others, including mission leaders, however, firmly believed that the NDWF, derived exclusively from African sources, should not be used to purchase land but rather that central government funds, derived from both African and European sources, should be used.

When papers on land were prepared for the April 1954 meeting of Executive Council, it was said that, on the basis of two shillings and sixpence an acre – which was what was being offered in some cases, for example to the ALC – some £37,550 would be required to purchase 300,000 acres, and Council was to be asked to advise whether protectorate funds should again be used. Colby, presumably aware that two shillings and sixpence an acre was far too low a price to contemplate realistically, and reluctant to use NDWF monies, knowing that the Africans would resent paying from their own funds for land to which they were convinced they had a right, made a note

CONCLUSION 185

in regard to financing: 'I do not want to take to Ex.Co: please put in a token £25,000 in the Estimates.' He was keeping his counsel and making some provision for land purchases, as a holding move whilst he tried again to secure money from the British government's CDWF.[25]

Although Colby's request for CDWF assistance received some support in the Colonial Office, it received more opposition. Officials in London took refuge in Colby's projected budgetary surplus – which was slightly greater than the sum then needed for land purchases – and in the potential, but unspecified, support from federal sources. This gave the British government a temporary respite but – presumably once it was apparent both that the Nyasaland surplus would be run down rapidly and that the federal government would not provide the support needed for land purchases – eventually they supplied the grants from the CDWF needed to solve the problem of Africans on private estates.

In 1957 and 1958, following requests from Armitage, three linked grants, totalling £300,000, were made for land purchase and resettlement;[26] this was precisely the sum estimated and requested ten years earlier as being required to purchase the estates which the Land Planning Committee had recommended for immediate or early acquisition. In 1959 and 1960, another grant was received totalling £120,000, to complete transactions of land already agreed for acquisition.[27] In 1961, the Governor announced that a further £108,000 was to be received from the CDWF to purchase 32 blocks of private land and reduce the number of families on estates to 14,000.[28] The government's development plan for 1962–5 provided £450,000 for further acquisitions and nearly all of this was spent, or committed, by the end of 1964.[29]

Colby knew that the money for land acquisition would eventually be forthcoming since both he and the Colonial Office placed the very highest priority on abolishing *thangata*. He himself had said that 'the settlement of this problem is worth a lot of money', and the Colonial Office had said that 'this has in one way or another simply got to be done' and the money found. The important point about finance was not that it would not be forthcoming but that there might be too long and too damaging a delay in it being provided. It was this delay which rendered the political security aspects extremely worrying.

Colby was deeply conscious of the prospect of politically motivated violence, which would hamper economic development, lead to individual suffering, consume resources, and put his personal reputation at risk. The possibility of violence had been raised as early as 1892, when Hetherwick told Johnston that the land situation could not 'fail to produce friction between natives and Europeans which will end in catastrophe one day';[30] the 1915 Chilembwe rising gave a very clear indication of the inherent danger; Fiddes in 1917 had warned of the use which 'agitators' might make of the Native Rents Ordinance; Jackson in 1920 referred twice to the 'numerous dangers' and spoke of 'real anxiety' and of the probability that mass evictions would cause 'serious disturbances'; Ormsby-Gore in 1925 said that the state of affairs was 'likely before long to lead to agitation'; Hailey in 1939 referred to the 'many possibilities of friction'; in 1942 and 1943, there were serious incidents in the Blantyre District, and even more serious incidents were only narrowly avoided in Cholo in 1945; Abrahams himself in 1946 wrote of the 'poisoned relationships' between estate owners and their tenants, and warned that the relationships and those between Europeans and Africans generally contained 'the seeds of many forms of trouble'.

Colby himself, from the earliest days of his governorship, tried to bring before the public the inevitability of rising nationalism and pleaded for attempts to be made to 'guide and harness' it. Few paid sufficient attention to his warnings, and even the fears raised by the 1953 disturbances soon abated in the European public's mind as they anticipated that federation would support their cause, protect their property and persons, and stem the tide of nationalism. Not only was Colby already convinced otherwise, but the political intelligence reports early in 1954 reinforced this conviction, and he determined to renew the attack on *thangata* and to do so vigorously and relentlessly. First, he needed to get the British government publicly to commit itself to his policy and to back him in implementing it, and second, he needed to crack the BCA Company nut. These he set about doing in the early months of 1954, building on the fears raised by the 1953 disturbances, not so much in the Nyasaland European mind as in the mind of the Colonial Office.

Colby realized from the outset that Nyasaland did not have much time in which to solve the problem of Africans on private estates before it became a dangerous grievance in the hands of African nationalist activists opposing powerful and inflexible Europeans, and he knew that, with an initial five-year appointment, he personally had little time: he had hoped to move on to a larger colony to complete his service before retiring after a further three years.[31] In the event, Colby solved, or sufficiently solved, the problem in the nick of time, if one takes the relevant 'time' to be 1959–60.

1959 opened with riots in Zomba in January and February; followed by the declaration of a State of Emergency, with many hundreds of arrests and political detentions, and the appointment of the Devlin Commission in March; the boycotting of produce markets and the publication of the Devlin Report in June; interim constitutional arrangements giving Africans a majority of non-official seats in Legislative Council, and the setting up of the Monckton Commission in August; and the appointment of the first African members of Executive Council in October.[32]

The next year opened with Prime Minister Macmillan's visit to Nyasaland, the accompanying disturbances and massively unfavourable press coverage in January, which led to the appointment of the Southworth Commission and Macmillan's summary dismissal of the Chief Secretary in February. In March, Macleod, Colonial Secretary, arrived to discuss revisions to the constitution, and on 1 April, Dr Banda was released from detention. June saw a number of industrial strikes and the enactment of security and detention legislation prior to ending the State of Emergency, and the Lancaster House Nyasaland Constitutional Conference the same month. In July, Macleod told the Governor that his period of office would not be extended and nine months later Armitage left. In September, October and November, there was a series of disturbing incidents of arson, assault, strikes, unlawful assembly and stabbings. In September, all the remaining political detainees were released, and in October, the Monckton Report was published. 1960 ended with the Federal Review Conference at Lancaster House in December.[33]

The period 1959–60 was, then, one of intense political activism and activity. In none of this was the question of land in general, or of Africans on private estates in particular, a live grievance or a worrying political issue.[34] That cudgel with which to beat the colonial government, so readily available and dangerous only a few years earlier, had by this time been whittled down to insignificant political proportions.

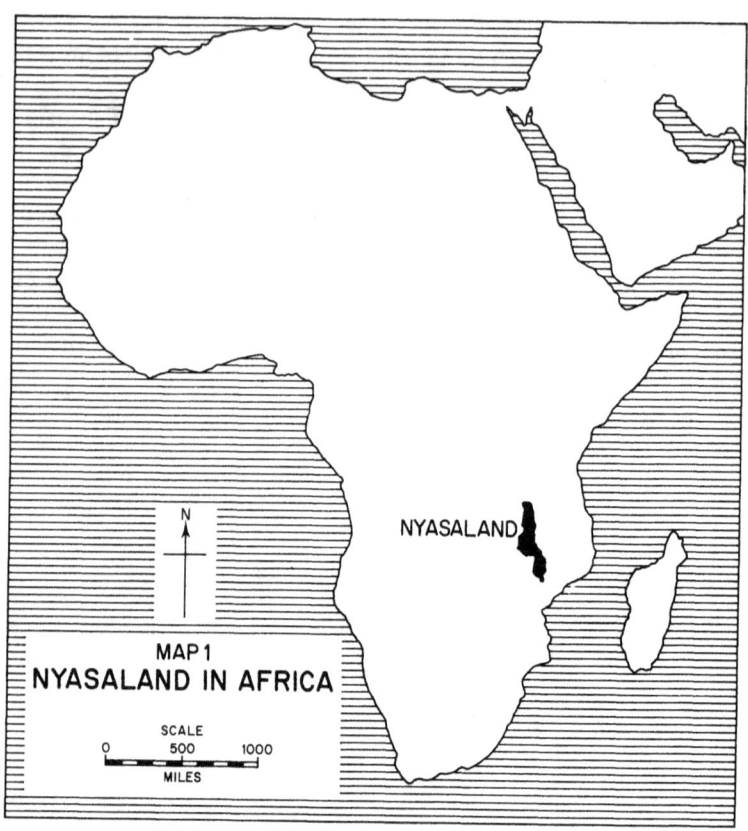

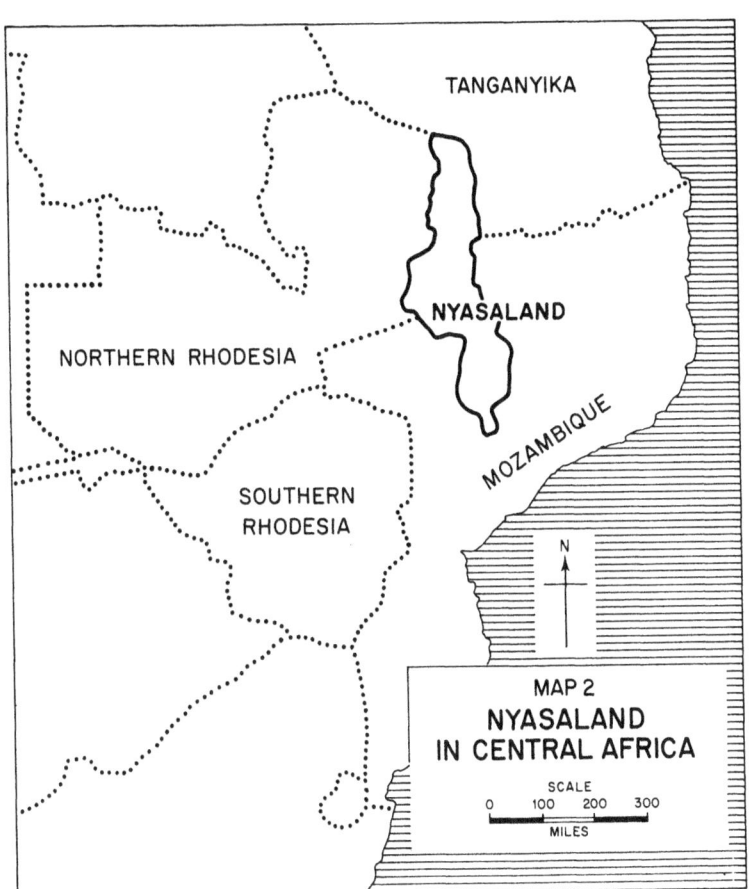

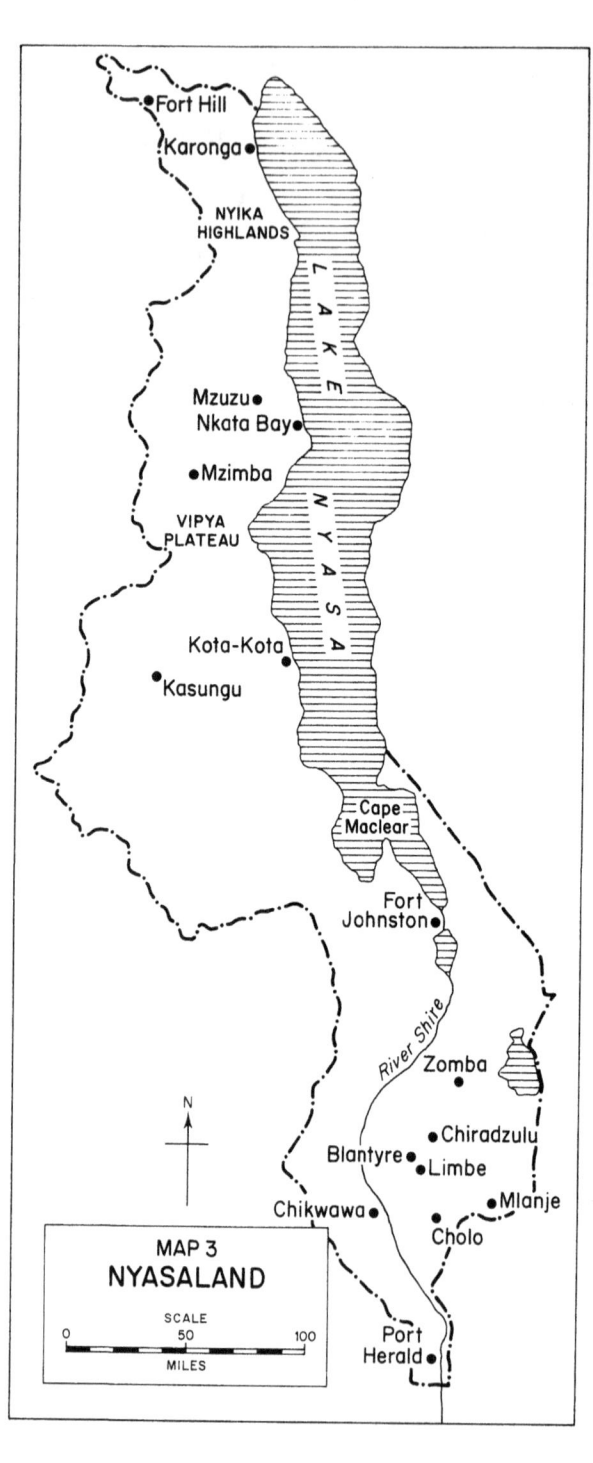

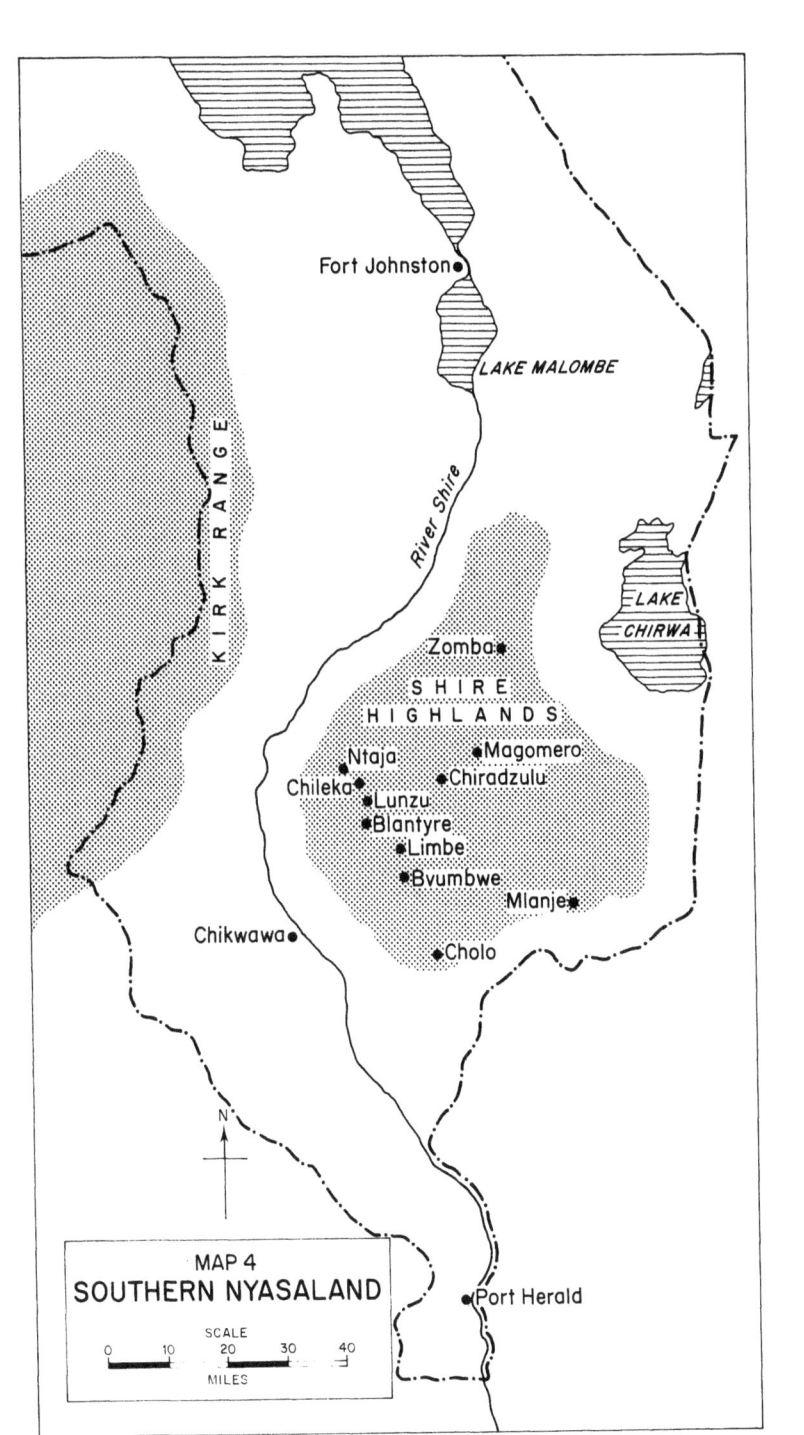

Notes

Preface
1. Malawi Government, *Proceedings of Parliament*, 1st Session, 2nd Meeting, 8 September 1964, IV.XNA, Speech by Dr Banda, pp.10–19, *passim*.

Chapter 1
1. For studies on the geography of Malawi, see J. G. Pike and G. T. Rimmington, *Malawi, A Geographical Study* (London, Oxford University Press, 1965), and S. Agnew and M. Stubbs, *Malawi in Maps* (University of London Press, 1972). See also R. W. Kettlewell, *Agricultural Change in Nyasaland: 1945–1960* (Stanford University Press, 1965), pp.229–39.
2. C. A. Baker, 'Malawi's exports: An economic history' in G. W. Smith *et al.*, *Malawi Past and Present* (Blantyre, Claim, 1971), chapter 6.
3. The British Central Africa Order in Council, 1902, *The Laws of Nyasaland, 1933* (London, Roworth, 1934), pp.1033–42; The Nyasaland Protectorate (Native Trust Land) Order in Council, 1936, *The Laws of Nyasaland, 1946* (London, Roworth, 1947), pp.1566–71.
4. C. A. Baker, *Johnston's Administration* (Zomba, Government Press (hereafter referred to as GP), 1970), chapter 1.
5. *Nyasaland Government Gazette*, (1907–1964), (hereafter referred to as *Gazette*, whether of British Central Africa, Nyasaland or Malawi), *passim*.
6. H. H. Johnston, *British Central Africa*, (London, Methuen, 1897), dedication page.
7. *Report on the Census of 1945* (Zomba, GP, 1946), Tables 1, 3 and 5.
8. Lord Hailey, *Native Administration in the British African Territories* (London, HMSO, 1950), vol. II, p.48.
9. C. A. Baker, 'Malawi's Early Road System', *Society of Malawi Journal*, 24:I (1971), pp.7–21.
10. Brief details of the early acquisitions are given in B. Pachai, *Land and Politics in Malawi, 1875–1975* (Kingston, Ontario, Limestone Press, 1978), chapter 3.

11. L. White, *Magomero: Portrait of an African Village* (London, Cambridge University Press, 1987), pp.77–81; National Archives of Malawi (hereafter referred to as NAM), SMP.12405, Memorandum by McDonald, n.d., probably late 1948. Hereafter the British Central Africa Company is referred to as BCA Company, the Blantyre and East Africa Company is referred to as B&EA Company, and the African Lakes Corporation or Company is referred to as the ALC.
12. Pachai, *op. cit.*, p.32.
13. Johnston, *op. cit.*, pp.107–8.
14. *Ibid.*
15. Memorandum by F. Moir, 14 May 1891, quoted in CO.525/104, Memorandum on Land Matters in the Nyasaland Protectorate by S. S. Murray, 9 October 1942 (hereafter referred to as the Murray Report), pp.1–3. See also Pachai *op. cit.*, pp.33–4.
16. Murray Report, p.4 and p.6.
17. Johnston, *op. cit.*, pp.112–3.
18. Murray Report, *passim*.
19. For an example, see R. C. F. Maugham, *Nyasaland in the Nineties* (London, Lincoln Williams, 1935), pp.61–2.
20. This is the view of Roland Oliver, *Sir Harry Johnston and the Scramble for Africa* (London, Chatto and Windus, 1964), p.221.
21. A. Hetherwick, *The Romance of Blantyre* (London, James Clarke, n.d., probably 1931), pp.85–6.
22. The traditional system of land allocation is dealt with in J. C. Mitchell, *The Yao Village* (Manchester University Press, 1956), pp.62–3; H. Rowley, *Africa Unveiled* (London, SPCK, 1876), pp.109–10; W. H. Rankine, *A Hero of the Dark Continent* (London, Blackwood, 1896), pp.175–6. See also T. O. Elias, *The Nature of African Customary Law* (Manchester University Press, 1956), chapter IX; and J. O. Ibik, *Restatement of African Law, Vol. 4, Malawi II, The Law of Land, Succession, Movable Property, Agreements and Civil Wrongs* (London, Sweet and Maxwell, 1971).
23. P. Mitchell, *African Afterthoughts* (London, Hutchinson, 1954), p.146.
24. Johnston, *op. cit.*, p.113.
25. *Ibid.*
26. *Ibid.*
27. 'Supervisor of Native Affairs versus Blantyre and East Africa Company', *Gazette*, Supplement, 30 April 1903.
28. FO.84/2197, Johnston to Rosebery, 13 October 1892.
29. A. C. Ross, 'The Blantyre Mission and the Problems of Land and Labour, 1891–1915' in R. J. Macdonald, *From Nyasaland to Malawi* (Nairobi, East Africa Publishing House, 1975), p.90; Pachai, *op. cit.*, p.xii.
30. A list of Certificates of Claim is given in Pachai, *op. cit.*, pp.37–40.
31. Johnston, *op. cit.*, p.113.
32. Nyasaland Protectorate Legislative Council, *Proceedings of the Select Committee of the Whole Council Appointed to Consider and Report what Legislation if any is Required to Ensure the Fullest Possible Agricultural Development of the Protectorate: the Position of Natives on Private Estates*

194 SEEDS OF TROUBLE

(hereafter referred to as *Select Committee Report*, 1934) (Zomba, GP, 1934), Paper 6, p.2.
33. R. Gray, *The Two Nations: Aspects of the Development of Race Relations in the Rhodesias and Nyasaland* (London, Oxford University Press, 1960), p.73.

Chapter 2

1. 'Supervisor of Native Affairs versus Blantyre and East Africa Company', *Gazette*, Supplement, 30 April 1903, pp.1-8.
2. *Ibid.*, p.5; L. Bandawe, *Memoirs of a Malawian* (Blantyre, Claim, 1971) pp.46-7; White, *op. cit.*, p.87; C. A. Baker, 'A Note on Nguru Immigration to Nyasaland', *Nyasaland Journal*, 14:I, January 1961, pp.41-2.
3. NAM, SMP.12405, Memorandum by McDonald, n.d., probably late 1948.
4. The following details of the agreements and of the judgment in 'Supervisor of Native Affairs versus Blantyre and East Africa Company' are from *Gazette*, Supplement, 30 April 1903, pp.1-8.
5. White, *op. cit.*, p.100.
6. Gray, *op. cit.*, p.76.
7. NAM, SMP. S/1/385/25, Land Commission Report, 6 May 1903; Pachai, *op. cit.*, pp.88-90.
8. *Ordinances of the Nyasaland Protectorate* (London, Stevens, 1913), chapter 48: The Lands (Native Locations) Ordinance, No.5 of 1904.
9. *Ibid.*, s.3.
10. *Ibid.*, s.6.
11. *Ibid.*, s.9.
12. R. S. Hynde, *et al.*, to Governor, 28 May 1925, repeated in *Report of the Land Commission, 1946* (Zomba, GP, 1947), Appendix XI.
13. CO.525/73, Smith to Secretary of State for the Colonies (hereafter referred to as SS), 16 April 1917, p.4.
14. *Blue Book* (hereafter referred to as *BB*), 1905 (Zomba, GP, 1906), p.124, p.136, p.137.
15. Land Commission to Pearce, 6 May 1903, cited in Pachai, *op. cit.*, p.84.
16. Hereafter the Shire Highlands Railway Company is referred to as SHR Company.
17. Pachai, *op. cit.*, p.72.
18. *Report of the Commission Appointed to Enquire into the Financial Position and Further Development of Nyasaland* (hereafter referred to as *Bell Report*) (London, HMSO, 1938), p.283; *Central Africa Times* (hereafter *CAT*), 18 January 1908, p.4.
19. Pachai, *op. cit.*, pp.76-7.
20. Hereafter, the Associated Chamber of Agriculture and Commerce is referred to as Chamber of Commerce.
21. *CAT*, 11 January 1908, p.7.

22. *CAT*, 6 February 1908, pp.4–6.
23. *Handbook of Nyasaland* (Zomba, GP, 1908), p.99.
24. *Ibid.*
25. *Proceedings of the Legislative Council of Nyasaland* (hereafter referred to as *LCP*), 4th Session, 2–5 November 1909, pp.22–4.
26. *Ibid.*
27. *LCP*, 13th Session, 10 December 1914, pp.12–16.
28. *LCP*, 5th Session, 24–26 May 1910, pp.6–10.
29. *LCP*, 8th Session, 7–9 November 1911, pp.10–13.
30. One of the directors of SHR Company was V. Oury, who was also a director of BCA Company. The BCA Company land referred to here is the Chingale estate which was much later purchased by the government (see chapter 4).
31. *LCP*, 10th Session, 5–8 November 1912, pp.20–3.
32. *Ibid.*
33. Ordinance No. 18 of 1912, ss.7(3) and 10(1)(p), *Ordinances of the Nyasaland Protectorate* (London, Stevens, 1913).
34. *BB* 1905, p.89 and *BB* 1913, p.R.1.
35. *Bell Report*, pp.281–2.
36. *Gazette*, 31 March 1914, General Notice No. 60 of 1914, p.57, and Native Tenancy Agreement Bill, pp.57–8; *LCP*, 13th Session, 10–12 March 1914, pp.12–16.
37. White, *op. cit.*, p.111.
38. *Report of the Commission Appointed by His Excellency the Governor to Inquire Into Various Matters and Questions Concerned with the Native Rising within the Nyasaland Protectorate*, Supplement to *Gazette*, 31 January 1916. See also G. Shepperson and T. Price, *Independent African: John Chilembwe and the Origins, Setting and Significance of the Nyasaland Native Rising of 1915* (Edinburgh University Press, 1958), *passim*.
39. CO.525/68, Smith to SS, 7 August 1916.
40. *Gazette*, 30 September 1916, pp.248–9.
41. *Life and Work in Nyasaland*, No.3, December 1916, pp.1–3, cited in Shepperson and Price, *op. cit.*, p.393.
42. CO.525/73, Smith to SS, 16 April 1917.
43. *Ibid.*
44. *Ibid.*
45. CO.525/73, Minutes by H. A. Bartles, 16 April 1917 and Sir G. Fiddes, 7 July 1917.
46. *Ibid.*
47. Governor's Circular No.6. of 1918, quoted in CO.525/109, Murray Report.
48. White, *op. cit.*, p.152.
49. *LCP*, 21st Session, 15 July 1919, pp.4–5.
50. *Gazette*, 31 July 1920, pp.191–2 and 30 September 1920, p.247.
51. *Report of a Commission to Enquire into and Report on Certain Matters Connected with the Occupation of Land in the Nyasaland Protectorate* (hereafter referred to as the *Jackson Report*) (Zomba, GP, 1920), pp.14–15.

52. *BB*, 1905, p.89 and *BB*, 1920, p.O.1; *Jackson Report*, p.12.
53. *Jackson Report*, p.12.
54. *BB*, 1919, p.R.1; 1921, p.O.1; and Gray, *op. cit.*, p.73.
55. *Jackson Report*, p.15.
56. *Ibid.*, p.14.
57. *Ibid.*, p.15.
58. *Ibid.*, pp.16–17.
59. *Ibid.*, p.20.
60. Colonial Reports – Annual, Nyasaland, 1921 (No. 1156) p.9, 1922 (No. 1162) p.10, 1923 (No. 1204) p.10, 1924 (No. 1257) p.11, 1925 (No. 1296) p.9, (London, HMSO).
61. L. P. Mair, *Native Policies in Africa* (London, Routledge, 1936), pp.110–1; and Jackson Report, Part VII, sections 5 and 7. Mair's figures (6,000,000 acres) and Jackson's figures (2,500,000 acres) approximately tally only if one assumes that Mair believed that Jackson had intended to include the 2,731,000 acres of British South Africa Company land in the North Nyasa District as being available – like Crown Land – for opening up to European occupation.
62. CO.525/104, Bowring to SS, 10 November 1924.
63. CO.525/109, Bowring to Ormsby-Gore, 12 November 1924.
64. *Select Committee Report*, 1934, Paper 1, p.7.
65. Reprinted in *Report of the Land Commission 1946* (hereafter referred to as the *Abrahams Report*) (Zomba, GP, 1947), Appendix vi.
66. Details are given in Pachai, *op. cit.*, p.117.
67. *LCP*, 32nd Session, 19 April 1926, p.7; *Select Committee Report*, 1934, p.7.
68. *LCP*, 34th Session, 11 and 20 May 1927, p.5.
69. *LCP*, 35th Session, 22 August 1927, p.4.
70. *Ibid.*, p.3.
71. Executive Council (hereafter referred to as Ex. Co.) Minute No. 71 of 14 March 1927, No. 96 of 4 April 1927, No. 227 of 29 August 1927.
72. *LCP*, 35th Session, 22 August 1927, p.9.
73. It is probable that Governor Smith in 1917 knowingly overstated the availability of Crown Land in order to reassure the Colonial Office and thereby secure their support for the 1917 Ordinance.
74. *LCP*, 35th Session, 22 August 1927, p.10.
75. *Select Committee Report*, 1934, Paper 3, p.5.
76. *Ibid.*, Paper 1, p.7.
77. *Laws of Nyasaland, 1933* (London, Roworth, 1934), chapter 43.
78. *Ibid.*, s.21(7).
79. *Select Committee Report*, 1934, Paper 2, p.6; *Annual Report of the Provincial Commissioners 1939* (Zomba, GP, 1940), p.12.
80. *Select Committee Report*, 1934, Paper 4, p.2.
81. *Ibid.*, Paper 1, p.8.
82. *Ibid.*, Paper 2, p.1.
83. *Ibid.*, Paper 2, p.2.
84. *Ibid.*, Paper 1, p.1, p.8.
85. *Ibid.*, Paper 1, p.7.

86. *Abrahams Report*, para. 36; see also *Select Committee Report*, 1934, Paper 3, p.6.
87. *Select Committee Report*, 1934, Paper 3, p.6. See also *Report on Native Affairs, 1932* (Zomba, GP, 1932), p.24.
88. *Report on Native Affairs, 1933* (Zomba, GP, 1934), p.9. The estimate of 3,124 people is calculated on the basis of four people per tenant family.
89. *Annual Report of the Provincial Commissioners 1934* (Zomba, GP, 1935), p.9.
90. *Select Committee Report*, 1934, Paper 2, p.4.
91. *Ibid.*, Paper 4, p.2.
92. *Ibid.*, Confidential Appendix: draft letter of instruction to the Commissioner.
93. SS to Kittermaster, 24 October 1934, quoted in *Abrahams Report*, paras. 43 and 44. A distinguished commentator said in 1946 that the Ordinance was 'an attempt to give equal treatment all round', C. K. Meek, *Land Law and Custom in the Colonies* (London, Oxford University Press, 1946), p.118.
94. Kittermaster to SS, 15 December 1934, quoted in *Abrahams Report*, paras. 46 and 47.
95. SS to Kittermaster, 20 September 1935, quoted in *Abrahams Report*, para. 48.
96. Kittermaster to SS, 23 January 1937, quoted in *Abrahams Report*, paras. 49–52.
97. For an outline of the nature and quality of management on the Magomero Estate under the General Manager, Kincaird-Smith, in the 1930s, see White, *op. cit.*, pp.194–8.
98. *Annual Report of the Provincial Commissioners 1939*, (Zomba, GP, 1940), p.13.
99. *Annual Report of the Provincial Commissioners 1938* (Zomba, GP, 1939), p.18.
100. *Annual Report of the Provincial Commissioners 1936* (Zomba, GP, 1937), p.14.
101. The Nyasaland Protectorate (Mineral Rights) Order in Council, 1936, *The Laws of Nyasaland, 1946* (London, Roworth, 1947), p.1561; *Bell Report*, p.23; LCP, 52nd Session, 19–20 October 1936, p.5.
102. *BB*, 1936, p.0.2.
103. Minute by Kittermaster, 15 November 1937, referred to in *Abrahams Report*, para. 54.
104. SS to Kittermaster, 22 September 1937, referred to in *Abrahams Report*, para. 53
105. *Annual Report of the Provincial Commissioners 1937* (Zomba, GP, 1938), p.16.
106. *Bell Report*, pp.34–7. Debenham later expressed this policy point as: 'With the Government must rest the last word on what is expedient. It can claim that there is no case of injustice ... it is rather a question of policy and that is to a large extent the prerogative of the Government.' F. Debenham, *Nyasaland: Land of the Lake* (London, HMSO, 1955), p.103.

107. *Annual Report of the Provincial Commissioners 1938* (Zomba, GP, 1939), p.18. 123 applications from the Bruce Estates is the figure given in this Report White, *op. cit.*, p.196, gives a figure of 127 applications, possibly following Pachai, *op. cit.*, p.127, who gives 127 as the number of actual evictions from the whole of the Southern Province.
108. *Confidential Report on Native Administration and Political Development in British Tropical Africa* (London, HMSO, n.d. probably 1943), pp.257–8.
109. *Memorandum on Native Policy in Nyasaland* (Zomba, GP, 1939), p.19.
110. White, *op. cit.*, pp.192–4.
111. *Annual Report of the Provincial Commissioners 1940* (Zomba, GP), p.16.
112. White, *op. cit.*, pp.192–3 and pp.197–8.
113. LCP, 56th Session, 3 December 1940, p.6.
114. Alistair Horne, *Macmillan, 1957–1986*, Vol. II of the *Official Biography* (London, Macmillan, 1989), p.187.
115. *Abrahams Report*, paras. 57–9.
116. LCP, 60th Session, 5 December 1944, p.64.
117. LCP, 59th Session, 7 December 1943, p.8.
118. CO.626/24, *Annual Report of the Provincial Commissioners 1946*, p.5, 1947, p.6.
119. *Abrahams Report*, para. 60. Details of the Mpezo applications for eviction are from NAM, SMP.11967, 4a.Ec.151278 *et seq.*, Confidential Appendix to the Draft Report of the Land Planning Committee, 1948.
120. *Gazette* 31 July 1946, p.152, General Notice No. 215.

Chapter 3

1. Abrahams to Richards, 31 October 1946, incorporated in *Abrahams Report*, p.3; *Abrahams Report*, Appendices I and II; and J. H. Ingham to author, 19 November 1991.
2. *Abrahams Report*, paras. 63–9.
3. *Ibid.*, para. 65.
4. *Ibid.*, para 20.
5. LCP, 13th Session, 10–12 March 1914, p.12. Gray, *op cit.*, p.77 and p.81, believed that Abrahams 'was the first to recognise that this was not a legal question so much as a conflict of basic assumptions' and 'a conflict of ideas'.
6. *Abrahams Report*, paras. 70–1.
7. *Ibid.*, para 75.
8. *Ibid.*, para. 75.
9. *Ibid.*, paras. 76–8.
10. *Ibid.*, paras. 79–81.
11. *Ibid.*, para. 83.
12. *Ibid.*, paras. 86–7.
13. *Ibid.*, paras. 90–4.
14. *Ibid.*, para. 95.
15. *Ibid.*, para. 99.
16. *Ibid.*, para. 102.
17. *Ibid.*, para. 107.

18. *Ibid.*, para. 106.
19. *Ibid.*, para. 105.
20. *Ibid.*, paras. 107, 113, 114, 116, 117, 125 and 126.
21. For example, CO.626/5 and CO.626/8, Ex.Co. Minutes 21, 74, of 1924; 31, 103 of 1925; 186, 187 of 1926; 230, 243 of 1927.
22. *Gazette*, 17 February 1947, General Notice No.56.
23. *LCP*, 62nd Session, 20 February 1947, p.4.
24. *Gazette*, 31 March 1947, General Notice No.107.
25. NAM, SMP.11967, Draft Report of the Land Planning Committee (hereafter referred to as DRLPC), para. 8.
26. NAM, SMP.10521/I, Report of the Land Planning Committee 1948 (hereafter referred to as RLPC).
27. RLPC, paras. 3–6.
28. *Ibid.*, para. 8.
29. *Ibid.*, para 9.
30. *Ibid.*, paras. 11–12.
31. *Ibid.*, paras. 13–16.
32. Abrahams to Richards, 31 October 1946, incorporated in *Abrahams Report*, para. 8.
33. *Abrahams Report*, para. 91.
34. Abrahams to Richards, 31 October 1946, incorporated in *Abrahams Report*, para. 8.
35. RLPC, para. 17.
36. *Ibid.*, para. 18.
37. *Ibid.*, para. 19.
38. DRLPC, para. 21.
39. RLPC, para. 20.
40. RLPC, para. 21; DRLPC, para. 22.
41. DRLPC, para. 22.
42. RLPC, Appendix I.
43. DRLPC, para. 23. The Magomero Estate had first been put on the general market in January 1945: *East Africa and Rhodesia*, 4 January 1945, cited in White, *op. cit.*, p.199.
44. RLPC, paras. 22–5.
45. *Ibid.*, Appendix I.
46. RLPC, para. 33; DRLPC, para. 35.
47. RLPC, paras. 34–40.
48. *Ibid.*, para 41.
49. *Ibid.*, paras. 43–4.
50. *Abrahams Report*, paras. 172–4.
51. RLPC, para. 45.
52. NAM, SMP.11967.
53. CO.626/24. *Annual Report of the Provincial Commissioners 1946*, p.5, *1947*, p.6.
54. DRLPC, Confidential Appendix, Section 5.
55. *Ibid.*, paras. 6–9.
56. 'Supervisor of Native Affairs versus Blantyre and East Africa Company', *Gazette*, Supplement, 30 April 1903, p.8; *Abrahams Report*, para. 120.

57. DRLPC, paras. 10–11.
58. *Ibid.*, para. 12.
59. *Ibid.*, para. 13.
60. *Ibid.*, para. 14.

Chapter 4

1. Details of Colby's career are based on interviews with Lady Colby, 15 March 1983 and 18 June 1983, and from correspondence with his former colleagues, 1979–90, undertaken as part of the research for a biography of Colby and privately held. This correspondence includes that with members of his family: Lady Colby (widow), Marcus Colby (brother), Carol Dudgeon (daughter), and Nancy Tallents (cousin). It also includes that with his former colleagues from Nigeria: Sir Rex Niven, Sir James Harford, Sir Arthur Weatherhead, Sir Thomas Shankland, Sir Frederick Pedlar, Sir Eric Tansley, Lord Grey, R. Peel, D. A. Pott, M. J. Davies, R. Varvill, Mrs F. C. Cann, A. A. Shillingford, J. E. B. Hall, and M. J. Bennion. It includes that also with those from Nyasaland, primarily Sir Roy Welensky, Sir Henry Phillips, Sir Hugh Norman Walker, W. J. R. Pincott, R. W. Kettlewell, D. A. G. Reeve, J. H. Watson and A. H. Mell. Correspondence with colleagues from the Colonial Office includes that with Sir Hilton Poynton, Sir John Martin, Sir William Gorell Barnes, Sir John Cartland, Sir Leslie Monson and John Martin.
2. C. E. Lucas Phillips, *The Vision Splendid* (London, Heinemann, 1960), pp.264–5.
3. Interview with Sir David Hunt, May 1975; James Robertson to author, 10 March 1992; J. R. T. Wood, *The Welensky Papers* (Durban, Graham, 1983), p. 1232.
4. *Nyasaland Times*, (hereafter referred to as *NT*), 8 July 1948, p.7.
5. *LCP*, 63rd Session, 19 July 1948, p.8.
6. *Ibid.*
7. NAM, LANCOM.14, Colby to Cohen, 28 April 1948.
8. *Ibid.* (Details in the following paragraphs, unless otherwise stated, are from this source.)
9. Nyasaland Protectorate Estimates for 1949, Head 14, item 24, p.40.
10. *LCP*, 64th Session, 29 November 1948, p.5. and p.62.
11. Drafts on NAM, LANCOM.14, April 1948.
12. Chief Secretary (hereafter referred to as CS) to Chairman, Tea Association, 1 June 1948, reproduced in *NT*, 24 June 1948, p.7.
13. *Ibid.*
14. *NT*, 15 July 1948, p.7.
15. *LCP*, 63rd Session, 19 July 1948.
16. *Ibid.*, p.6.
17. *Ibid.*, p.8.
18. *Ibid.*, p.14.
19. *Ibid.*
20. NAM, SMP.10521/I, Colby to CS, 23 October 1948.

21. *Ibid.*
22. NAM, SMP.10521, Minute by Colby, No.68, 23 October 1948.
23. NAM, SMP.10521/I, Minute by Edwards, 26 October 1948.
24. NAM, SMP.10521/I, Minute by Colby, 26 October 1948.
25. NAM, SMP.10521, Minute by Colby, No.48, 31 August 1948.
26. NAM, SMP.12258, McDonald to CS, 12 December 1948. The following details are from this source.
27. See also Pachai, *op. cit.*, p.18.
28. NAM, SMP.10521, Minute by Colby, No.63, 12 October 1948; SMP. 12258, Minute by Colby, 22 December 1948.
29. NAM, SMP.10521/I, Minute by Colby, 23 October 1948.
30. NAM, SMP.10521, Minute by Colby, No.74, 5 November 1948. It is not clear what lay behind Colby's question since it was in an isolated and unexplained minute in the Secretariat Land files.
31. NAM, SMP.12664, Note of Discussion with Secretary of State at Government House, 26 April 1949.
32. Ex.Co., 8 June 1949, Minute 305; NAM, SMP.12258, McDonald to CS, 12 December 1948.
33. Ex.Co., 4 July 1949, Minute 361.
34. NAM, SMP.I.10521, Minute by Colby, No.87, 24 November 1948.
35. NAM, SMP.I.12501, Barrow to Colby, 24 June 1949.
36. NAM, SMP.10521, Ex.Co., 13 April 1949, Minute No. 193, and 8 June 1949, Minute No.41.
37. CO.1015/707, referred to in Minute by Marnham, 14 October 1953.
38. *Abrahams Report*, para. 119.
39. CS to Secretary of the Convention of Associations, 24 June 1949, cited in *NT*, 4 August 1949, p.3.
40. *Report on the Nyasaland Protectorate for the Year 1950* (London, HMSO, 1951), p.14.
41. *Ibid.*
42. *Report on the Nyasaland Protectorate for the Year 1951* (London, HMSO, 1953), p.18.
43. CO.1015/848, Colby to SS, 7 October 1955.
44. *Report on the Nyasaland Protectorate for the Year 1952* (Zomba, GP, 1953), p.19; *Report on the Nyasaland Protectorate for the Year 1953* (Zomba, GP, 1954), p.18.
45. Reeve to author, privately held.
46. White, *op. cit.*, p.199 and pp.202–11.
47. Reeve to author, privately held.
48. *Report on the Nyasaland Protectorate for the Year 1954* (Zomba, GP, 1955), p.14; *Report on the Nyasaland Protectorate for the Year 1955* (Zomba, GP, 1956), p.13.
49. *NT*, 18 December 1950.
50. Nyasaland Protectorate Estimates for 1953, Head 22, item 106, note 2, p.69.
51. NAM, SMP.10719, Proposed Acquisition of Freehold Land Belonging to the British South Africa Company (BSAC): Edwards to Robbins, 9 October 1947; Report by Rangeley, 10 April 1948.

202   SEEDS OF TROUBLE

52. *Ibid.*, Edwards to Robbins, 9 October 1947.
53. *Ibid.*, Robbins to Edwards, 17 November 1947.
54. *Ibid.*, CS to Robbins, 6 May 1949.
55. *Ibid.*, Robbins to CS, 25 May 1949.
56. *Ibid.*, Robbins to CS, 29 August 1949.
57. *Ibid.*, CS to Secretary BSAC, 15 July 1950.
58. *Ibid.*, MacDonald to CS, 23 October 1950.
59. *Ibid.*, Robbins to CS, 28 November 1950.
60. *Ibid.*, Feeny to Robbins, 20 December 1950 and Robbins to Feeny, n.d., probably end December 1950.
61. *Ibid.*, note attached to Mell to D. C. Blantyre, 15 January 1953.
62. *Ibid.*, Robbins to CS, 8 June 1954.
63. *Ibid.*, Barnes to Feeny, n.d., probably early 1954.
64. *Ibid.*, Barnes to CS, 12 February 1955.
65. *Ibid.*, CS to Robbins, 19 February 1955.
66. *Ibid.*, Robbins to CS, 28 February 1955.
67. *Ibid.*, CS to Robbins, 10 March 1955.
68. *Ibid.*, Robbins to CS, 29 March 1955.
69. *Ibid.*, General Manager BSAC to CS, 12 June 1956.
70. *Ibid.*, NAM, SMP.18950, Report of the Committee Appointed to Consider the Amendment of the Natives on Private Estates Ordinance, 4 April 1951.
71. *Ibid.*, the following details are from this source.
72. Ordinance No.8 of 1952, Laws of Nyasaland, 1957, chapter 78.

Chapter 5

1. NAM, Minutes of Convention of Associations, Special Session, 11 February 1953.
2. NAM, Ex.Co., 22 April 1953, Minute No.195.
3. D. Taylor, *Rainbow On The Zambezi* (London, Museum Press, 1953), p.77; see also p.98.
4. C. Sanger, *Central African Emergency* (London, Heinemann, 1960), p.213.
5. NAM, Ex.Co., 22 March 1953, Minute No. 195.
6. *Report on the Nyasaland Protectorate for the Year 1953* (Zomba, GP, 1954), p.5.
7. NAM, Ex.Co., 8 September 1953, Minute No. 523.
8. CO.1015/707, Colby to SS, 2 October 1953. See also CO.1015/707, Colby to Gorell Barnes, 20 November 1953.
9. CO.1015/707, Marnham to Colby, 9 November 1953; Minute by Marnham, 13 October 1953.
10. Hereafter referred to as CDWF.
11. CO.1015/707, Minute by Abrahams, 15 October 1953.
12. CO.1015/707, Minute by Bourdillon, 16 October 1953.
13. CO.1015/707, Minute by Johnston, 23 October 1953.
14. CO.1015/707, Gorell Barnes to Colby, 24 October 1953.
15. CO.1015/707, Minute by Marnham, 14 October 1953.

16. CO.1015/707, Colby to Gorell Barnes, 20 November 1953.
17. CO.1015/707, Minute by Marnham, 13 October 1953.
18. CO.1015/707, Colby to Gorell Barnes, 20 November 1953.
19. *Ibid.*
20. CO.1015/707, Minute by Williams, 27 November 1953. Similar views were expressed in CO.1015/707, Minute by Marnham, 27 October 1953.
21. CO.1015/707, draft, Gorell Barnes to Colby, December 1953.
22. CO.1015/847, Vernon to Drake, 11 March 1954.
23. CO.1015/707, Minutes by Marnham, 27 October 1953, Williams, 27 November 1953, Gorell Barnes, 22 December 1953, Melville, 15 December 1953, Bourdillon, 10 December 1953.
24. CO.1015/707, Marginal note by Lloyd on Minute by Gorell Barnes, 22 December 1953.
25. CO.1015/847, Colby to Gorell Barnes, 26 February 1954.
26. CO.1015/847, Vernon to Drake, 7 May 1954.
27. CO.1015/707, Colby to Gorell Barnes, 20 November 1953.
28. CO.1015/707, Note, Gorell Barnes to Marnham, 14 December 1953.
29. CO.1015/707, referred to in Brief for the SS: Land Policy in Nyasaland, n.d., probably early 1954.
30. CO.1015/707, Colby to Gorell Barnes, 26 February 1954.
31. CO.1015/707, Colby to Colonial Office, 16 March 1954.
32. CO.1015/707, Colby to Gorell Barnes, 26 February 1954.
33. CO.1015/707, SS to Colby, 26 March 1954.
34. CO.1015/707, Colby to Colonial Office, 29 March 1954.
35. CO.1015/707, Minute by Marnham, 18 March 1954.
36. NAM, SMP.25282.K, Note of a Meeting in the Secretary of State's Room, House of Commons, 14 April 1955.
37. NAM, SMP.20767/43, Colby to SS, 16 March 1954.
38. NAM, SMP.20767, Minute by Graham-Jolly, 17 June 1954.
39. NAM, SMP.20767, Minute by Colby, 26 October 1953.
40. NAM, SMP.20767, Minute by Graham-Jolly, 17 June 1954.
41. The draft memorandum is in NAM, SMP.20767, folio 15, and a copy of the final version was reprinted in *East Africa and Rhodesia*, 10 June 1954, pp.1287–8.

Chapter 6

1. NAM, SMP.20767, Colby to SS, 16 March 1954. See also NAM, Ex.Co. Precis, Ref.26127, April 1954.
2. NAM, SMP.20767, SS to Colby, 16 April 1954.
3. NAM, SMP.62531, SS to President, Nyasaland Protectorate African Council, n.d., probably late May 1954.
4. CO.1015/847, Minute by Marnham to Gorell Barnes, 18 March 1954.
5. *East Africa and Rhodesia*, 27 May 1954, p.1219.
6. CO.1015/707, Colby to SS, 2 October 1953.
7. *East Africa and Rhodesia*, 27 May 1954, p.1219.
8. CO.1015/847, Note by Colby, 20 April 1954.

9. NAM, SMP.25282.K, and CO.1015/847, Dixon to SS, 1 May 1954. Details of the Memorandum are from this source.
10. Ordinances No. 19 of 1948 and No. 34 of 1952; *NT*, April–September 1952, *passim*; *LCP*, 66th Session, 27 November 1950, 67th Session, 17 December 1952 and 68th Session, November 1953.
11. *East Africa and Rhodesia*, 27 May 1954, p.1215.
12. NAM, SMP.25282.A. and CO.1015/847, Record of a Meeting held at Government House on 6 May 1954. See also CO.1015/849, Colby to SS, 7 May 1954, and Colby to Brook, 7 May 1954.
13. NAM, SMP.25282.K, Note of a Meeting in the Secretary of State's Room, House of Commons, 14 April 1954.
14. *NT*, 2 February 1950, p.7.
15. NAM, SMP.20767/43, Colby to SS, 16 March 1954.
16. NAM, SMP.25282.A and CO.1015/847, Record of a Meeting held at Government House on 6 May 1954.
17. NAM, SMP.25282.A, Note on Points of Policy to be Made to the Secretary of State, n.d., probably very early May 1954.
18. NAM, SMP.25282.K, Note of a Meeting in the Secretary of State's Room, House of Commons, 14 April 1954.
19. CO.1015/847, Footman to Gorell Barnes, 22 May 1954.
20. CO.1015/848, Note of a Meeting with Sir Geoffrey Colby, 12–13 October 1954, dated 15 October 1954.
21. *Gazette*, 13 May 1954, General Notice No. 231.
22. CO.1015/707, Gorell Barnes to Footman, 16 August 1954; NAM, SMP.25282.A, *passim.*; CO.1015/848, Minute, Marnham to Gorell Barnes, 20 October 1954; NAM. SMP.25282.A, Footman to Gorell Barnes, 7 September 1954.
23. CO.1015/847, Colby to Gorell Barnes, 21 August 1954.
24. CO.1015/848, Note of a Meeting with Sir Geoffrey Colby, 12–13 October 1954, dated 15 October 1954.
25. CO.1015/707, Colby to Gorell Barnes, 21 August 1954.
26. CO.1015/848, Minute, Marnham to Gorell Barnes, 20 October 1954.
27. CO.1015/848 Minute, Gorell Barnes to Lloyd and SS, 21 October 1954. See also CO.1015/848, Gorell Barnes to Colby, 22 November 1954, and Minute, Gorell Barnes to Lloyd and SS, 17 February 1955.
28. CO.1015/707, Gorell Barnes to Colby, 22 November 1954.
29. NAM, SMP.25282.A, Gorell Barnes to Footman, 27 May 1954.
30. NAM, SMP.25282.A, and CO.1015/847, Record of Discussion in Executive Council, 9 June 1954. See also NAM, SMP.25282.A, Minutes 14, 21, 25, 54, 115, 116, 119.
31. *Nyasaland Government Staff List, 1955*, p.70.
32. NAM, SMP.25282.A, *passim.*
33. CO.1015/848, Minute by Williams, 6 August 1955.
34. NAM, Ex.Co. 10 December 1954, Minute 561.
35. Colby Papers, Colby to Milverton, 23 December 1948.
36. NAM, Ex.Co. 10 December 1954, Minute 561.
37. CO.1015/848, Minute, Williams to Gorell Barnes, 9 February 1955.

38. CO.1015/847, unsigned minute, 'The Abolition of the Tangata System', 30 June 1955.
39. NAM, SMP.25282.A, Gorell Barnes to Colby, 14 March 1955; CO.1015/848, Minutes Lloyd to SS, 18 February 1955 and SS to Lloyd 27 February 1955.
40. CO.1015/848, Minute, Williams to Lloyd, 16 April 1955.
41. *Ibid.*
42. CO.1015/707, and NAM, SMP.25282.A, Footman to Gorell Barnes, 5 January 1955; Gorell Barnes to Colby, 14 March 1955; Colby to Gorell Barnes, 25 March 1955; SS to Colby, 28 March 1955; Colby to SS, 30 March 1955; SS to Colby, 5 April 1955; Colby to SS, 6 April 1955.
43. CO.1015/848, Minutes on Colonial Office file, 26 March 1955.
44. CO.1015/851, Colby to SS, 6 April 1955; NAM, SMP.25282, Colby to SS, 6 April 1955.
45. CO.1015/848, Colby to SS, 7 October 1955.

Chapter 7

1. CO.1015/847, Footman to Gorell Barnes, 22 May 1954.
2. CO.1015/849, Footman to Raynor and Tennett, 10 May 1954.
3. V. L. Oury to author, 30 October 1987, enclosing Extract from the Chairman's Statement in BCA Company's Annual Report for 1953.
4. CO.1015/707, Colonial Office to Colby, August 1954.
5. CO.1015/848, Note of a meeting held at the Colonial Office on 12 and 13 October 1954.
6. CO.1015/848, Minute, Gorell Barnes to Lloyd and SS, 21 October 1954.
7. CO.1015/848, Minute by Lennox-Boyd, 18 November 1954.
8. CO.1015/848, Minute, Gorell Barnes to Lloyd and SS, 21 October 1954.
9. CO.1015/848, Footman to Colonial Office, 15 October 1954.
10. CO.1015/848, Note of a meeting held at the Colonial Office on 5 November 1954.
11. NAM, SMP.25282.A, Draft Despatch to the Officer Administering the Government of Nyasaland, n.d., probably mid 1954.
12. CO.1015/856, Note of a Meeting held at the Colonial Office on 5 December 1954.
13. *Ibid.*
14. CO.1015/851, Colby to Brook, 22 November 1954.
15. CO.1015/851, Colby to Brook, 27 February 1955.
16. CO.1015/851, Colby to SS, 19 November 1954.
17. CO.1015/851, Colby to SS, 20 November 1954.
18. CO.1015/851, Gorell Barnes to Colby, 24 November 1954; CO.1015/851, Colby to Gorell Barnes, 26 November 1954.
19. CO.1015/851, Colby to SS, 20 November 1954.
20. CO.1015/851, Colby to Brook, 22 November 1954.
21. CO.1015/851, copy enclosed in Colby to Gorell Barnes, 29 November 1954.

22. CO.1015/851, Colby to Gorell Barnes, 29 November 1954.
23. *Ibid.*
24. CO.1015/851, Summary of Discussions between Mr Brook and His Excellency, the Governor, 26 November 1954.
25. CO.1015/851, cited in CS to Gorell Barnes, 24 December 1954.
26. CO.1015/851, Footman to Gorell Barnes, 24 December 1954.
27. CO.1015/851, Harris, Hearn, Smith and Hadlow to Footman, 25 December 1954.
28. CO.1015/851, Footman to Harris, Hearn, Smith and Hadlow, 31 December 1954.
29. CO.1015/851, Colby to Marnham, 6 February 1955.
30. CO.1015/851, Minute, Marnham to Williams, 31 January 1955.
31. CO.1015/851, Brook to Colby, 7 February 1955.
32. CO.1015/851, Harris, Hearn, Smith and Hadlow to Footman, 9 February 1955.
33. NAM, SMP.11967, Confidential Appendix to DRLPC, para. 16.
34. CO.1015/851, Brook to Colby, 7 February 1955.
35. CO.1015/851, Footman to Harris, Hearn, Smith and Hadlow, 21 February 1955.
36. CO.1015/851, Colby to Brook, 27 February 1955.
37. CO.1015/851, Colby to Gorell Barnes, 27 February 1955.
38. CO.1015/851, enclosed in Footman to Gorell Barnes, 4 March 1955.
39. CO.1015/851, Minute, Marnham to Williams, 31 January 1955.
40. CO.1015/851, Colonial Office to Colby, 1 April 1955.
41. CO.1015/707 and CO.1015/848, Colby to SS, 5 April 1955; NAM, SMP.25282.A. Colby (from Colonial Office) to Footman, 29 April 1955.
42. CO.1015/851 and CO.1015/848, SS to Colby, 7 April 1955.
43. CO.1015/848, Colby to SS, 13 April 1955.
44. *Ibid.*
45. *Ibid.*
46. CO.1015/848, SS to Colby, April 1955.
47. CO.1015/848, Minute, Gorell Barnes to Lloyd and SS, 30 April 1955.
48. CO.1015/848, Minute, Morgan to Gorell Barnes, *et al.*, 19 May 1955.
49. CO.1015/851 and CO.1015/848, Note of a meeting in the Secretary of State's Room, 4 May 1955.
50. CO.1015/851 and CO.1015/848, Colby to Brook, 11 May 1955.
51. *Ibid.*
52. CO.1015/848, Colby to SS, 20 June 1955.
53. Chairman's Statement, BCA Company Annual Report for 1954.
54. Chairman's Statement, BCA Company Annual Report for 1955.
55. Brook to Members, BCA Company, 21 September 1955, copy enclosed in Oury to author, 30 October 1987.
56. NAM, SMP.28698, Reeve to Provincial Commissioner, Southern Province, 28 September 1955.
57. Brook to Members, BCA Company, 21 September 1955, copy enclosed in Oury to author, 30 October 1987.
58. CO.1015/848, Colby to SS, 7 October 1955.

NOTES 207

59. CO.1015/848, Nyasaland Political Intelligence Reports (hereafter referred to as PIR), August 1955, paras. 13–14; September 1955, paras. 6–7; November 1955, paras.14–16; December 1955, para. 9; January 1956, para. 3; February 1956, paras. 5 and 13; March 1956, paras. 4–5; April 1956, paras. 10 and 14; June 1956, paras. 18 and 23; July 1956, para. 15; August 1956, paras. 15 and 17; September 1956, para. 16.
60. CO.1015/848, Armitage to SS, 14 September 1956.
61. CO.1015/848, SS to Armitage, 22 September 1956.

Chapter 8
1. CO.1015/848, Colby to SS, 7 October 1955 and SS to Colby, 28 December 1955.
2. CO.1015/1337, Annual Report on the Progress of Land Acquisition and Resettlement in the Southern Province of Nyasaland, 1957–8, para. 3.
3. *Ibid.*, 1956–1957, para. 5.
4. Armitage Papers, 1956, p.51.
5. CO.1015/1337, Armitage to SS, 24 January 1958; Armitage to SS, 10 February 1958; Armitage to SS, 25 February 1959, enclosing the Annual Report on the Progress of Land Acquisition and Resettlement in the Southern Province of Nyasaland for 1957–1958, from which the following details are taken.
6. CO.1015/1337, Footman to SS, 8 June 1959.
7. *Ibid.*
8. CO.1015/1337, Armitage to SS, 25 February 1959.
9. CO.1015/1337, Armitage to Morgan, 17 April 1957.
10. *Ibid.*
11. CO.1015/1408, Armitage to SS, 24 April 1958 and Armitage to Monson, 5 November 1959.
12. CO.1015/1337, Armitage to SS, 25 February 1959.
13. CO.1015/1337, Extract from Nyasaland Situation Report No.5. October 1958, para. 19.
14. *Nyasaland Protectorate Report for the Year 1956* (London, HMSO, 1957), pp.140–1.
15. CO.1015/1952, Records of the Visit of Secretary of State to Central African Territories, January 1957 – Nyasaland, para. D.
16. *Ibid.*
17. *LCP*, 71st Session, 5 February 1957, pp.19–32. The following details of the debate are from this source.
18. *The Colonial Office List, 1955* (London, HMSO, 1955), p.263; *The Daily Telegraph*, 13 June 1990, p.21; and CO.1015/2116, Armitage to Macpherson, 4 October 1957.
19. *The Colonial Office List, 1955*, p.307.
20. CO.1015/1337, Annual Report on the Progress of Land Acquisition and Resettlement in the Southern Province of Nyasaland, 1956–1957, para. 7.
21. CO.1015/1337, Gorell Barnes to Armitage, 17 March 1959.

22. CO.1015/852. This file is devoted to correspondence to and from Gardiner.
23. CO.1015/852, Gardiner to Lennox-Boyd, 9 October 1955.
24. Acknowledged by Gardiner in CO.1015/852, Gardiner to Colby, 6 December 1954.
25. CO.1015/852, Gardiner to Colby, 6 December 1954.
26. CO.1015/852, Colby to Gorell Barnes, 11 January 1955, signed by Footman.
27. *Ibid.*
28. CO.1015/852, Minute, Morgan to SS, 11 July 1955.
29. CO.1015/1337, Armitage to SS, 10 February 1958.
30. CO.1015/1406, Note of a Discussion with the Governor of Nyasaland on Land Matters at the Colonial Office on 17 April 1958.
31. CO.1015/1337, Extract from Nyasaland Situation Report, No.5, October 1958, para. 18.
32. CO.1015/1337, Gorell Barnes to Armitage, 17 March 1959.
33. CO.1015/1337, Armitage to Gorell Barnes, 17 April 1959, from which source the following details are taken.
34. CO.1015/848, Armitage to SS, 3 December 1956.
35. CO.1015/1337, Armitage to SS, 25 February 1959.
36. CO.1015/1337 and CO.1015/1466, Note of Discussion with Governor of Nyasaland on Land Matters, 17 April 1958.
37. Armitage Papers, 1958, p.53.
38. CO.1015/1337, Minute Simpson to Hall, 16 April 1958.
39. CO.1015/1337, Minute by Gorell Barnes, 25 May 1959; Minute by Gorell Barnes to Armitage-Smith, 4 June 1959.
40 CO.1015/1337, Morgan to Armitage, 4 September 1959.
41. CO.1015/1337, Annual Report on the Progress of Land Acquisition and Resettlement in the Southern Province of Nyasaland, 1957–1958, para. 3.
42. *Nyasaland Protectorate Estimates 1959/60* (Zomba, GP, 1959), p.142.
43. V. L. Oury to author, 30 October 1987, enclosing Extract from the Chairman's Statement in BCA Company's Annual Report for 1956.
44. CO.1015/848, Minute, Gorell Barnes (?) to Hudson, n.d., probably December 1956; see also CO.1015/848, Armitage to SS, 3 December 1956.
45. V. L. Oury to author, 30 October 1987, enclosing Extract from the Chairman's Statement in BCA Company's Annual Report for 1957.
46. V. L. Oury to author, 30 October 1987, enclosing Extract from the Chairman's Statement in BCA Company's Annual Report for 1960.
47. *Ibid.*, reports for 1954–63.
48. V. L. Oury to author, 30 October 1987, enclosing Extract from the Chairman's Statement in BCA Company's Annual Report for 1963.
49. CO.1015/1337, Armitage to SS, 24 January 1958, and Armitage to SS, 25 February 1959.
50. CO.1015/1337, Armitage to SS, 25 February 1959.
51. CO.1015/848, Armitage to SS, 3 December 1956. Almost 30 years earlier Sir Frank Stockdale had also made the point that the system was

NOTES 209

popular with the tenant share-croppers: *Colonial Advisory Council of Agriculture and Animal Husbandry* (London, HMSO, C.A.C. 75, 1930–31), cited in V. Liversage, *Land Tenure in the Colonies* (Cambridge University Press, 1945), p.40.
52. CO.1015/1337, Armitage to SS, 25 February 1959.
53. CO.1015/1337, Annual Report on the Progress of Land Acquisition and Resettlement in the Southern Province of Nyasaland, 1957–1958, para. 2; *Report on the Census of 1945* (Zomba, GP, 1946), para. 51 and Table 5.
54. CO.1015/1337, Armitage to SS, n.d., probably late 1959; and Malawi Government Archivist to author, 8 August 1990 enclosing 30386/II/71, Armitage to SS, 9 February 1961.
55. *Nyasaland: Report for the Year 1961* (London, HMSO, 1962), pp.174–5.
56. *LCP*, 76th session, 4th Meeting, 29 May–1 June 1962, pp.266 *et seq.* Details of the Bill and the debate on it are from this source.
57. *Annual Report of the Lands Department, 1966* (Zomba, GP, 1967), p.3.

Chapter 9

1. Cited in Gray, *op. cit.*, p.8.
2. Welensky, interview with author, 12 June 1982.
3. R. Welensky, *Welensky's 4,000 Days* (London, Collins, 1964), p.28.
4. CO.1015/848, Note for Secretary of State's Meeting with Sir G. Colby, 28 April 1954, prepared by Williams.
5. Colby to Armitage, 20 March 1956, Armitage Papers.
6. Armitage Papers 1956, p.50.
7. Armitage to Lennox-Boyd, 30 July 1956, NAM, SMP.29079.
8. Armitage Papers 1956, p.38.
9. W. J. R. Pincott to author, 12 May 1990.
10. Pachai, *op. cit.*, p.70.
11. Pachai, *op. cit.*, p.63.
12. NAM, SMP.10282, Vols. I and II, and 12385; Ex.Co. Minutes Nos.251, 23 May 1951, 317, 4 July 1951, 331, 17 July 1951, and 374, 25 June 1953; Rene Philip to author, 4 January 1983, 3 February 1983, 22 May 1983.
13. Pachai, *op. cit.*, p.14 and p.41.
14. See, generally, A. H. M. Kirk-Greene (Ed.), *The Transfer of Power* (Oxford, University of Oxford Inter-faculty Committee for African Studies, 1979), especially chapter II.
15. CO.1015/707, Minute by Marnham, 14 October 1953.
16. Instructions passed under the Royal Sign Manual and Signet, to the Governor and Commander-in-Chief of the Nyasaland Protectorate: Nyasaland Order-in-Council, Instruction XXXIV, *The Laws of Nyasaland, 1933* (London, Roworth, 1934), Vol. II, p.1071.
17. G. Hodgson to author, August 1979.
18. *LCP*, 76th Session, 4th Meeting, 29 May 1962–1 July 1962, p.269.
19. Armitage Papers 1956, p.78.
20. *Nyasaland Protectorate Report for the Year 1955* (London, HMSO, 1956), p.136.

21. Abrahams Report, paras. 121–6. For a note on the Native Development and Welfare Fund (hereafter referred to as NDWF), see Hailey, *Native Administration in the British African Territories* (London, HMSO, 1950), Part II, p.60.
22. NAM, LANCOM.14, Colby to Cohen, 28 April 1948.
23. *Report on the Nyasaland Protectorate for the Year 1952* (London, HMSO, 1953), p.43; *Report on the Nyasaland Protectorate for the Year 1957* (London, HMSO, 1958), p.50.
24. NAM, SMP.26127, McDonald to CS, 23 March 1954.
25. NAM, SMP.26127, Minute by Colby, 16 April 1954.
26. Nyasaland Protectorate Annual Estimates, 1957/8, p.184, and 1958/9, p.247.
27. *Ibid.*, 1959/60, p.246.
28. *Ibid.*, 1960/61, p.254, and 1961/62, p.258.
29. *Nyasaland Development Plan, 1962–1965* (Zomba, GP, 1962), p.122.
30. Hetherwick to Johnston, 12 February 1892, Blantyre Mission Papers, cited in Pachai, *op. cit.*, p.34.
31. Interview with Lady Colby, 18 June 1983.
32. *Nyasaland Report for the Year 1959* (London, HMSO, 1960), pp.1–20.
33. *Nyasaland Report for the Year 1960* (London, HMSO, 1961), pp.1–28.
34. In his discussions with the Governor in the latter part of 1958, following his return to Nyasaland and during the build-up to the turmoil of 1959–60, Banda made representations about federation, independence and agricultural education, but not about land or Africans on private estates.

Sources

I. Publications

Books

Agnew, S. and Stubbs, M. *Malawi in Maps*, University of London Press, 1972
Baker, C. A. *Johnston's Administration*, Zomba, Government Press, 1970
Bandawe, L. M. *Memoirs of a Malawian*, Blantyre, Claim, 1971
Boeder, R.B. *Alfred Sharpe of Nyasaland, Builder of Empire*, Blantyre, Society of Malawi, 1980
Brelsford, W. V. (ed.), *Handbook to the Federation of Rhodesia and Nyasaland*, Salisbury, Cassell, 1960
Buchanan, J. *Shire Highlands (East Central Africa) As Colony and Mission*, London, Blackwood, 1885
Clegg, E.M. *Race and Politics; Partnership in the Federation of Rhodesia and Nyasaland*, London, Oxford University Press, 1960
Debenham, F. *Nyasaland: The Land of the Lake*, London, HMSO, 1955
Duff, H. L. *Nyasaland Under the Foreign Office*, London, George Bell, 1903
Elias, T. O. *The Nature of African Customary Law*, Manchester University Press, 1956
Franck, T. M. *Race and Nationalism: the Struggle for Power in Rhodesia-Nyasaland*, London, George Allen and Unwin, 1960
Gelfand, M. *Lakeside Pioneers*, London, Blackwell, 1964
Gray, R. *The Two Nations: Aspects of the Development of Race Relations in the Rhodesias and Nyasaland*, London, Oxford University Press, 1960
Lord Hailey, *Native Administration in the British African Territories*, London, HMSO, 1950
Hanna, A. J. *The Beginnings of Nyasaland and North-Eastern Rhodesia, 1859–1895*, London, Oxford University Press, 1956
Hanna, A. J. *The Story of the Rhodesias and Nyasaland*, London, Faber and Faber, 1960
Hetherwick, A. *The Romance of Blantyre*, London, James Clarke, 1931
Ibik, J. O. *Restatement of African Law*, vol. 4, Malawi II, London, Sweet and Maxwell, 1971
Johnston, A. *The Life and Letters of Sir Harry Johnston*, New York, Cape, 1929

Johnston, H. H. *British Central Africa*, London, Methuen, 1897
Johnston, H. H. *Handbook to British Central Africa*, London, British Central Africa Company Ltd, 1905
Johnston, H. H. *The Story of My Life*, London, Chatto and Windus, 1923
Jones, G. B. *Britain and Nyasaland: A Study of the Political Development of Nyasaland under British Control*, London, George Allen and Unwin, 1964
Kettlewell, R. W. *An Outline of Agrarian Problems and Land Policy in Nyasaland*, Zomba, Government Printer, 1955
Kettlewell, R. W. *Agricultural Change in Nyasaland: 1945–1960*, Stanford University Press, 1965
Liversage, V. *Land Tenure in the Colonies*, Cambridge University Press, 1945
Lucas Phillips, C. E. *The Vision Splendid*, London, Heinemann, 1960
Lugard, F. D. *The Dual Mandate in British Tropical Africa*, 4th edn, London, Blackman, 1929
MacDonald, D. *Africana, or the Heart of Heathen Africa*, London, Dawsons, (reproduced) 1962
Macdonald, R. J. *From Nyasaland to Malawi: Studies in Colonial History*, Nairobi, East Africa Publishing House, 1975
Macmillan, W. M. *Africa Emergent*, Harmondsworth, Penguin Books, 1949
Mair, L. P. *Native Policies in Africa*, London, Routledge, 1936
Mason, P. *Year of Decision: Rhodesia and Nyasaland in 1960*, London, Oxford University Press, 1960
Maugham, R. C. F. *Nyasaland in the Nineties*, London, Lincoln Williams, 1935
Maugham, R. C. F. *Africa As I Have Known It*, London, J. Murray, 1929
Mitchell, P. *African Afterthoughts*, London, Hutchinson, 1954
Moir, F. L. M. *After Livingstone: An African Trade Romance*, London, Hodder and Stoughton, 1924
Murray, S. S. (ed.), *Handbook of Nyasaland*, London, Crown Agents for the Colonies, for the Nyasaland Government, 1931
Norman, L. S. *Nyasaland Without Prejudice*, East Africa (journal), London, 1934
Oliver, R. *Sir Harry Johnston and the Scramble for Africa*, London, Chatto and Windus, 1964
Pachai, B. *The Early History of Malawi*, London, Longman, 1972
Pachai, B. *Malawi: The History of the Nation*, London, Longman, 1973
Pachai, B. *Land and Politics in Malawi, 1875–1975*, Kingston (Ontario), Limestone Press, 1978
Pike, J. G. and Rimmington, G. T. *Malawi, A Geographical Study*, London, Oxford University Press, 1965
Pike, J. G. *Malawi, a Political and Economic History*, London, Pall Mall, 1968
Pollock, V. H. *Nyasaland and Northern Rhodesia: Corridor to the North*, Pittsburgh, Duquesne, 1971
Rankine, W. H. *A Hero of the Dark Continent*, London, Blackwood, 1896
Rowley, H. *Africa Unveiled*, London, SPCK, 1876
Sanger, C. *Central African Emergency*, London, Heinemann, 1960
Schatz, S. P. *South of the Sahara: Development in African Economics*, London, Macmillan, 1972

SOURCES 213

Shepperson, G. and Price, T. *Independent African*, Edinburgh University Press, 1958
Smith, G. W. et al., *Malawi Past and Present*, Blantyre, Claim, 1971
Taylor, D. *Rainbow On The Zambezi*, London, Museum Press, 1953
Welensky, R. *Welensky's 4000 Days*, New York, London, Collins, 1964
White, L. *Magomero: Portrait of an African Village*, London, Cambridge University Press, 1987
Wills, A. J. *An Introduction to the History of Central Africa*, London, Oxford University Press, 1964

Journals
Baker, C. A. 'Chigaru's: A Study of its Population (Blantyre District)', *Nyasaland Journal*, vol.11 (January 1958), 60–4
Baker, C. A. 'Blantyre District: A Geographical Appreciation of the Growth, Distribution and Composition of its Population', *Nyasaland Journal*, vol.12 (January 1959), 7–35
Baker, C. A. 'A note on Nguru Immigration to Nyasaland', *Nyasaland Journal*, vol.14 (January 1961), 41–2
Baker, C. A. 'Nyasaland, the History of its Export Trade', *Nyasaland Journal*, vol.15 (January 1962) 7–35
Baker, C. A. 'Malawi's Early Road System', *Society of Malawi Journal*, vol.24, 1 (1971), 7–21
Brietzke, P. H. 'Rural Development and Modification of Malawi's Land Tenure System', *Land and Labour in Rural Malawi*, Rural Africana, Current Research in the Social Sciences, 20 (Spring 1973), part I, 53–68
Cardew, C. A. 'Nyasaland in 1894–95', *Nyasaland Journal*, vol.1 (January 1948), 51–5
Dixey, F. 'Distribution of population in Nyasaland', *Geographic Review*, (1928), 274–90
East Africa and Rhodesia
Hadlow, G. G. S. J. 'The History of Tea in Nyasaland', *Nyasaland Journal*, vol.13 (January 1960), 21–31
Kandawire, A. K. 'Thangata in Pre-colonial and Colonial Systems of Land Tenure in Southern Malawi with Special Reference to Chingale', *Africa*, vol.47, 2 (1977), 185–90
Lamport-Stokes, H. J. 'Land Tenure in Malawi', *Society of Malawi Journal*, vol.23, 2 (1970), 59–88
Nyasaland Times
Life and Work in Nyasaland, Blantyre, Church of Scotland Press.
Pachai, B. 'Land Policies in Malawi: an examination of the colonial legacy', *Journal of African History*, vol.XIV, 4 (1973), 681–98
Pachai, B. 'The Issue of "Thangata" in the History of Nyasaland', *Journal of Social Science (Malawi)*, vol.3 (1974), 20–34
Rangeley, W. H. J. 'A Brief History of the Tobacco Industry in Nyasaland – Part I', *Nyasaland Journal*, vol.10 (January 1957), 62–83; Part II, vol.10 (July 1957), 62–83

Rangeley, W. H. J. 'A Brief History of the Tobacco Industry in Nyasaland – Additional Notes', *Nyasaland Journal*, vol.11 (July 1958), 24–7
Withers, F. M. 'Nyasaland in 1895–96', *Nyasaland Journal*, vol. 2 (January 1949), 16–34

Government publications
British Central African Gazette (1894–1907)
Nyasaland Government Gazette (1907–1964)
Ordinances of the Nyasaland Protectorate, London, Stevens, 1913
Report of the Commission Appointed by His Excellency the Governor to Inquire Into Various Matters and Questions Concerned With the Native Rising Within the Nyasaland Protectorate, Supplement to *Gazette*, 31 January 1916
Report of a Commission to Enquire into and Report on Certain Matters Connected with the Occupation of Land in the Nyasaland Protectorate, Zomba, Government Press, 1920
The Laws of Nyasaland, 1933, London, Roworth, 1934
Report of the Commission Appointed to Enquire into the Financial Position and Further Development of Nyasaland, London, HMSO, 1938
Memorandum on Native Policy in Nyasaland, Zomba, Government Press, 1939
Confidential Report on Native Administration and Political Development in British Tropical Africa, London, HMSO, n.d., probably 1943
Report on the Census of 1945, Zomba, Government Press, 1946
Report of the Land Commission, 1946, Zomba, Government Press, 1947
The Laws of Nyasaland, 1946, London, Roworth, 1947
The Colonial Office List, 1955, London, HMSO, 1955
Report on an Economic Survey of Nyasaland, 1958–1959, Salisbury, Government Press, 1959
Nyasaland Development Plan, 1962–1965, Zomba, Government Press, 1962
Malawi Government Gazette (1964)
Annual Report of the Lands Department, 1966, Zomba, Government Press, 1967
Annual Report of the Provincial Commissioners, Zomba, Government Press
BCA Company Annual Reports
Blue Book, Zomba, Government Press
Nyasaland Protectorate Estimates, Zomba, Government Press
Proceedings of the Legislative Council of Nyasaland
Report on Native Affairs, Zomba, Government Press

II. Unpublished material

Public Record Office, London
CO.525/68, 73, 104, 109.
CO.626/5, 8, 24.
CO.1015/707, 847, 848, 849, 851, 852, 1337, 1408, 1446, 1952, 2116.

SOURCES   215

National Archives of Malawi, Zomba
NAM, SMP.10282, 10521, 10521/I, 10719, 11967, 12258, I/12501, 12664, 18950, 20767, 20767/43, 25282, 25282.A, 25282.K, 28698, 62531.

Theses
Baker, C. A. 'The Development of the Civil Service in Malawi, 1891–1972', University of London, Ph.D, 1981
Krishnamurthy, B. S. 'Land and Labour in Nyasaland, 1891–1914', University of London, Ph.D, 1964
Myambo, S. S. 'The Shire Highlands Plantations: a socio-economic history of the plantation system of production in Malawi, 1891–1938', University of Malawi, M.A., 1973
Page, M. E. 'Malawians in the Great War, 1914–1925', Michigan State University, Ph.D, 1977
Ng'ong'ola, C. H. S. 'Statutory Control of Land and the Administration of Agrarian Policies in Malawi', School of Oriental and African Studies, University of London, Ph.D, 1983

Seminar papers
University of Malawi Chancellor College History Seminar Papers:
Chidzero, C. Z. 'Thangata in Thyolo District: a socio-economic study in Chimaliro and Bvumbwe area', 1980/81, Paper no. 13
Paskar, M. G. L. 'Towards a History of Thangata in Chief Chikowi's area from 1880s to 1915', 1980/81, Paper no. 14
Vaughan, M. 'Food production in early colonial Southern Malawi', 1981/82, Paper no. 2

Oxford University Development Records Project
Transcript of a Colloquium on Land in Nyasaland, Rhodes House Library, 22 November 1980

Armitage Papers
These are a collection of papers, some of which are deposited at Rhodes House Library, Oxford, and others lent by Armitage's son to the author. References in this book are to typescript memoirs by Armitage included in the Papers

Colby Papers
These are a collection of papers, lent to the author by Colby's daughter, now deposited at Rhodes House Library, Oxford